COMMUNITY LIBRARY
Y0-BWU-113

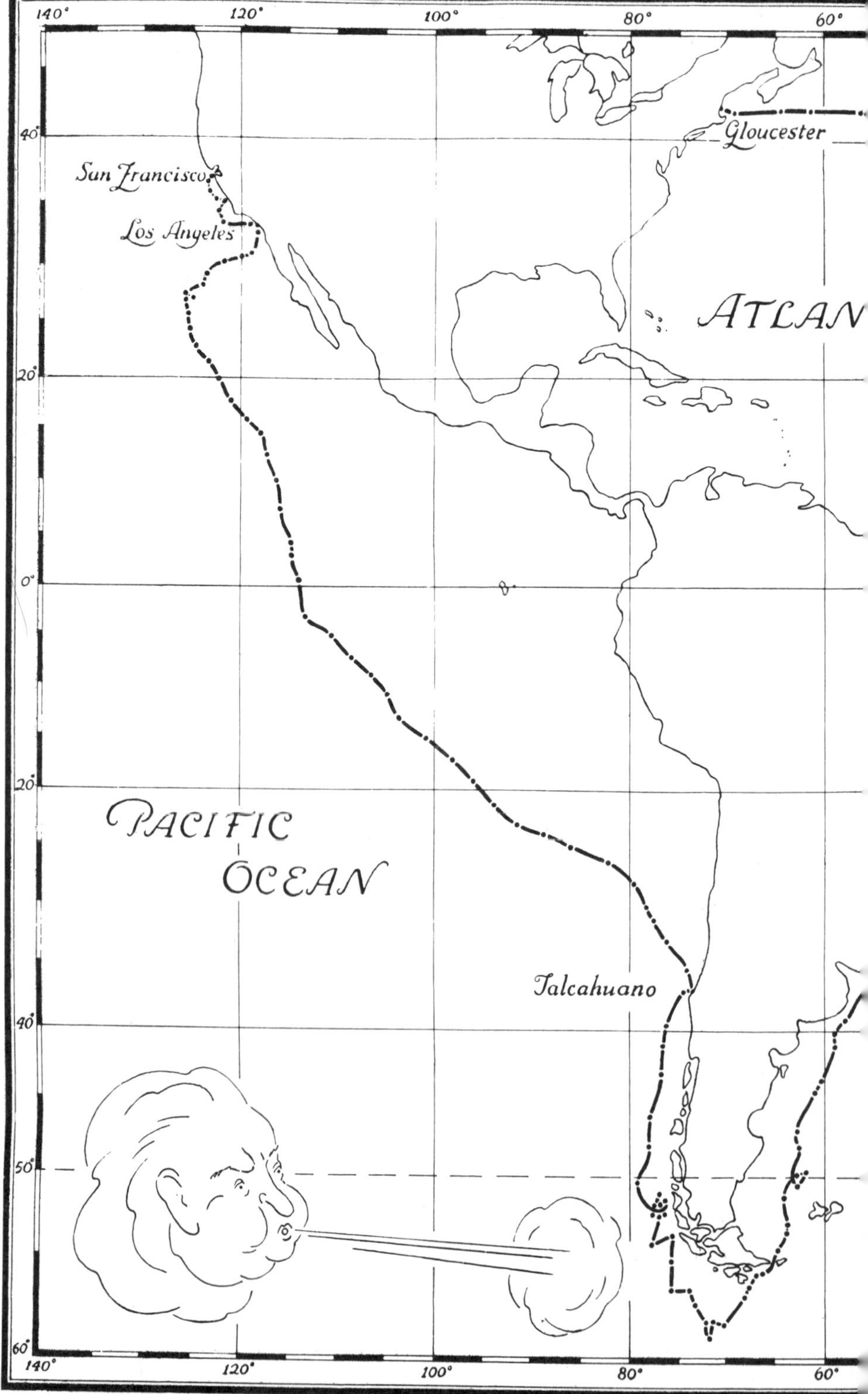
140°
120°
100°
80°
60°
40°
20°
0°
20°
40°
50°
60°
Gloucester
San Francisco
Los Angeles
ATLAN
PACIFIC
OCEAN
Talcahuano

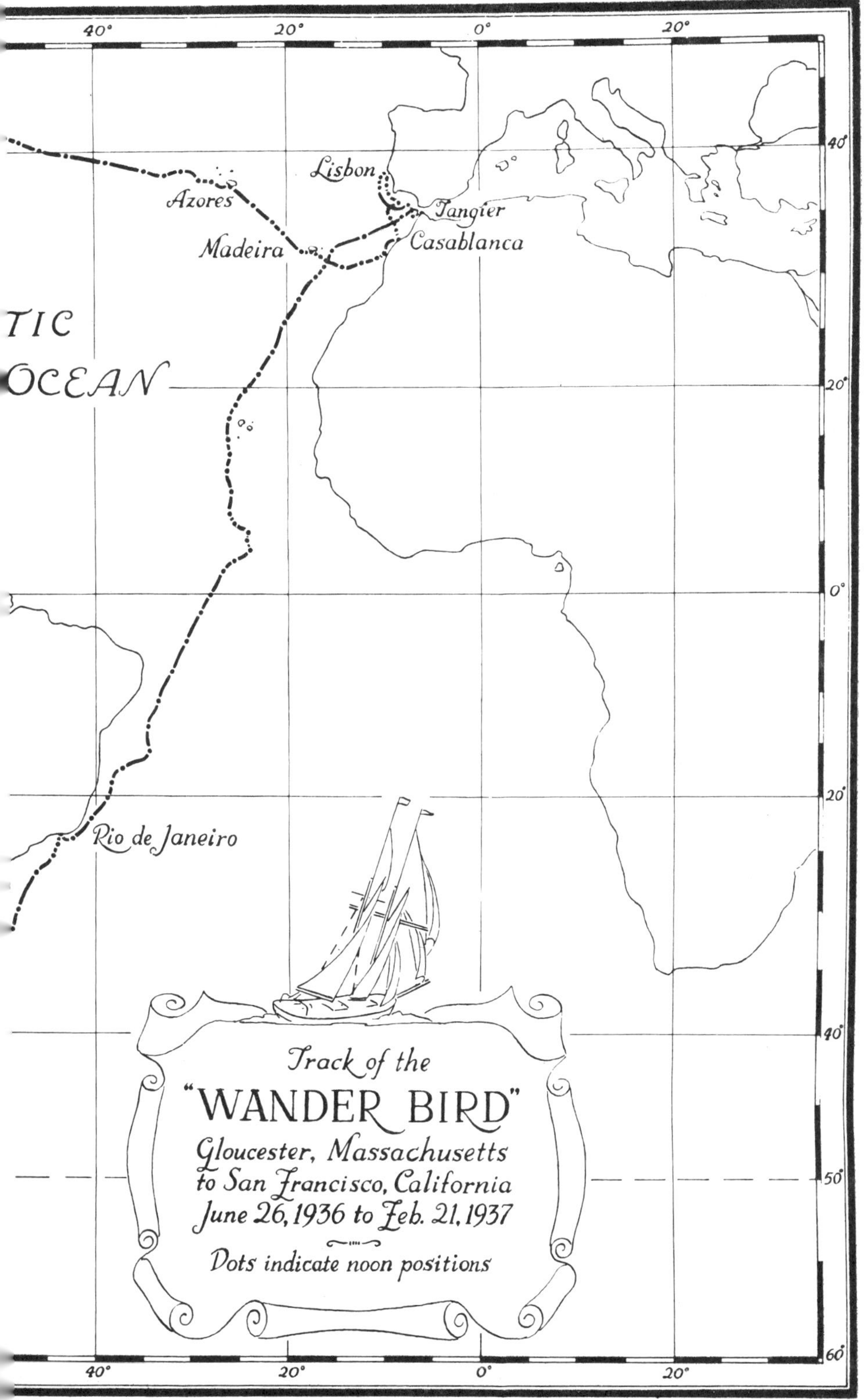
40°
20°
0°
20°
40°
20°
0°
20°
40°
50°
60°
TIC
OCEAN
Lisbon
Azores
Tangier
Madeira
Casablanca
Rio de Janeiro
Track of the
"WANDER BIRD"
Gloucester, Massachusetts
to San Francisco, California
June 26, 1936 to Feb. 21, 1937
Dots indicate noon positions

Fifty South
to
Fifty South

Fifty South
to
Fifty South

The story of a voyage west around Cape Horn in the schooner *Wander Bird*

by Warwick M. Tompkins

Ox Bow Press • Woodbridge, Connecticut

First published, 1938

2000 Reprint published by
OX BOW PRESS
P.O. BOX 4045
WOODBRIDGE, CONNECTICUT 06525
Telephone Number: 203-387-5900
Fax: 203-387-0035
E-mail: oxbow@gte.net

Illustrated with pictures from the author's moving -picture films and
additional photographs made by members of the ship's company

ISBN 1-881987-16-7 (Paperback)
Library of Congress Catalog Card Number: 00-103234

Printed in the United States of America
on acid-free paper

To
My Mother
and the memory of
My Father
This Book Is Dedicated

CONTENTS

ACKNOWLEDGMENTS

THE time has come to write the last line of this book, and it is a privilege here to thank the good shipmates, *Wander Birders* all, who let me reproduce their superb photographs found herein. It is exceedingly pleasant to look over the pictorial record and to know that every photograph and every drawing is the work of a man who has lived at sea with me and my ship. It makes the entire work a singularly close family affair.

The chart, end-papers, and all the line drawings are the work of Robert Freeman. The others to whom credit is due are: Dr. John Barr Tompkins, John North, Wells Morss, John Wright, Frank Vining Smith, Chadwick Wiggin, Hillard Russell, Thomas W. Laffee, Jr., Capt. Irving Johnson, and Richard Danforth.

Warwick M. Tompkins.

New York.
1938

Grim, gray, cold. Whipped bare by the unceasing savage westerly winds. Hammered by sleet. Shrouded in scud. Echoing to Pacific surges, the screams of penguins, albatross and seals. Unlighted. Uninhabited. Unfriendly.

CAPE HORN!

There it is, a 1500-foot marker over the graves of seamen, marker between two great oceans, coccyx of the continent's Andean spine.

This photograph, from the only moving picture ever made of the Cape, which is usually hidden in mist or is given a wide berth, shows Wander Bird coming up fast on the Horn which lies seven miles west still. The sea at the moment is smooth, but beyond the Horn are fast-gathering storm clouds. Thirty minutes after this picture was made the ship was hove-to in a wind of hurricane violence. She never got so near to the Horn again, and it was eighteen days later when she crossed FIFTY SOUTH in the Pacific and completed the rounding.

I. WHAT WENT BEFORE

SHIPS and the sea I have loved passionately longer than I can recall. Why this should be is hard to say, for my ancestors, sturdy landsmen who made excellent teachers, engineers and farmers, knew and cared nothing for the sea. Welsh-English they were, and happily they left me a measure of their proverbial tenacity. Without it I should never have cherished for so long my fond and possibly foolish dream of a conquest of Cape Horn in my own ship.

Undeniably a Cape Horn voyage today, east to west, under sail, is a ridiculous anachronism. Time there was when a California-bound vessel *had* to round the Cape, but the ditch at Panama changed all that. In the bitter winds and angry seas of the Cape there is the same old measure of anxiety and discomfort. Along the old, forsaken trail there is some danger, though not as much as most people believe. What is to be gained? Wealth? Of that there is not enough down there to support the wiliest Chinese trader. Fame? Stouter and bolder fellows years ago exhausted that stock. Of Fame's modern sister, Publicity, even, there are but minuscule favors to be won, and Publicity is a cheap bawd whose caresses are more bitter than ashes.

I knew all this before we sailed, yet I count the high cost of the voyage a small price to pay for the unquenchable glow, the thrill of deepest satisfaction which is mine forever, regardless of buffets Fate may have in store for me. Aye, though the voyage left me poorer in dollars than I had been before, though I planted no flag on new lands, laid nothing of importance on the altars of Science, even though accomplishment has robbed me of a motive greater and more vital than I suspected—despite all this the voyage, in its conception, planning and execution, was worth far, far more than its price.

A man who loves the sea and ships can aspire to no more searching test than a Horn passage. It is the last word in the lexicon of sailormen. There Nature has arranged trials and tribulations so ingeniously that in the van of all synonyms for sea cruelty and hardship is the ironbound name of Cape Horn. Winds blow elsewhere at times as strongly as they do south of fifty. Seas elsewhere may pyramid as high, break as heavily. There may be places equally remote and as bleakly lonely. Currents in other regions may be as adverse. These foes the sailorman may encounter separately or in pairs here and there, aye, encounter and best, but always in his heart he will wonder if he could face all combined. If he glories in the unequal contest of human muscles and artifices with the ocean, if the sea shouts an insistent challenge, he can never be truly content until he has voyaged from Fifty South in the Atlantic to Fifty South in the Pacific in his own command. This is the ultimate test, given to very few to know.

Memory does not focus sharply on the awakening of my determination to round Cape Horn. It was an old dream ten years ago when I found *Wander Bird*. Probably it stirred vaguely before I ever set foot on a deck, when I was just another reader of sea stories, following in books the reeling clippers.

Cape Horn is not to be approached lightly or carelessly. Actually the greatest part of its conquest must be accomplished long before the ship nears the fiftieth parallel in the South Atlantic. First there must be the unshakable determination to go, then the long and arduous struggle for essential experience to oppose the Cape's brutality. The ship must be fitted, tested, refitted and tested again. All of this takes time, much time, and much money which is often hard to come by.

My schooling in sea lore started when I joined a miserable fifty-five-foot yawl, the *Eleanor*, in the steaming port of Davao, a jungle-hedged village on the Island of Mindanao in the Philippines. Previous years in the war-time Navy and months in the merchant marine can be almost entirely discounted. What one can learn of the real ocean—my ocean—in those services is little indeed.

The *Eleanor* proved a hard school. She was a sea-going monstrosity whose general unfitness for the sea was exceeded in quality only by the lamentable dilapidation of such scanty gear as she had. Fortunately I for long did not suspect just how frowsy she was, my first ship. In her I voyaged perilously for just one year. Ardently I pursued self-taught mastery of navigation. Of necessity I learned to splice parted hemp and wire, how to patch sails so rotten that a sneeze, almost literally, split them. By dint of eternal patching and a truly tropical disregard of time's flight we worked *Eleanor* from the Philippines to Jolo, Borneo, Celebes, Bali, Lombok, Timor, Thursday Island (filthy spot!) and on to Port Moresby, capital of British New Guinea.

Two weeks after leaving Moresby we had won only 150 miles of easting despite constant sailing. There the breaking monsoon squalls caught us, stripped us of every rag of canvas, blew us away from our only anchors and but for a miracle would have pounded us to bits on the barrier reef. Scudding before the blow we ran back those hard-won miles to Port Moresby in just twenty-four hours!

Lying without a master in Moresby's turquoise harbor was a comparatively smart, well-found schooner, the *Sir Arthur*, a vessel engaged in the somewhat questionable business of labor recruiting. This activity is the modern equivalent of slaving, although there is no rough stuff connected with it, a more subtle and effective technique having been found to lure jungle men to labor in mines and plantations. I was offered command of the schooner and jumped to take it.

At twenty-three I had my first vessel, my own quarterdeck. *Sir Arthur*, named after an egotistical Australian knight who had built her, was once a fast yacht and she retained the weaknesses common to the breed, though her glories were long since memories alone. She was long-ended, without sufficient freeboard, sadly whittled away in the body. She was sixty-five feet over-all and her gross tonnage was twenty-eight. To gain cargo space an original centerboard had been removed. Her one little cabin aft housed a brute of a motor which, when hot and running, definitely relegated the master to life on deck. She was my first command, and in my eyes she was grand even with scarred, dirty decks, the reek of gasoline and rails blackened and ruined. She wouldn't go to windward without the engine, naturally, but she'd run at dizzy speed with the monsoon winds.

Marine laws were lax in Papua. No one seemed to care when I'd take the ship to sea with twenty-five tons of cargo and nearly sixty souls—sixty souls with their accumulated luggage. On those runs our freeboard, until we'd landed cargo, mail and passengers through the surf here and there, was measurable in inches.

Our voyages always took us finally into the deep jungle, up the vast New Guinea rivers. From the forests came my paying cargoes of contract laborers. When the ship was filled, often a matter of three or four weeks of exploring and the disposal of much cheap tobacco and trinkets, we returned across the Gulf of Papua to Port Moresby where the volunteer laborers were signed up by a paternal government to one, two or three years of servitude at a wage of about $2.50 a month.

My crew numbered seven fuzzy-headed Papuans, who looked every inch the cannibals they had been and probably were on suitable occasions. Old Wagi, my mate, was a splendid chap, loyal and able, a sailorman with real instinct for leadership. He spoke the common dialect with which one can converse with nearly any Papuan regardless of his tribal tongue. Wagi was principally responsible for successful palaver with the natives. My job was to keep an eye on the ship and her cargo, to get her safely in and out of the rivers, across the bars where South Pacific rollers broke in majestic thunder, and then on across the debris-strewn Gulf. It was a lonely, interesting job. It left me with a horror of jungles and an intense dislike of auxiliary power.

I learned how to handle a whale boat in surf, how to cross bars and how to coax a sullen and alien crowd into a good humor by tact and kindness. I learned the value of the hand lead and how to carry out kedge anchors when an unsuspected river bar reached up to grip the ship in sucking embrace.

There was a lot of money to be made as master of the *Sir Arthur*, but loneliness and calling memories of a girl half the world away outweighed the lure of cash, the tarnished fascination of a vast wilderness and even the pride of youthful command.

Homeward-bound, a Sydney beachcomber, it was my fortune to be signed as acting second mate of a big American freighter sailing for San Francisco. A British Coastal Master's license and a knowledge of navigation, tangible souvenirs of two ships, sent me home in pleasant style.

By now I knew that neither the mechanized navy nor the stupidly dull merchant marine held anything for me. The hopeless death struggles of the last commercial sailing ships were everywhere to be seen. Where to turn now? Where find anodyne for the consuming sea fever?

Perforce I turned to yachting and naturally enough to the most rugged and interesting sort of yachting, ocean racing. There were berths waiting for a man who could navigate and command even though he had no money or social position.

In 1926 I sailed as navigator of the forty-foot schooner *Harlequin* in the Bermuda Race. My job quickly expanded when her young owner proved incompetent. Despite the fact that we had next to the smallest boat, that I sailed a totally unorthodox sort of course, that our crew was completely green, we very nearly won in our class and were close enough at the finish to see the two boats which led us across the finish line.

The next month I was in England trying to find a berth in the second annual Fastnet Race. How I rowed through that neglected, rain-drenched little fleet petitioning for any job from peeling spuds to command, all that is irrelevant here except that it shows how bent I was on gaining experience under sail. A great-hearted Irishman finally hauled me aboard his fifty-foot cutter, the *Gull*. We sailed her smashing down Channel, around the bold Fastnet Rock and very nearly to Davy Jones' locker in a buster of a gale. Yes, *Gull* very nearly foundered that dirty night off the Stag Rocks, but we got her safely past the Old Head of Kinsale (how I love those great names!) and into Cork harbor before she cradled her weary frame on the mud. Thank you, Captain Donegan, for your well-remembered and splendid example of leadership that night! Your cool courage and decisiveness will always be a stirring memory and example.

That autumn young Fred Ames, of Boston, asked me to be one of his crew the following summer when he wanted to take his husky *Primrose IV*, winner of second place in the Fastnet

Race, back to Boston over the far northern route, calling at the Faroes, Iceland, Greenland and Labrador. No yacht had ever made that voyage blazed by the Vikings. Somewhere along that lonely course, only a few years before, had vanished the *Lief Ericsson* sailed by Bill Nutting and Arthur Hildebrand and their Scandinavian shipmates.

Here was a challenge to my liking, and I waited impatiently through a Paris winter for the coming of spring when I could start refitting the ship for this ambitious undertaking.

That was a glorious voyage; from departure in Bembridge (Isle of Wight) to the sunlit afternoon when we reached Newport it was very nearly perfect. The ship was right, her crew congenial to a rare degree. The knowledge that we were embarked on a hard voyage knit us very closely together.

Brave little *Primrose IV!* It is a pity space forbids telling all her story, of the hard slog to windward in the North Sea, of the race into a Scottish port to hospitalize a shipmate. He was suffering the agonies of what we diagnosed as acute appendicitis but which proved to be an obstructed kidney. We found little we could do for him but drive the ship. The hours he groaned and sweated in torture remain possibly the longest in my life. We got him to an Edinburgh hospital in time, thank God, and months later—when *Primrose* was leagues away—he was discharged, a well man. (Where are you now, laughing Fred Rearden? Possibly it was your stories of the Horn and your Irish courage, forged down there, which sent me to follow you to the Cape!) If space allowed we could well tell these things, and how we found the Faroes and bleak Iceland, why we skipped Greenland because two-inch pine planking did not seem fit to oppose field ice, how we were run down by a blundering, fog-blind steamer which miraculously left us virtually undamaged off Cape Sable.

Primrose IV, her owner-master and her crew were awarded the Blue Water Medal by the Cruising Club of America for this cruise which was deemed the outstanding yachting voyage of 1927.

In 1928 I was married and my sailing curtailed, not because of my wife, oh, no! It was high time, we two decided, for me to stop sailing boats for other people and to get one for us. Nevertheless this year I sailed as navigator in the famous racing schooner *Niña* when she won the Fastnet Race through no particular or brilliant efforts of her navigator. When I left her I set my face resolutely toward owning my ship, toward Cape Horn.

We were poverty poor in everything except enthusiasm and determination. How we pinched the sous in our seventh heaven Paris garret, hoarding the few francs to be salvaged from a newspaperman's meager salary, how our dream ship took shape slowly from adventure stories churned out by night for pulp magazines, this is again another story.

By this time I knew I wanted a boat built for and tested in arduous pilot service. I wanted a ship which could go to sea and keep the sea in comfort and safety regardless of the season, a ship smart in sailing and easily handled, a vessel which could run forever with a fair wind and lie snugly and quietly hove-to with a gale ahead. These are the functions of pilot boats. Architects say, "FORM FOLLOWS FUNCTION"—afloat or ashore—and this law of evolution has produced the finest sea boats known in the world.

I'd have no *Eleanor*, sluggish, hideous as sin; no tiny and cramped *Harlequin* of Bermuda memory. Affection could not blind me to the fact that the undercanvased *Primrose IV* had been a sluggard to windward and that she hove-to miserably. That pitching fool *Niña*, with her cut-away forefoot! She was a dangerous, exhausting devil to steer before real wind and sea.

Wander Bird. *From a painting by Frank Vining Smith.*

In her 57th year the old pilot boat prepares for Cape Horn in Rockland, Maine.

No one could have given me a *Niña* with her toplofty Bermuda rig and multitude of staysails. Likewise no narrow-gutted *Gull* nor no long-ended *Sir Arthur* would lure our little savings.

No yacht, no summer season butterfly; no converted fisherman with hull and rig compromised for commercial efficiency—nothing like these would do.

We wanted a pilot boat. Alone of all the world's working craft they are designed to sail on a fixed water line. They are shaped, framed, planked and fastened to meet any test of the sea. They are virtually super-yachts, born of centuries of trial and error, fruit of immeasurable sea experience, unquestionably the ablest craft afloat.

Ultimately—slighting months of such breathless living as they alone know who challenge destiny armed only with a vision—we found THE SHIP.

If this were not fatalism, the work of kind, directing gods who knew how well we would mate with this old ship, it is difficult to believe that events could have occurred so perfectly. How otherwise could we have stumbled upon the perfect ship?

Her name, when we brushed aside the accumulated grime of Hamburg, was *Wandervogel—Wander Bird*. Vandals had shattered her hatches and skylights. Rain water rose brown to the floors. The filth of four Hamburg years lay thick everywhere. Thieves had stolen every belaying pin, every item of gear in the lazarette. Aye, she was sad, dishevelled. But she was sound; and it is astounding what soap and water, paint and varnish and new gear will do to any ship so long as she is sound!

Wander Bird was built in 1879. At this time the cut-throat competition among pilots in the world's great ports was reaching intolerable conditions. The races—often four or five hun-

She is big-bodied underwater, but sharp and clean as a racer must be.

650 pounds of copper nails hold the copper sheathing in place over heavy felt. Note how copper is lapped so the sea cannot rip it off.

dred miles long—staged by rival pilot boats of New York, San Francisco, Boston and Hamburg had produced ever bigger, faster, smarter vessels. Such competition was of necessity bringing the modern era of co-operative pilotage and compulsory fees. These were the twilight hours of the great age of sail. Men knew more about sail and the sea than ever before, more than they will ever know again. Their racing pilot boats reflected their cunning, in them they produced the most superb small sea-going vessels ever launched.

Wander Bird is a schooner readily distinguished by a stem raked slightly aft from the perpendicular, by sharply raked masts (raked for staying strength) a matchless sheer and the same beautiful rounded, lifting stern developed in the clippers.

She gives the impression of being much larger than she is with an over-all length of 85 feet, a slender beam of 18 feet 6 inches and a draft of nearly 11 feet.

She cost her builders $40,000. Twice that today might duplicate her were there available such white oak, Swedish iron and greenheart. Elsewhere I give dimensions of scantlings, lines and sail plans and those technically interested can learn there much of interest. Here I will point out only a few achievements which have made *Wander Bird* in the fifty-ninth year of her life one of the world's outstanding craft.

"I consider *Wander Bird* the best-designed and best-built vessel of her size in America." The quotation is from John Alden, great designer of yachts. He refers to the art evident in every line of her hull, the entry—not too full, not too sharp; the satiny-smooth run aft which rejoins parted waters so gently that the ship's wake is smooth and quiet. He points out how cleverly a displacement of 138 tons has been distributed along

"Looks O.K. to me, William." The "Commodore" checking up on his ship with the Bosun.

a waterline length of 76 feet so the critic is unaware of massive weight.

Contrary to modern yachting practice *Wander Bird* has a deep, straight forefoot drawing seven feet. This great amount of forward lateral plane—a vivid technical phrase—insures the ship a vital grip on the water. This prevents the head from being blown off to leeward when she is hove-to and likewise eliminates wild, dangerous yawing when running before heavy weather. She does not tack with the speed of a cut-away modern hull, of course, but even so comes about very smartly in forty-five seconds when making five knots in smooth water. At sea no one wants a ship spinning like a lady of the ballet.

The schooner is astonishingly dry, which means comfort and safety for those on deck, and added efficiency and speed in handling of gear. Bulwarks on many small craft are a menace, holding aboard tons of water at critical times and making

Oakum driven into a ship's V-shaped deck seams and—

Payed with hot marine glue prevents leaks below.

the ship dangerously loggy. Nearly threescore years at sea have proven that *Wander Bird's* bulwarks—priceless adjunct to safety and comfort, both—present no such peril to her.

We added topmasts to the original pilot boat rig and permanently fixed the formerly housing jibboom which was set off-center, European fashion, from the bowsprit. We gave the ship all of a yacht's light sails, since such kites are the reply to calm weather, the antidote for slow passages through areas of calm. We would have no motor; we'd need all the cloth we could hang up at times.

There are many, brought up to aero-dynamic manners of yachting days since popularization of the Bermuda rig (improperly called the Marconi rig), who do not hesitate to point out how hopelessly outmoded are *Wander Bird's* fidded top-

Tons of stores come aboard and—

masts, her gaff-headed sails, her iron rigging. Without engaging in pointless controversy with them I'd like to make one point, irrefutable, in favor of the gaff rig. I'd like them also to remember that my eyes and thoughts were always on waters where they will never go.

Some day designers *may* make their Bermuda masts and sails as trustworthy and as accident-proof as the gaff rig. But the new rig can never have the centuries of world-wide testing out of which the gaff rig painfully evolved. No Sound racing, no summer ocean races, no occasional world cruise, no laboratory tests can simulate the tens of thousands of struggling ships and men,

Are checked by the cook and then snugly stowed below.

the countless gales, the gradual, cautious experiments of our grandfathers and their forefathers. Where I was going I *must know* my gear; where it was a matter of life and death we could not brook a doubt. Here are Achievement and Record, demonstrated Practice against Theory, and the gaff wins every time on wild blue water.

Just because something is new that which is tried and old is not necessarily bad. Iron rigging, well stretched, is still the most enduring rigging there is and it is not subject to unforeseeable changes in quality which still afflict the alloys of the present-day metallurgists.

But we must defer such technical details to an end chapter where they won't bore those whom they little concern.

Wander Bird, stripped, soiled, bruised superficially, cost me $1,500.00. (Her copper fastenings and sheathing cost $6,000.00 alone in 1879!) Before we got her away from the shipyard she had cost $15,000. Eight years of voyaging—always with the Horn looming nearer—and the wear and tear incident to hard driving passages, the mistakes made and rectified, the experiments successful and unsuccessful which we tried, all these things must have taken another $40,000. Where did it come from?

I still owe friends almost all of that first $15,000. It was generously and readily lent in those affluent days of 1928 and 1929. It was lent to make possible an idea which, by producing those many other dollars and bringing the ship through the depression, proved it was no wild fantasy.

Everywhere about us men and women, for a multitude of

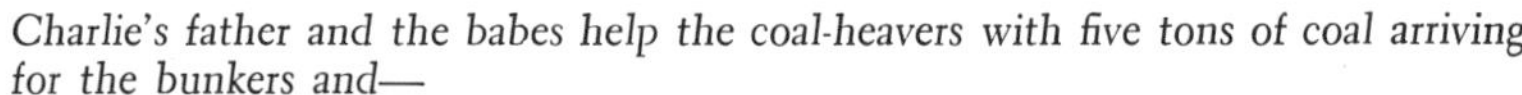

Charlie's father and the babes help the coal-heavers with five tons of coal arriving for the bunkers and—

William and Charlie discover urgent work aloft bending the squaresail.

reasons, are yearning for the sea and its romance and color. The sea of the sailing ship of which they dream is now but a dream. It occurred to me that possibly a man who could supply in himself leadership, organizing ability and sea experience, a man who could provide the right ship—such a man might rally about him enthusiasts who would work the ship and pay her expenses too.

This was no novel thought. There is a pathetically long and growing list of similar ventures which have failed dismally. Their promoters did not have friends the caliber of mine; some were so foolish as to seek money by this means (it is so easily made, too, on paper!) and almost all of them lacked experience in an effort demanding a thousand answers to as many problems.

Oh! All you bright-eyed romantic dreamers who read this! Do not lightly follow my example, glamorous as it probably seems to you! Possessed of all the courage you may have, all the determination, all the fervor, even so, how can sheer good fortune such as mine possibly be yours? Mine gave me not only staunch friends but a thousand incredible, essential coincidences! Would Lady Luck again be so open-handed?

A medal commemorating our voyages must have a reverse which is a grim picture of financial difficulties. Months and years of great uncertainty, anxiety and worry would be shown. The devil of Self-Doubt would be there, constantly indicating the beauty of a regular pay check and the enviable calm of those whose working day stops with a whistle. Had we foreseen these days and fears and struggles in some crystal before we were committed to our venture we should never have embarked on it. Had I alone faced the impacts I must have been worn and discouraged long ago. My wife's unflagging and quiet faith and her growing delight in a truly rich and adventurous life kept me going ahead many times when another single step forward seemed impossible.

Wander Bird, flying our flags, has made thirteen North Atlantic passages. She has been deep into the Mediterranean. Twice she has sailed the length and breadth of the Baltic. She has traversed our eastern seaboard from Florida to Labrador and been sighted at most of the West India islands. Her criss-cross tracks in the North Sea and English Channel defy plotting on any but a large-scale chart. Diamond Head and the volcanoes of Hawaii have looked down upon her and the shadow of Rio's Sugar Loaf has fallen across her deck. Dream come true, her crowning achievement, is the zig-zag track around Cape Horn.

Three hundred men and boys and half-a-dozen adventurous

The forward end of the main cabin, looking into the forecastle and galley. The curtained recesses are built-in bunks which the pilots used and there are fourteen of them in this cabin. The table is so suspended and counterweighted that its top is free to swing and thus maintain its level at sea. Only in very heavy going are the down-folded strips along its edges raised to catch sliding dishes. Colorful individual drinking mugs salvaged from Gloucester's old barber shops gleam under the skylight. Stores are kept under the long benches running the length of the cabin on both sides and under the bunks as well. The water tanks are under the flooring shown, and a corner of the medicine chest is visible under the table and behind the door. The ship's limited but excellent library is darkly seen against the bulkhead.

women supplied the cash and the muscle. To critics who sometimes say I have lived selfishly and pointlessly I refer these sailormen and sailorwomen of *Wander Bird*. Neither the ship nor her master has failed entirely if it be worth while to broaden perspectives, cultivate latent abilities, endow human beings with confidence and courage and make them more appreciative of the simple and beautiful things about us.

Now, to support extreme but well-considered claims for the ship, examine but briefly the highlights of her history these last nine years.

The stupidity of a Belgian tugboat skipper once broke the leg of one of my boys. That has been our only injury. Seasickness has been the only illness aboard. No hungry sea has ever claimed one of us.

In 1935 *Wander Bird* sailed in 16 days 21 hours from Gloucester to Pentland Firth. This is believed to be the fastest passage ever made by a vessel of one hundred feet or less in length. Her best day's work, made on this cruise, is 246 miles, noon to noon. In nine of those blowy days she covered 1809 miles. Remembering the quality and quantity of Western Ocean competition it is truly a remarkable feat. The ocean racing yachts sail a shorter course (to Plymouth, generally, from Newport) and they take longer. They are smaller, it is true, but opposed to our schoolboy crew (average age eighteen) they present veteran ocean racing men and every known gadget and device which money can buy to make a boat go faster. Also they race from the start; we drove the ship when we got the westerly blow, but until then, five days out of port, we had cruised leisurely.

This same year saw *Wander Bird* triumphant, if not without scars, amidst the historic autumn gales which flogged the North Sea and Channel. England recorded tides three feet higher than ever before as the westerlies piled the Atlantic onto Europe's shores. Shrubbery *sixty miles inland* was damaged by salt spray. The old schooner was out in all those swiftly recurring gales. The North Sea broke her main boom and thrice tore off the battened hatch of the bosun locker (and this when the ship was hove-to!) and uprooted the binnacle. A sea threw some wreckage against the bobstay so violently a new ⅞-inch shackle broke under the shock. It sent a lowering hurricane squall before which the ship drove for six hours at nine knots, carrying only a single storm jib.

A man may live his life out on the ocean and never meet a "chance" sea. If he's lucky he won't. We saw and were smashed by one off the Lizard. The sea hit us on the weather side and exploded, carrying away our stout bulwarks for twenty-three feet. The timber disappeared like smoke. With that injured starboard side to leeward we then drove for the smooth water in the lee of Lizard Point. Those ensuing hours we sailed a ship whose pumps couldn't spew out water as fast as it came in. Here is another story which must be skipped and used only to point out the lesson it taught: that *no* ship and *no* man can withstand the full might of the ocean and its winds.

In 1934 Gwen, my Negro bosun William, a Swede workaway and I were the entire deck force bringing the ship from Stockholm to the Bahamas. Harrison, unequaled seacook, managed meals and helped below to care for our two sea babies. That was a small enough crew, but it was even smaller when the Swede left the ship in Nassau and we had to get her home with the three left. So, with two men and a girl on deck, we sailed in mid-December for ice-bound Boston. That was a pleasant voyage, in all sincerity, thanks to a ship whose consummate ease of handling it so strikingly demonstrated.

We were thirteen days making 1300 miles, many of them

to windward. With watch-tackles and hand winches the bosun and I set almost every sail we had. We set them, took them in, reefed them when necessary and stowed them. We got home in fine health and spirits. It takes a marvelous vessel to treat her people so well!

Wander Bird, to conclude this proud category, has sailed through the notorious Woods Hole. She has beaten through the slender Great Bras d'Or of Cape Breton. She sailed fifty miles to windward in fourteen hours through Stockholm's Skargaard when the boarding pilot opined it was a forty-eight-hour job without the motor he had expected to find aboard. She has picked her way in and out of many crowded harbors. She has never met any ship anywhere near her size she couldn't leave running or reaching. In smooth going only the smartest and sleekest yachts will point appreciably higher on the wind, and when they have been scoured from the sea by rising wind and waves the old pilot boat will still be serenely going ahead about her business. Countless tests have proven that here is a ship which can do everything well and many things so superbly as to challenge comparison.

With every good wish I have made of all these things which went before our arrival at Fifty South only a hasty and incomplete tale, but we must advance now, to meet at the very threshold of the Horn the first of its welcoming gales.

The preceding pages will indicate, I hope without arrogance, that we went to the adventure prepared, equipped and forewarned. We knew that *There Is No Substitute for Experience.* We knew *The Best Gear Is None TOO Good.* We had as much of both experience and gear as we could accumulate.

The ship's eighth annual cruise, in 1936, ended for all but one of my schoolboy crew at Tangier, Morocco. Two new hands, John North and Julian Howell, joined the ship there as did Gwen and the two children.

A Spanish Government destroyer, stripped for the action which subsequently soon destroyed it, was our last contact with a distrait Europe as we sailed for Rio de Janeiro. In Rio we replenished our larder and refilled our water tanks. On October 26, 1936, we sailed out of Rio and into the south, not without tenseness in our hearts and many reinforced anxieties.

Was our ship good enough? Were we?

Cape Horn would soon answer us on both counts!

After years of preparation Wander Bird *leaves Gloucester June 26, 1936, outward bound for San Francisco via way ports.*

II. THE SHIP'S COMPANY

THERE is in America a virtually religious belief that we are an adventurous and sporting people.

It is reasonable to reckon that 300,000 Americans knew, by word of mouth, the whisper of a little advertisement and such occasional newspaper stories as appeared—that *Wander Bird* was to round Cape Horn. They knew the ship had a long and proud record. They knew the advertised cost of a share in the voyage, $1300.00, was no more than many of them would spend if they remained ashore. For this relatively small sum a bold spirit could have had five months crowded with romance, action and adventure.

Thirty of the 300,000 were interested enough to write for particulars.

Three of the 300,000 sailed with the ship. Beside these three we had my brother, my wife and our two children and two professionals—cook and sailor—who had been with me for six years.

Americans like adventure. Regard the gaudy burdened news-stands! Americans like their adventure to meet them on a familiar corner, neatly packaged at a dime a bundle; they embrace it avidly when it is cheap, comfortable, safe and quite vicarious.

It is a pity we didn't find the other two hands we wanted.

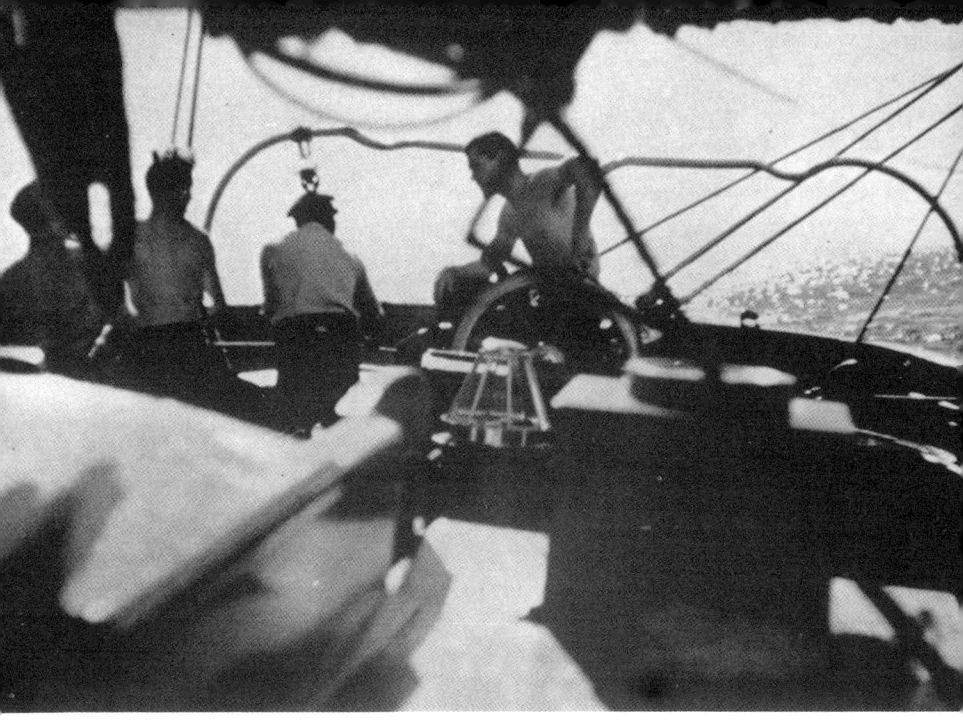

Taking in some mainsheet on an afternoon of pleasant wind and sunshine.

They would have made work lighter down south. With their contributions to the strongbox the voyage would have broken even financially, as I had planned it should.

Much could be written about any ship's company and the necessity of considering it well before putting to sea. On the loyalty, congeniality, courage and willingness of the crew, on its stamina and obedience, depend the safety and happiness of the voyage. In the triumvirate of Master, Ship and Crew the ship's company shares equally in honor and responsibility.

On a ship such as *Wander Bird* obedience is enforced by none of the traditional sanctions provided for naval commanders. *Wander Bird's* sailors make voyages possible with sinews of cash as well as muscle. No system of petty checks or severe punishments is applicable where hurt feelings and bad blood are insupportable. Discipline, nowhere more essential

Gwen B. Tompkins

than at sea, must be effected solely by shared enthusiasm, common understanding of the risks entailed without it, by unremitting subordination of self to the common cause.

These vital things are mentioned briefly in the hope that those who read may better comprehend the sterling quality of the men who worked the ship from Fifty South to Fifty South. They never complained. They never hesitated at an order. In our little oak-walled world, beset by violence, there wasn't a quitter, a shirk or a coward. The achievement of that crew is an enduring monument to the ship's company.

These were *Wander Bird's* people:

1. GWEN BOHNING TOMPKINS: Gwen is a Texan, daughter of a Fort Worth family, graduate in the Class of '27 of Smith College. She didn't like the idea of sailing around Cape Horn. The vicissitudes of 60,000 miles in the *'Bird* had given her keen appreciation of smooth water and gentle breezes. She asserts two things only persuaded her to go: the unhappy

prospect of having to listen for the rest of her life to our salty tales, and a housewifely desire to keep her eye on the ship's silverware, china and other treasures. Actually Gwen is more vital to this ship than its very spars. Her great tact, patience, good humor and courage (and she's not undecorative, either!) vastly altered this cruise for the better.

Good helmsman, best of shipmates, I'm glad we met that long ago day in Paris!

2. ALBERT HARRISON, Cook: Rubies and precious stones abound compared to honest, able and cheerful seacooks. It is pleasant to pay tribute here to this shipmate who has played a major part in so many cruises. Harrison had cooked for the ship five years before we sailed for the Horn. His meals have come punctually to the table. They have been savory, steaming hot and splendidly varied regardless of the weather. His galley at times is a hideous, bouncing hell. To see him then lashing pots to the stove, propping pans to the crazy heeling angles and taking from the oven perfect golden lemon meringue pies—well, that is to witness at work a stout-hearted, consummate artist. In a pinch Harrison can be a very useful hand

Albert Harrison

William S. Palmer

heaving and hauling on deck. He could be as excellent a seaman as he is a chef.

3. WILLIAM PALMER, Bosun: William carried the weight of forty-one years with tigerish ease. He is a sailorman of the age of sail with but few faults and many great virtues—honesty, patience, cleanliness, pride of craft and fierce love of his ship. He is a teacher of ability who likes nothing better than helping a novice. With little faculty for leadership he is machine-like in the relentless manner he will carry out a superior's order. William had been the ship's careful bosun for six busy years. He knew every inch of her gear. No finer sailorman ever lived before a mast. It is the world's great loss that such men are a breed nearly extinct.

4. JOHN BARR TOMPKINS: Barr sailed to Labrador with *Wander Bird* in 1930. He came back to the schooner in 1936

Dr. John Barr Tompkins

with ink drying on a Ph.D. in Anthropology and his thirtieth birthday just passed. He could have stayed in comfort at home, teaching in the cloisters of some university, doubtless, but because he was terrified at the very thought of our voyage he knew he must go. Reeling mastheads, big winds, big seas, these he feared. Feeling no essential kinship with the sea, lacking great physical ruggedness, Barr came to us in search of self-knowledge and self-confidence. He gained both, and in so doing set an inspiring example of unwearying intelligence and courage. He gave much, and in return the sea steeled his muscles, bred stamina and steadied his soul with the comforting knowledge that it *was* brave.

5. CHARLES VAN SICKLEN: Charlie, nineteen, was ripe for the polishing grind of the voyage. His temper was as burly as his heavy-set stroke-oar's body, as difficult to keep plastered smooth as his unruly curls. Charlie was the one hand among my 1936 summer crew who was allowed to remain with me.

Charles Van Sicklen

By the time we reached Fifty South he was a good hand, better even than I knew, for I had not appreciated how joyously that Dutch pugnacity would blaze at the taunts of Cape Horn. Here is a grand sailorman whether the job is to be done high aloft or head-under on the lancing jibboom. Charlie gets my highest praise for his completely splendid service. In a world shaken by doubts and griefs such boys are bright lights leading one to hope yet again that all is not lost.

6. JOHN NORTH: For twenty years a fine, efficient factory had claimed John's every day. From it pours forth a stream of

bright tools known wherever skilled hands clutch cunningly-shaped steel. John could have taken any holiday money can buy. His Cadillac-Sixteen, his good looks, his Princeton background, Philadelphia social eminence, above all his inspiriting zest for life—these ensure him instant warm welcome anywhere. It is an illuminating measure of the man that he should have joined his lot with ours.

Years of good living had covered his oarsman's muscles generously, but neither they nor success in business had atrophied his imagination or sporting spirit.

It is amusing to recall that he stepped from the finest suite in the *Normandie* to exalted possession of a shelflike six-foot-six bunk in the *'Bird's* main cabin, and that for nearly five months he cheerfully stood his watch, took his turns waiting on table and scrubbing toilets.

John North was a grand shipmate, and higher praise than that for another no sailor can bestow.

John North

Julian Howell

7. JULIAN HOWELL: Julian had never sailed until he left Tangier with us. His bent was mechanical. He spoke with subtle and pleasing good humor in the soft accents of Georgia. Julian was intelligent, kindly always, quick and eager to learn. He soon made a good hand and pulled his full weight. He ran our lighting plant and did countless little odd jobs demanding cleverness of hand and eye.

His life had not been entirely happy; it pleases us who were his shipmates to believe that with us in the closing days of that life he was more content, better understood and better loved than ever before. His heart stopped abruptly only a little while after *Wander Bird* was home. Sleep well, sailorman! Your shipmates will always remember you fondly.

8. ANN TOMPKINS: Ann, six, crossed the Atlantic eight times in *Wander Bird* before she came to Fifty South. To this young lady the fixed world was this vessel, movable and changeable were the shores and ports which she found successively moored to her ship. "Daddy, when will Stockholm tie up to us again?" had been a recent question indicative of her idea of relativity. Cape Horn was nothing to her but just another migrating promontory entertainingly supplied with seals, albatross, and penguins.

Ann assumed the duties of mess-boy as the hard days closed

Ann Tompkins

"Commodore" Warwick M. Tompkins, Jr.

around us. Agilely she ferried dishes between the galley and the cabin in weather when adults were taxed to keep their feet.

9. "Commodore" WARWICK M. TOMPKINS, JR.: "Commodore" is one of those almost pre-natal nicknames which stuck and, thanks to hereditary and environmental influences, proved most suitable for a young man of four, veteran of six Atlantic passages under sail, certified a "Shell-back" by Father Neptune himself.

"Commodore" knows every line on the ship and its function. He can slack away a halliard, lowering a spar or a sail thirty times his weight, as smartly as anyone. Even at four he was a hand, not a passenger.

10. THE OLD MAN.

The Old Man

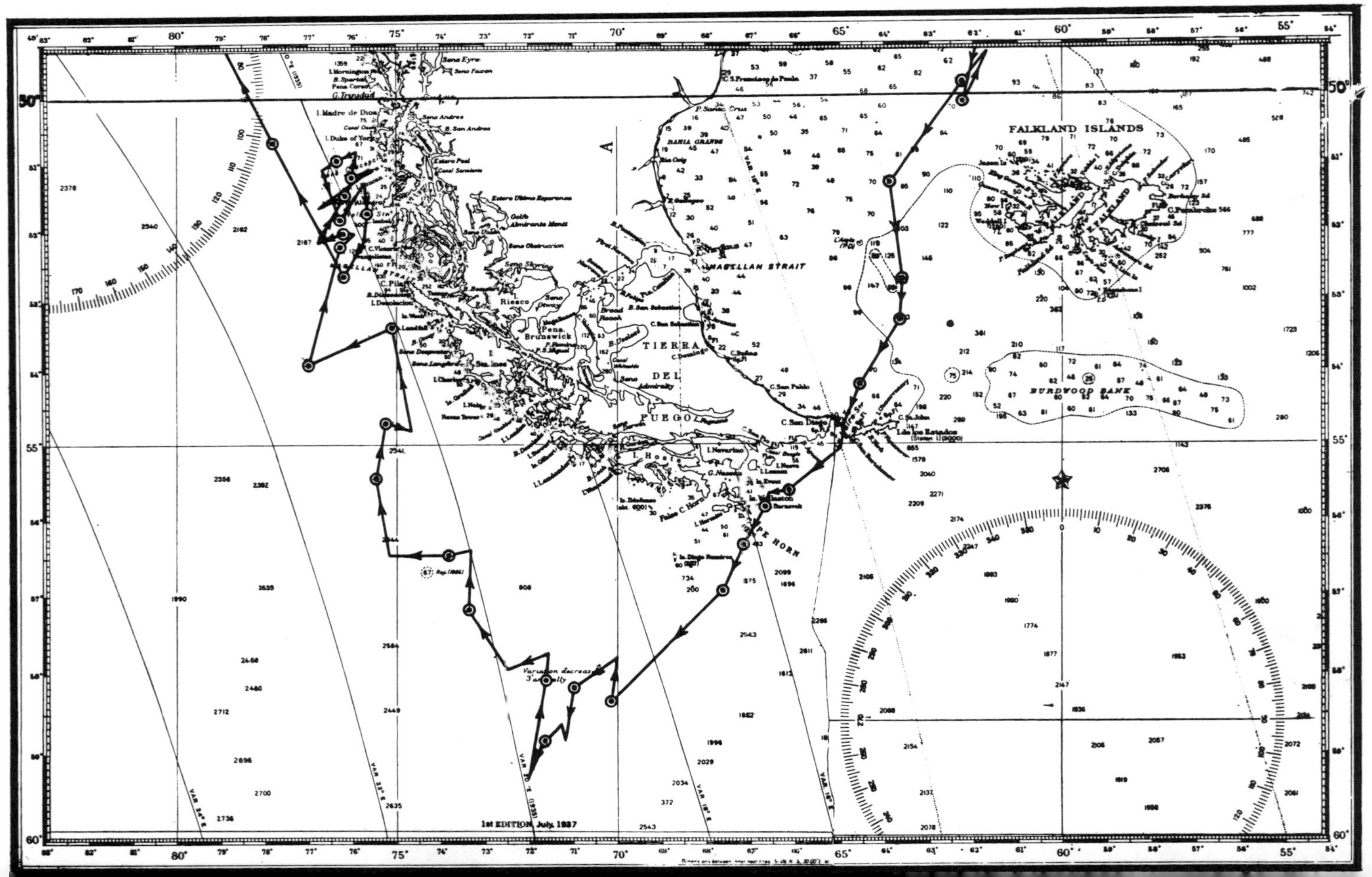
FALKLAND ISLANDS
BURDWOOD BANK
MAGELLAN STRAIT
TIERRA DEL FUEGO
CAPE HORN
BAHIA GRANDE
Riesco
Pena. Brunswick
1st EDITION July 1937

FIFTY SOUTH *To* FIFTY SOUTH

TRACK CHART LEGEND

Circled dots indicate Wander Bird's *noon positions from November 13, 1936—when she was just south of Fifty in the Atlantic—until December 11, 1936, on which date she crossed Fifty South in the Pacific. Where it has been feasible to do so courses sailed from noon to noon have been indicated, but many tacks were so short the plotting of them proved impracticable on a chart of such small scale as this.* Wander Bird's *course covered 2215 miles. The shortest possible distance from Fifty to Fifty is 1000 miles.*

III. THE TWENTY-EIGHT DAYS

BETWEEN Fifty South in the Atlantic and Fifty South in the Pacific, along the shortest possible track, lie one thousand sea miles of ocean. *Once* a lucky ship covered them in a single week. The average passage, mean of thousands, demanded 17.8 days. Many vessels, bruised and beaten by two, three and even four *months* of Horn weather within these boundaries, have ultimately turned east and circumnavigated the world to enter the Pacific.

"From fifty degrees south, east of Cape Horn, to the same parallel west, lies the rub—"

"So it appears that the passage from England to New York (3000 miles) under canvas in winter time is nearly as difficult as the passage around the Horn (1000 miles)." (Parentheses by author.)

Quotations from *Findlay's South Atlantic Directory*, Fifth Edition, Published 1867, Pages 149-150.

"From my experience of winds and weather during the opposite season (summer) at Port Famine I preferred the winter passage (of Cape Horn)—easterly and northerly winds prevail in the winter off the Cape whilst southerly and westerly winds are constant during summer months; and not only are the winds more favorable in winter but they are moderate in comparison to the fury of the summer gales."

Capt. Robert Fitzroy, R.N.

"Indeed our sufferings, short as has been our passage, have been so great I would advise those bound into the Pacific never to attempt the passage of Cape Horn if they could get there by any other route."

CAPT. DAVID PORTER, U. S. Frigate *Essex*. 1814.

"August, September and October are the coldest months at Cape Horn. Westerly winds, rain, snow, hail and cold weather then prevail. December, January and February are the warmest months; the days then are long and there is some fine weather, but westerly winds, which often increase to very hard gales, with much rain, are frequent even throughout this season which carries with it less of summer than in almost any part of the globe."

South Atlantic Pilot by CAPTS. KING and FITZROY. Page 154, Fifth Edition, 1860.

"In the winters of Cape Horn and its vicinity wind, accompanied with rain, sleet, snow or hail, is the prevailing characteristic. The humidity is excessive for, besides that arising from the vast expanse of ocean by which it is surrounded, rain, more or less, falls every night. The rain is so violent and incessant that one might suppose the waters of the firmament were falling in the shape of a second deluge."

Findlay's South Atlantic Directory. Page 77, Fifth Edition, 1867.

In the old days, before the hot ditch provided easy escape, when the Horn was a brooding antagonist on the sailing routes, men gave the best years of their lives to the study of its moods and villainies. I quote from their superb writings which remain as true today as when set down by scratching quills. What is a fleeting century to the Horn's winds, snows, rains and seas? Will man's sly evasion sober their rages?

From Fifty South to Fifty South, *EAST to WEST*; these are the old, established boundaries of a Horn passage. There are those today who would capitalize on a name and legend of iron. Generally as passengers these scriveners blow into the Atlantic from the Great Southern Ocean and their ships are scarcely docked before the world is apprised of the suffering of these pseudo Cape Horners.

Turn again to Findlay's yellowed pages and see what the great Fitzroy has to say about the west-to-east passage:

> "The summer months, December and January, are the best for making a passage from the Pacific to the Atlantic, although *that passage is so short and so easy that it hardly requires the choice of time.*" (Italics mine.)

These quotations, which could be augmented a hundredfold, bear out the assertion that the Horn presents a truly diabolical problem to the seaman. Some like it best—or, rather, fear it least—in the dark of winter when there are fair winds at times, fair winds offset by long nights and the menace of bergs. Others think the violent summer gales preferable, since they blow through long days and over an ocean barren of ice.

But, in very truth, it is a desolate, lonely, hard corner. Winter or summer there is little to recommend it.

The currents, seas and winds of Cape Horn contested *Wander Bird's* way for twenty-eight long days. To win the thousand coveted miles she sailed 2215.

The story is told in precise detail in her battered and stained log where the very paper is salty with oilskin drip. Logs, alas, are all too terse, matter-of-fact and difficult reading for the layman. Here, then, is an effort to dramatize, honestly and legitimately, the story of those days. It is not an easy task. Stowing a flogging jib in one gale is very much like stowing it in another. For all their true variety both big winds and seas cannot command widely differing descriptions.

My desire is to impart the feeling, the sense of struggle, the omnipresent burden of loneliness and uproar rather than each single maneuver where so many were repetitious.

Gibberish though it probably sounds to landsmen, the sailor's language is one of the most beautifully precise and meaningful of tongues. Circumlocutions are fatal to a sea story. If you do not know the sea words and wish to read with comprehension, reference to the glossary is urged.

In the following pages courses sailed, directions of the winds and bearings are TRUE. In the transcribed log at the end of the book all courses, directions and bearings are MAGNETIC.

FRIDAY, November 13, 1936.

Cape Horn welcomes us with a gale. Its first puff, with ambassadorial chill and might, springs from the southwest when the day is not ten minutes old. The mid-watch is given over to shortening down. Before breakfast the ship is sailing herself, helm lashed, under foresail and headsail.

The brave west winds from the Argentine send the ship south, but the next day—

she lies idle on a vast mirror which imperceptibly melts into the sky.

Well, we are ready! The maintopsail was sent down yesterday. The skylights are dogged and their covers battened into place. A high storm-sill guards the main companionway. Reefing gear is to hand. Oil and oil bags are convenient in the wheel-box.

The ship slashes boldly ahead. Now that we are actually in Horn territory the crew shakes off uncertainty and tenseness, proving yet again that it *is* waiting for the unknown which men fear most. We are heartened by the grand ship under us.

Before noon we cross Fifty South; the noon sight establishes us five miles within the frontier of the Cape. It is a day of vivid color. The hard sky is so blue it hurts the eyes and fairly drowns the high, piled ocean with indigo. Compact white clouds, rolled tight by the flowing wind, fly past seeming scarcely to clear the maned seas and our reeling trucks.

Noon Position: 50°—05′ S., 62°—14′ W.
1000 Miles to go to 50° South in the Pacific.

At three o'clock we abandon the struggle. The ship never complains but she is thrusting her jibboom through the tumbling crests and the jibs are escaping their lashings. The whine of the wind, too, is increasing and the storm is plainly working to a higher pitch.

We run off, dead to leeward, while Charlie relashes the jibs. They are board-stiff, tormented by wind, hard indeed to handle, and his task is made more difficult by the hampering weight of heavy clothing and oilskins.

The schooner flies. Her speed planing down the seas is breath-taking. The horizon is alternately a saw-edged line distant a dozen miles and then, as we lie relatively becalmed in a spume-paved trough, only a ship-length away.

We run yet another mile, hunting a smooth where we can quickly bring the ship a-gybing onto the safe port tack. It won't do to broach-to in the path of one of these breaking seas. Their charge is merciless and irresistible.

Now, hove-to under a reefed foresail, the ship heads north-west-by-west, six points from the wind. There is real threat in these seas. The crests are breaking four feet deep. The wind picks up one dollop and tosses it aboard, a free sample. It slaps ponderous John across the shoulders and lifts him lightly as a feather right across the deck.

We break out the storm oil, surely cheapest and most potent of elixirs. It is the dregs of cod-liver vats in Gloucester. Viscous, brownish as morning-taste after a wild party, it stinks to the heavens. We pour a quart into each of three small canvas bags and hang these over the weather side. The effect is immediate and astonishing.

This is indeed a fragile, shimmering and iridescent buckler to raise against giant seas! But look! Now the seas break with their clamorous WHOOOSH under our bowsprit, pass with venomous S-S-S-RRRAAAH under the counter, but no longer do they assault our side. Miraculously shielded the ship lies safe and snug. The deck dries spottily.

At dusk lights are hung in the rigging. A lookout makes frequent rounds, noting wind, sea and gear. A small tear is found at the clew cringle of the foresail. Evidently the clew lashing wasn't hauled tight enough when we reefed—and this may cause trouble. We watch this anxiously. It grows no larger. The sail is safe apparently as long as the strain remains constant.

"Have you seen the barograph lately?" someone shouts in a peculiarly inflected voice.

"No, what's it doing?"

"You'd better look yourself. S'elp me Gawd, I'd say the thing is running backward!"

"What? How can a clock run backward!"

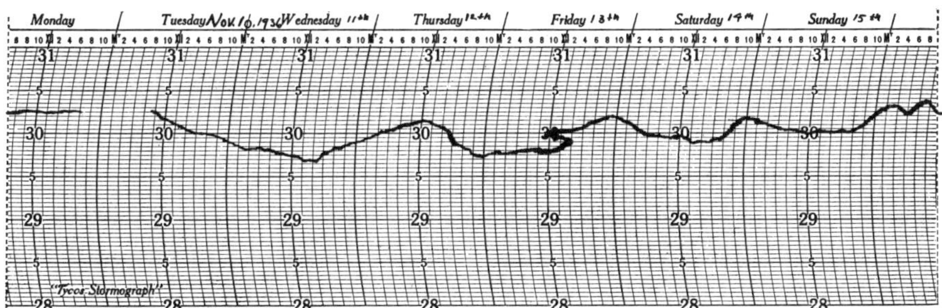

"Offhand I'd say it couldn't, but just take a look yourself!"

Dammit! The barograph *is* in reverse, too! For six years the instrument has plodded phlegmatically along from day to day. Now, possessed of incomprehensible frenzies, it is headed back for Thursday. Well, if the gale is enough to scare a thing of brass and steel into utter rout we have done well indeed to heave-to!

Perplexity is heaped upon perplexity as Friday marches further and further away from the barograph's retreating pen. Precisely at the hour when we notice the gale is moderating the seemingly sentient instrument faces about with new courage and resumes its accustomed direction.

For two weeks we shall remain mystified, certain only that we have the finest heavy-weather story ever born of a Horn dusting. On November 29th, however, the barograph will again go on such a jag that we shall investigate its innards, discovering the worn and loose spindle which henceforth invalidates its attempts at marking time. Ah, well! Who'd otherwise have believed even the documentary evidence of this astounding aberration? Nevertheless, it has the makings of a gorgeous sea legend, one so monstrous it deserved perpetuation.

Raffee and squaresail drawing nicely as the ship stands south through fluky autumnal northeast trade winds.

The ship quiets for the night. Below decks she is dry, snug, serene. The night penetrates only as a lulling, sustained roar dampened to a musical monotone. The babes, all unconcerned, tumble into their bunks. The crew, mindful of a tiring day passed, roll happily into blankets and peaceful dreams.

I read about the nearby Falklands and ponder the grisly and effective hoax played on Von Spee who sleeps with his sailors in these very waters. Hereabouts the German squadron (which escaped from the Orient in 1914) was finally found and sunk. Few know the story of that finding.

The British Admiralty was in possession of the German naval codes almost from the outbreak of the War. After the battle of Coronel, when Von Spee sank a weak British squadron off the Chilean coast, the British knew he would round the Horn to harass vital Atlantic commerce. They knew, too, he would have to get coal, and that Port Stanley in the Falklands would be the best place to get it.

So Von Spee received radioed orders to proceed direct to Stanley.

As his ships approached the islands they were sighted by an old woman. She hiked up her petticoats and slithered into Stanley, carrying the alarm to the British fleet sent there by the Admiralty.

Von Spee had not the slightest inkling of the presence of the British, just as he was never to know that his seemingly bona fide orders had issued from Whitehall and not the Wilhelmstrasse. He steamed past the blanketing headlands and suddenly opened Stanley harbor. He was virtually within that commodious port before the grim gray shapes of the enemy were visible against the gloomy background of the hills.

News of the Germans' approach brought near-pandemonium

Sometimes the variable winds were not only light but from ahead. In going like this no one complained very much, however.

to the British. Von Spee was days earlier than he'd been expected. After a race the length of both Atlantics the British were coaling. Barges were alongside, crews up to their ears in grime, and weary. Battle stations were all secured. Anchors were down.

"Clear for action" bugles were still shrilling when the *Scharnhorst* and the *Gneisenau*, with their weaker consorts, stood in, and discovered the trap.

While Sturdee's ships frantically slipped their cables, cast colliers adrift and got underway, Von Spee chose to make a disastrous tactical blunder, little realizing his foe's unreadiness.

The British ships were bigger, faster, more heavily armored and armed than his; Von Spee realized this the moment he sighted them. Had he taken advantage of their disarray the battle of the Falklands would be a vastly different story. At point-blank range his guns would have played with deadly

Crystal sea and porpoises

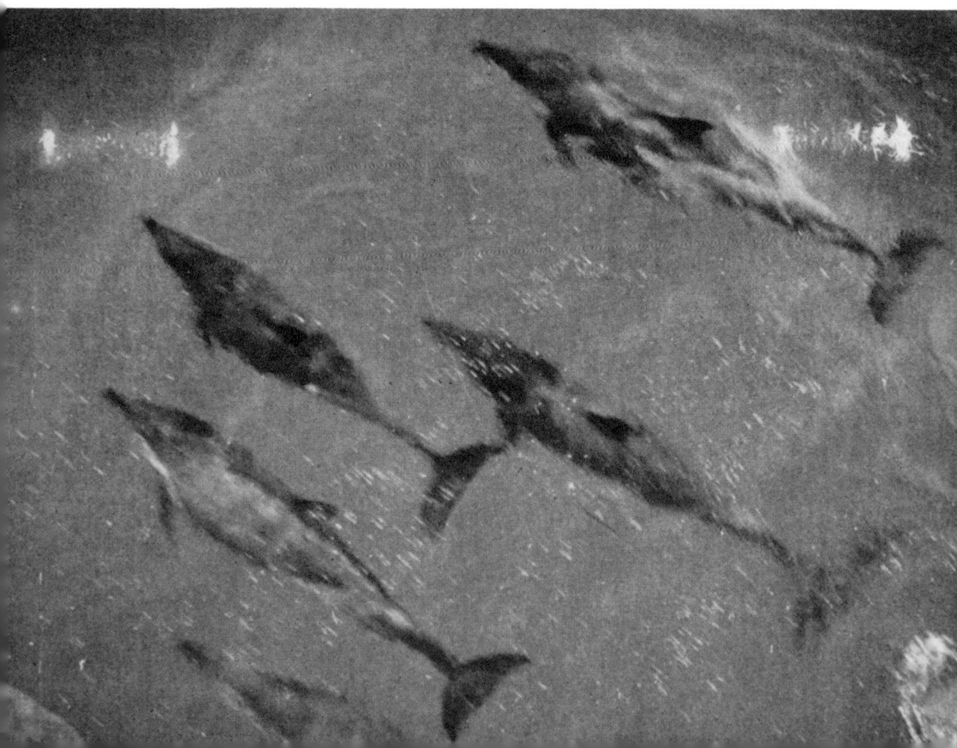

effect. His ships could have shot, rammed and slashed in ship-to-ship, old-style warfare. Quite possibly such an attack would have destroyed every British man-o'-war and left Von Spee stunningly supreme.

Von Spee chose to run. Running he was easy prey for the now reorganized enemy. The British took full advantage of superior speed and power. They fought according to the unsporting catechism of modern naval war, remaining comfortably beyond range of the enemy, and from there calmly pounding him to junk. Von Spee and all but one of his ships went to the bottom.

The weather is moderating at eight bells, but the sea still runs so heavy that there is no question of getting underway before morning. The relieving lookout comes sleepy-eyed to welcome in

SATURDAY, November 14.

The wind has worked to the westward and throughout the early morning hours the sea has smoothed out. The white crests are gone altogether at five when we are up making sail. All have profited from a comfortable rest and refreshed spirits are indicated by the cheery shouts with which the jibtopsail goes aloft.

The westerly, very gentle at first as it cross-ruffles the long and lazy storm rollers, soon strengthens. The sky is overcast and there is a feeling of snow in the air. The pump sucks air and suds out of the bilge in four short minutes. The old ship is tight as a bottle.

At a smooth seven knots we drive for the Straits of Le Maire. Our position is uncertain, although a morning sight indicates we are considerably east of our reckoning. This is not surprising when we study the pilot chart. Doubtless we are feeling the current which sweeps northeastward around the Horn, making a huge eddy whose rim washes the Falklands.

For days we have sought the protection of Argentina. In the lee of the plains we would probably have far less current, certainly far fewer gales. But the winds have remained fixed in the west, thwarting us constantly. This latest blow very nearly left us no alternative but to go to the eastward of the Falklands. Just off the coast the gale percentage is seven; out here it is fifteen. Out here the current sets northeast at from five to twenty miles a day.

Noon Position: 49°—45′ S., 62°—13′ W.
To 50° South in the Pacific: 1045 Miles.
Made Good (Noon to Noon): Minus 20 Miles. Distance Sailed by Log: 34¾ Miles.

The sun, a worn, thin dime, shows fleetingly near the meridian, and computation shows for the day a loss of twenty miles. We are again at the threshold of Cape Horn, in latitude 49°—45′ S. Our storm drift was fifty-one miles dead to leeward. The current robbed us of what westing we'd normally make.

This morning we sight a northbound steamer, obviously one of the infrequent links between the Falklands and Buenos Aires. She passes within a mile and gives not the slightest indication she has even seen us. This snub hurts; a sign of comradeship would have been heart-warming in a bleak world. In the old days there was a brotherly feeling among seamen. Passing sailing ships invariably spoke one another. Often their commanders hove-to long enough to dine together while the crews fraternized and exchanged letters for posting. Do so many little ships dot this chill sea that the modern sailorman can't afford even the dip of a flag, the wave of a cap to a passing vessel?

Gliding ship and lifting sails—A study in effortless progress from the end of the main boom.

It is tinglingly cool this afternoon, 49° Fahrenheit in the shade, and under a suitably gray and forbidding sky we again cross the fiftieth parallel. Giant albatross convoy us, soaring tirelessly on our eddies, hanging at times within arm's reach and turning on us the jeweled glare of their alert eyes. On a signal, invisible to us, they slip sideways into a far sortie, dipping into sea valleys and rising just enough to let the marching seas clear their soft bellies. What superb poetry of motion!

The sun breaks through grandly at sunset, glinting on what appear to be vast clumps of oddly flapping sea weed. It is not kelp, just flippers and weaving heads of vast seal herds. They turn soft curious glances on us, but little disturbed by our intrusion.

Before midnight the wind has gone to the southward and we have tacked to gain coveted westing. We wish no glimpse of the Falklands. It is gloriously clear with the merest breath of a breeze, a pleasant contrast to last night.

Sunset Calm—Much such weather was encountered between Rio and Fifty South, and the passage was consequently disappointingly slow.

SUNDAY, November 15.

Out of this night's fickle zephyrs we finally get a wind which works from south to southwest and after breakfast necessitates a single reef in the mainsail. The day is clear and cold. Since it will probably be no finer we get the foresail down for repairs. The reef-cringle and the encircled bolt rope are tearing from the tabling. Punching a needle through the many layers of number two canvas is difficult, but the rip is eventually herring-boned together. To reinforce it we cut a slot in a new piece of heavy cloth and sew around it as though it were a buttonhole. The cringle is now slipped through the hole and the cloth strongly sewn onto the sail on both sides. It makes a strong-looking job.

Noon Position: 51°—11′ S., 63°—55′ W.
To 50° South in the Pacific: 911 Miles.
Made Good: 89 Miles. Sailed by Log: 126 Miles.

The foresail is now reefed and reset to a breeze too strong for the jibtopsail, which is accordingly stowed.

It starts to blow this evening. Alternately the world is dark and bright. The flamboyant sun sinks, wavers and dies as the reinforced westerly pipes up from a cloud cape flung over our mastheads.

The *'Bird* is dressed snugly; she can stand a lot of wind reefed this way, and she is going places like a champion. The sea is big and sharp, close-coupled, but we log eight knots and at that speed should swiftly run into the clear area we can plainly see just to the southward.

The night watch is John's and mine. With eyes fixed on the stars and blue of that luring sky we keep the schooner flying. Jagged seas slap us and spray flies green and red past the running lights, but what care we for spray! Our watch ends as the ship emerges from under the dark and lowering cloud. It is

Friday, Nov. 13, 1936, Wander Bird approaches Fifty South in the Atlantic. Under gray skies and over a gray sea she drives in the face of a mounting wind soon to be a hard gale.

blowing a full gale. The ocean challenges the firmament with its own fiery phosphorescent constellations and tailed meteors.

Charlie takes over. Gwen stands his watch with him since some upset has made Barr miserable this day and he needs rest and warmth.

Salt and weariness smart in my eyes as Gwen, concern in her face, joins me at the high-thrown windward rail. "Hadn't we better heave-to?" she asks. Ah, dear Gwen! Always ready to heave-to! Can't you see that the sky is clearing, that we've left the squall astern? Would you stop the careering ship now when she's eating the miles with racer speed?

"No, we'll carry on," I decide. "Call me if it gets worse. I don't think it will, but I'll turn in all-standing just in case."

So the ship lunges ahead. The paired musical bells welcome

MONDAY, November 16.

The Old Man is tired. The clear sky above banishes concern. The peace of the ship below is a lulling embrace. Where are those who cry out against sleep, labeling it sloth, waste, idleness? Have they ever wedged themselves into a narrow sea-berth, drawn warm blankets over their ears and fallen drug-deep into a sailor's slumbers? As warmth creeps over relaxing muscles I hear unconcernedly the crash of solid water overhead. Something in the cabin gets adrift and slides noisily to leeward. Still blowing hard, but it will certainly ease soon.

How ineffably luxurious to be out of wind and spray! How fine to know that every line, shackle, plank, bolt, knee and block is fit for this testing!

I am deeply asleep. The unresting part of my mind will recall forever the delicious warmth of these moments. It traitorously ignores the increasingly heavy and more frequent crashes of solid water on deck. It does not register as the ship is crushed farther and farther to leeward.

Friday, Nov. 13, 1936: immediately after crossing Fifty South in the Atlantic Wander Bird encountered the first severe gale and was driven far north again. The seas attained an estimated height of 50 feet and a length of 1/3 mile. Here the ship is running off before a typical monster while—

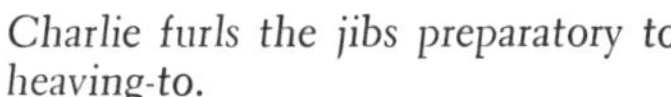

Charlie furls the jibs preparatory to heaving-to.

The ship runs dry with John at the wheel and Gwen looking apprehensively astern at a big fellow which—

hisses and roars menacingly as it bears high above us.

"I think you'd better come on deck—blowing terribly hard—too much water on deck—better heave-to—" Dimly I grow aware of Gwen's voice jerkily summoning me back to consciousness. Oh, dearly beloved but overly-cautious wife! Couldn't you let me sleep? Struggling resentfully from the depths I suppress my irritation. I am a ship master and have forfeited all right to unbroken rest.

"How does the weather look?" I ask, subduing annoyance.

"Very clear, the same," the soft voice replies. The hand on my shoulder is cold and wet. "But I think it is blowing much harder than it was."

I should get up at once, climb into boots, cast aside these seducing blankets and take the deck. Instead I lie wide-eyed in inky blackness, listening, wishfully thinking and rationalizing. The ship is sailing hard; but then she can. The sky is clear; this can't be more than just another hard dry squall. Gwen is too easily scared by a capful of wind.

The ship quivers to a shock. Flung spray drums on the mainsail. It's not the first time tonight that has happened by any means.

"It sounds no worse than before," I comfort the disturber. "We've got to drive hard to get away from here, honey. Make up your mind to that. Keep her going. This will blow out soon, surely!"

Gwen leaves, silently eloquent of disapproval. She gropes up the steep companionway and I can tell from her footfalls that she is having a struggle to get aft. Charlie howls a question; her reply is snatched away by the wind.

Sinking toward sleep again I irritably wish the girl wouldn't frighten so easily. It seems that whenever the ship really gets going she is clamoring to take in sail or to heave-to.

A chiding devil fixes me accusingly. "You stubborn, damned fool! Here you are carrying on again simply because *she* has affronted you by suggesting you do what you know damned well you should do! Oh, yes, I'll admit *you* are the Master, and, yes, there can't be two on any ship, but just the same, you know it's blowing like hell. Don't let silly male resentment at a girl's criticism lead you altogether into folly!"

And I cannot regain my treasured oblivion, deep though I snuggle under the blankets. My head seems as big, dark and strange as a vast cavern, peopled with ethereal fantastic shapes. Deep affection for Gwen wrestles with irritation at her interference. Recollections of many times when she has been right and I quite wrong people the darkness, mingling with perturbed semi-awareness of increasing turmoil above.

"YOU MUST COME! CHARLIE CAN'T HOLD HER LONGER!" This is no accusing phantasy shaking me and shouting alarums. It is Gwen back again to rout the half-conscious and bring me sharply to my senses. She speaks, pleadingly, "Come! Please, quickly, darling! I'm frightened!" Sharp are the spears of self-reproach. Fool! Fool! You've shirked your responsibility! Get out of this mess now, if you can! I am not pleasant company for myself as I thrust into the boots. The ship is limping, tripping and staggering. The lift and mastery are gone out of her.

"Call all hands," I assent.

No one has been sleeping very soundly. The lights snap on and swaying, balancing figures are climbing into oilers as I heave up the companion and out into the wild night.

How these stars blaze! Each appears conventionally star-shaped, and their criss-crossed needle points filigree the bottomless blue of the heavenly dome. The sea to weather is hidden momentarily by the high-lifted bulwarks, but a solid white smother to leeward has engulfed the lee rail.

"Down mainsail! Down jibs!"

The sea is leaping so erratically and unpredictably, its ranks are so close-packed, sharp and thin that it resembles nothing

Oil on troubled waters—Barr rigs the bow oil-bag.

The slick already formed by bow and midships bags is very apparent as he heaves third bag over from the quarter.

Sea is breaking very heavily everywhere but immediately to windward of the ship where oil has spread.

Note appearance of water under the oil and contrast it with the spray-covered ocean elsewhere. Barr contemplates his work with satisfaction.

so much as the up-jabbing, scalloped paper seas in the long windows of cash registers.

Charlie is in the lee main rigging, getting down the throat halliard which is lashed there. The scuppers and freeing-ports beneath him snarlingly free the decks as the *'Bird* rights herself and swings off before the gale. Her acceleration sensibly reduces the apparent wind. It will be but a moment now and the big sail will be stowed. John, William and even Barr—for all hands this time *means ALL*—winch in the main sheet, securing the boom on the gallows.

"HOLD TIGHT!" Gwen's scream rings sharp. Towering on our quarter is the poised menace of a great sea. It strikes the next second, a foul dirty blow sweeping up from below. The ship's stern is thrown high and, all unready, she crashes heavily far to port. The ocean floods aboard. Half the deck is under solid, rushing water. The three at the winch fight for their footing, the water waist-deep about them. Charlie, caught off-balance and burdened with the heavy halliard, is gone! "Charlie!" If he is over-side he is gone past all help of ours!

Seconds are long. No head appears in the streaming wake. The trio on the main sheet is still there, safe. The ship staggers up. The freeing-ports vomit.

"Charlie! CHARLIE!"

A strangled cough replies, how sweetly! Charlie, fouled by the halliard, drags himself from the gulping clutch of the main freeing-port. Breathless and shaken he is—this has been a close and desperate moment—but unhurt. "Give me a hand capturing this halliard!" he roars, rage in his voice. "Let's get this damned sail in, quick!"

It is hard work, and wet, but we get the sails in, mainsail and jibs. Under jumbo and reefed foresail the ship makes better than three knots untended. Below we get into dry clothes and gulp hot chocolate. The thermometer is down now to 43 and still slipping.

Noon Position: 52°—40′ S., 63°—37′ W.
To 50° South in the Pacific: 835 Miles.
Made Good: 83 Miles. Sailed by Log: 96 Miles.

From this night forward in heavy weather we stow both the main halliards amidships, lashed at the base of the mast and not in the rigging, and we nail guards across the yawning mouths of the freeing-ports. The wise sailor doesn't wait for the sea to reiterate a lesson.

We are just east of the Straits of Magellan now, and it is understandable, the appeal of their smooth landlocked waters, even if their navigation is complicated almost unbearably by tides, down-sweeping mountain squalls and tortuous channels. We could get through the Straits, in time, but it would be a desperately hard voyage and one actually far more hazardous—for the ship—than the Horn road.

By six o'clock we can no longer carry the jumbo and the seas are simply deadly. The ship faces saucily up into the gale, once more riding behind her oil slick. This wind is southerly, right from the Straits of Le Maire. We hope it soon blows out.

We begin to realize now, too, why sailors regard the albatross with such reverence. The first explorers down here doubtless killed the first of the great birds they saw and were seemingly punished for it by gales of such suddenness and fury as they had never known. Cause and effect, obviously!

About eight o'clock the glass rises sharply and the wind drops, but it is late afternoon before we can again get going. The wind is now southwest, fading so fast that we only slat and bang about when sail is made, making no miles in any direction. The night watch, idle, records a half-mile run, notes in capitals that there is "NO BREEZE ON OCEAN. ALL'S WELL," and it is

TUESDAY, November 17.

These days certainly do not lack variety. This one starts and ends in complete calm having afforded us meanwhile clear skies quickly overcast and dripping. Only the gentlest of westerly breezes have materialized. The glass falls with speed for some hours, levels and then rises precipitately, but nothing untoward happens. The electric bilge pump clogs and is dismantled. Equipped with a crude but efficient strainer it again settles down with a contented purr to spewing out what little water is in the bilge. Our progress south, west, east, up and down nets us a gain of only thirty-six miles, noon to noon.

Noon Position: 53°—16′ S., 63°—38′ W.
To 50° South in the Pacific: 799 Miles.
Made Good: 36 Miles. Sailed by Log: 29¾ Miles.

WEDNESDAY, November 18.

No more peaceful day was ever seen hereabouts. During the night we make some smooth miles with a gentle, fair wind through hours vocal with the barking of seals. At daylight, four o'clock, the peaks of Staten Island are faintly blue, sharply clear in the south. The fisherman is up long before breakfast, but neither it nor the whole mainsail suffice to move the ship. Even the shining folds of the ballooner hang limp.

At noon the sun strikes directly on the thermometer which has registered 54 degrees in the shade. It now climbs to an astounding 90 degrees and the helmsman sprawled atop the wheelbox divests himself of everything the law allows.

We are but thirty-four miles from the Straits of Le Maire. The flat-topped, long slope of the Tierra del Fuego highlands drops out of the west towards Staten Island.

Noon Position: 54°—10′ S., 64°—28′ W.
To 50° South in the Pacific: 729 Miles.
Made Good: 63 Miles. Sailed by Log: 70¾ Miles.

Fair wind in the dog-watch—The sun breaks through to silver a swell left by the Falkland gale and for a moment Wander Bird *again makes her course with sheets eased and wind free.*

No stratagems of ours effectively snare the tantalizing catspaws rippling the mirror on which we float. The ship lies inert, swinging slowly to the behest of the current, and we forsake the deck for a luncheon all together.

This afternoon we crudely determine the approximate depth into which we can see. An enameled plate is down 175 feet on a fishline before its last faint glimmer is perceptible.

Out of these pellucid depths rises the lazy bulk of a big shark. According to our tastes we rush for harpoons or cameras. The cameras click and whirr, a harpoon strikes home and the shark is convulsed. He gets away, away from a parted line, but the cameras have him. He is gone, and the hiding ocean obliterates the rusty-brown, smoky trail of blood which pollutes the royal blue. We little reckon, nor can his dull brain possibly foreshadow, what fame is to be his!

A year from this day formally-dressed people will be attending previews of Samuel Goldwyn's *Hurricane*. Millions will

Guns aren't dangerous if you know how to use them. Ann watches "Commodore" at the target practice which is part of their unusual education.

"Commodore" checks on his mother's steering.

then see this ill-fated, nameless actor of the deep South Atlantic. For thirty seconds, in all his sinuous, cruel, honest beauty and menace, he will monopolize the glittering screens. Sharply intaken breaths and a sweeping murmur of amazement will be his tribute.

The night watch takes over. It is cool and damp, clear. The ship is twenty miles from the Straits, ghosting along at two knots. Cape San Diego's light, on the western shore of the channel, beckons us at nine, and before midnight the weak Staten Island flame also is discovered. Current is under us and the ship is covering the ground far faster than the knot or two recorded every hour. The day coming in is

THURSDAY, November 19.

Current, augmented by an exceedingly strong tide, draws us furiously into the Straits. The wind comes abruptly from the east and veers to the northward, giving us commanding speed.

(It must be realized that in the Southern Hemisphere a veering wind, following the sun, goes from east to west through north, contrary to the rule in the Northern Hemisphere.)

We save fifty or sixty miles of priceless westing by using the Straits. It was something of a terror to square-rigger men and the more cautious of them habitually avoided its lure. For all of its thirteen miles of breadth they little liked its tumultuous tides, the paucity of anchorages on the Staten Island side and the risk of getting becalmed in mid-channel only six or seven miles from rocky shores. For a smart little ship like ours there is no risk at all in the Straits in moderate weather.

When Le Maire made his voyage of discovery he proceeded through here with breathless caution for fear of angering the vast whales which lay shoulder-to-shoulder as far as eyes could see. They were so huge and so numerous that there was more than a slight possibility of their wrecking his vessels if disturbed. Well, the bloody endeavors of New Bedford's hunters and their more efficient successors have at least eliminated this risk. We

Constant climbing from infancy has developed admirable confidence, fearlessness and strength in these sea-babes. Ann is on her way aloft here with simian-like agility and ease.

have not sighted a whale in a month, and shall not see another this side of Fifty South. The great herds whose geysers misted the sea are slaughtered; it is a pity.

The ship reels through the Straits. Despite five knots through the water she is twirled this way and that in the chattering, boiling tide.

At four, in broad daylight, we gybe and set the course for Cape Horn, distant now only 89 miles. The lights are gone, a small loss. These are the world's southernmost beacons, but they are all charted with the caveat U—unwatched, unreliable. No snug, inviting cottages snuggle under their rays, no patient tender watches the lenses and the waters they light, eager to signal passing ships. These lights blink from bare skeleton tripods, as coldly remote and detached as the very stars.

The sky changes; the north wind freshens on the quarter, giving us five, six and then seven knots. The sea is smooth, and the Fuegian peaks march past in steady procession. The ship is lifting, flying.

The babes, excused an hour early from school work, come on deck to romp in our first snow squall and to peer ahead for the imminent glimpse of the Cape. The snow turns to rain which in turn passes. Low clouds lift and the Wollaston Isles, adjacent to the Hermites, appear on the starboard bow.

Noon Position: 55°—37′ S., 66°—07′ W.
To 50° South in the Pacific: 624 Miles.
Made Good: 105 Miles. Sailed by Log: 74½ Miles.

We experience oddly mingled emotions. It is noon and the Horn is only forty-five miles away. We are eating that up at seven miles the hour. Can it be we are actually to make a *yachting* passage, all kites set? What luck! But do we want that? Have we sailed all this way, planned and prepared for Olympian antagonisms, only to find a fair wind and a mill-

"Commodore," a real sailor at four, keeps a critical eye on the job in hand, from which the camera has momentarily diverted Ann. The babes are taking in the tack of the maintopsail.

pond sea at the very Cape itself? What will they say at home when we tell of carrying a balloon jib west around the Horn? What anti-climax! We sail on, liking and disliking the fair wind.

Cape Horn! There, two points on the starboard bow, 2:15 o'clock! We haul up to bring it close ahead and discover we are eleven miles behind our reckoning. Horn currents have been opposing us strongly this morning.

At five the ship is flat becalmed, Cape Horn still west eighteen miles. We stow the fisherman. The ballooner goes to hibernate deep in the lazarette, buried under such ominous gear as reefing tackles, storm oil and heavy trysails.

The sunset, a gaudy display lasting hours; the painfully clear night, the vacuum-quiet atmosphere—all these flaunt a warning. WEATHER BREEDING!

Penguins swim about, yelling their harsh R-R-Raurrrk! R-R-R-Raurrrk! doubtless their equivalent to a Bronx cheer. Sleeping Cape pigeons and albatross chirp guttural protest when we move about the deck.

Eddying currents set us north during the night. Before the lingering twilight is gone the snaggle-toothed rocks of Deceit Island have obtruded and hidden the Cape.

All nature is eerily quiet and the ship mirrors the mood. The stars gaze at their reflections in the vast glass of the sea-bowl, and so perfect is the illusion that the schooner seems fixed in space, the focus of a celestial sphere. At long intervals the mainsail rustles and the reef points dance a tap-routine.

The Old Man keeps the night watch alone, reading for the dozenth time of the little schooner *Sea Serpent* and her pas-

The "Commodore" blithely descends to the deck from the crosstrees, sliding 60 feet on a halliard and at this somewhat breath-taking point is swung from it by the roll of the ship. He knows his way about so well he has never had a fall at sea.

sage west around the Cape a hundred years ago. It is the only account extant of a Horn voyage in a ship comparable to the *'Bird*. It was hereabouts, where this silence now lies thick as a quilt, that they cut away the *Sea Serpent's* bulwarks— "—it blew a perfect hurricane and soon created a mountainous sea—" recorded her master.

Coronet, probably the only registered yacht ever to precede *Wander Bird* here, passed this way in 1896. Her owner, Arthur Curtiss James, sent her with a professional crew around to San Francisco, from where she conveyed a party of astronomers to the study of an eclipse. *Coronet*, for all her 135 feet, so closely resembled the *'Bird* that Mr. James brought us, one day in Miami, the precious volume which records the voyages of that old ocean racer.

She came by here two months later. Captain Crosby noted "February 4, 1896, was very fine. It was almost calm, with the sea smooth as a kitten's eye. With the Islands of the Ramirez in the north about four miles and the high land of the Cape, the sky in the background, the scene was very handsome." A few sentences further on the old sailor succinctly damns the next fortnight with "—from this day on for fifteen days was very bad weather."

It is a place of extremes, apparently.

Just now it is grave-peaceful. There is no slightest breath of air. But from somewhere, from everywhere, there is a faint whisper. It is the warning trumpet of a rushing gale. Already the silvery cirrus lambs high overhead are stampeding before it.

"Rise and shine, Charlie! Your lookout trick. Call me at the slightest change of weather."

FRIDAY, November 20.

The sun slides diagonally out of the ocean at 3:50, taking unconscionably long to clear its rim from the horizon's razor-

Sheet home your jibs!—As Wander Bird comes about the headsails fill on the new tack and sailors quickly trim the sheets.

Wander Bird *drives through.*

edge. The calm holds until noon, teasing us with vagrant puffs which lure us into setting the fisherman. We drift close to Evout Island. The bleak Barnevelts lie between us and the Horn.

Julian and Charlie want badly to launch a boat and explore those rocks, and I am almost persuaded to let them. It would be fun to stretch the legs, even though on nothing more inviting than the guano-whitened Barnevelts, the nesting spot of bird millions.

But that eerie whisper, heard at midnight, is insistent and warns against such nonsense. We stand together and the dories are undisturbed under their doubled gripes. It is still calm, but no longer peacefully so.

Toward this battlesea of ships and wind the Valkyries ride fast. Before them color has fled. Yesterday's soft lavender peaks are black and hard. The sky droops, heavy, gray. The sea is ink, malignant with mounting rage.

The bitter loneliness of the Horn penetrates the stoutest jackets. Its smiling, peaceful mask is down and we are at last face to face with its true countenance. Call on no gods now, sailors! Expect no mercy! Scream—no one will hear. Fail—none will succor you. You are at the Horn!

The world is a tight smooth bomb about to shatter explosively.

The wind comes from the west, with one first blow pushing us far down and signaling release to a sea which leaps wolf-fast. The brittle calm breaks, shattered like a delicate glass smashed on a marble floor. All about us the unleashed storm furies shriek and scream to one another.

As we tend halliards and claw banging canvas we are galewrapt. Never have I seen a storm come so fast; this is a giant sprung full-grown from the womb.

For an hour we slog south-by-west under reefed foresail and jumbo, making three knots, helm lashed. By this time the gale is so violent even thinking is difficult. The senses are heavily oppressed by the incredible fury. One fixed idea remains—SAVE YOUR GEAR! (there's no more to be had hereabouts!) SAVE YOUR SHIP! (if you'd save yourself!) If we can get that jumbo off we must do it, and quickly!

Four of us creep forward. The sea is lashed and flailed until it is snow-white. Spray flies in unbroken sheets.

The ship lies down, quivering like a spent doe and urging us to speed. The halliard is cleared. Charlie starts carefully to ease it. Zing! It wrenches from his grasp and smokes about the pin as the sail takes charge. Three straining men pull their hearts out on the downhaul, shouting encouragement as the heavy canvas thunders in collapsing folds and comes down, intact.

The schooner, vastly relieved, swings closer to the wind while we pass the gaskets and imprison the sail. William heaves out oil bags, and we meet the storm with fortified challenge.

Noon Position: 55°—49′ S., 66°—29′ W.
To 50° South in the Pacific: 611 Miles.
Made Good: 13 Miles. Sailed by Log: 51 Miles.

The land is fading. We see sadly that we are going to leeward like a balloon.

This is the violence of a hurricane. Crouched under the weather bulwarks we watch with fascination the imperiled foresail. Beyond belief it still stands. Momentarily it must vanish down wind. Painfully, for every movement is laborious, we rouse out the storm trysail and secure it in readiness along the deck. It will replace the foresail if the foresail understandably blows to hell.

Senses reel under the impact of this force. One thing alone seems desirable—sleep, deep, dreamless sleep, sleep unbroken

Wander Bird sails herself under jumbo and reefed foresail through seas of a strong Horn gale whose combers sometimes break—

so close aboard that—

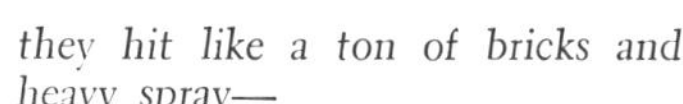

they hit like a ton of bricks and heavy spray—

rises like a springing ghost from the bow and—

all along the weather side to sweep inboard—

in a deluge which clears to show—

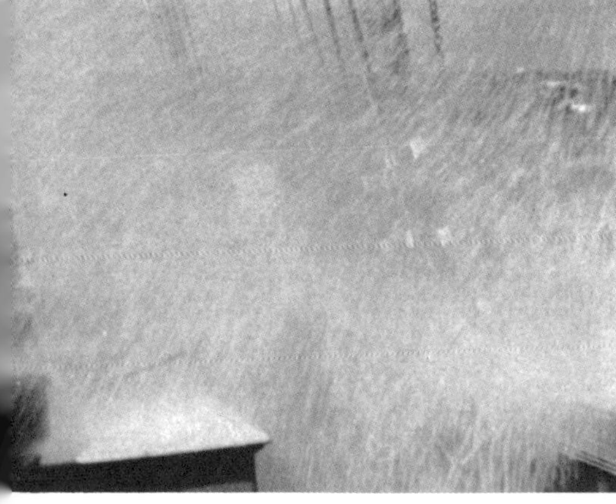

the ship nosing unconcernedly ahead at her work while everything (including the cameraman and his gear) drips gallons of salt-water (see it pouring from top of deck-house).

Wander Bird has never taken more solid water than this and hence is what sailors term "a very dry ship" even at such moments.

until a measure of sanity and reason has been restored to a maniacal world. Momentary panic, if felt at all, is soon allayed. With the ship behaving so splendidly and with no dangers to leeward it is physically impossible to be afraid of anything for long. Harrison's supper bell is greeted with yells by those hardy ones whose appetites are lusty regardless of the weather. All of us expend a vast amount of energy just waiting, waiting with more or less apprehension. We wait, tense, for the uproarious clatter of gear ultimately strained beyond its stoutest endurance, for the devastating shock of some untamable, monstrous sea, for the electrifying, ever-expected clarion "All Hands!"

The tempest penetrates even the insulated cabin, and the ship's strange new voices are clamant and wearying. Above the full-throated monody of the storm is the piercing soprano screeching of vibrating stays, the fifing of every hole the wind can discover, the applauding slap-slap-slap of halliards on bare masts and innumerable other unidentifiable tones all chorusing a chant of stress and fury unrestrained.

The too-vivid recollection of red-inked ledgers at home scourges me reluctantly to the taking of pictures. It is a task for which I have exceedingly little taste under these conditions, but there is in truth little point in fighting to save the ship here if it is only to deliver her to some callous sheriff's deputy. Even here, the old economic determinant! So I slip and slide from hand-hold to hand-hold, lugging the Eyemo, shielding its so-easily-fouled lens, manipulating the light meter and seeking to practice all the commandments of photography. This evening I will spend hours cleaning the machine which otherwise will be frozen beyond repair by tomorrow. Ah! Well do I know why Hollywood prefers bathtub storms to the real thing!

As abruptly as it began the storm moderates this evening. At once we set the jumbo and thereafter at intervals the inner and

Giant albatross snatch our garbage in the amazingly warm calm just north of Staten Island. The smaller birds are Cape pigeons.

outer jibs and the double-reefed mainsail. Midnight comes, finding us standing southwest-by-south, content to get away from the pitch of the Cape and its shallow waters.

SATURDAY, November 21.

Yet again wind and sea snatch brief midnight rest. Just so seven of the last nine days have been ominously stillborn. The early dawn of the southern spring finds the ship still north and miles east of the Horn, victim of eddying current, leeway and this new calm.

Refreshed and gleeful at new-planned deviltries the wind comes whistling from the northwest at three. It feints to the northward two full points and we are lured into setting the full mainsail. With eased sheets the *'Bird* romps for the Horn.

"Breakfast in the Pacific!" forecasts John. "We knocked off eight knots this last hour."

Close aboard the terminal ranges plunge sharply into the ocean. Anson named them Tierra del Fuego, Land of Fire. They have altered not at all since he, with loathing and dread, thus christened them. Blackly-blue, rent by deep, mysterious canyons, crowned with snow these mountains (contrary to popular opinion) know nothing of volcanic pyrotechnics or vaporing geysers. Even as it is today it has always been; not a single wavering smoky spiral climbs into the solid gray clouds.

And so long as Anson held his luck he saw no fires, either. They sprang up, leaping sparks blown from peak to peak, only when he started losing his ships and men on the plentiful dangers hereabout. Then each brief, bright signal rallied to slaughter and looting the hardy primitives who, for reasons beyond comprehension, are native to this region of eternal unkindness.

Such quick, brief flames may well leap again, and for us, if

The bleary-eyed and curious baby seal was greatly interested in the idle schooner. The teeming sea-life is much more evident in calms than otherwise.

we but touch the coast where sharp, peering eyes can appreciate our helplessness.

Missionary efforts have modified but slightly the barbarically simple manners of the Tierra del Fuegians. Our new charts print warnings to those trafficking with them; only twenty years ago they baldly stated these people were cannibals. Captain Joshua Slocum's most enduring bid to fame was made when he shrewdly planted his decks with big carpet tacks, points up, and effectively kept *Spray* clear of bare-footed, murderous visitors in the Straits of Magellan.

Barr, our anthropologist, tells of these people whose habitations are mere lean-tos fronting their campfires, who wear only the most rudimentary fur garments, and those with the fur outside. Their food is the meat of seals and the flesh of fish, stewed with edible sea plants and the local wild celery which has in times past saved so many mariners from scurvy.

Luffing sails abruptly terminate Fuegian speculations. The north wind shifts eight points. It puffs just once from the west and then drops to nothing. With her sails all emptied the schooner glides for a space, borne by her momentum. Before she can come to rest the unnaturally servile sea, aping the masterful wind, has itself settled into treacherous repose.

Entr'acte!

Our very cigarette smoke hangs heavily inert. The wind that is gone—or is it the wind which is to come, or perhaps both in duet?—whines faintly. From the swiftly altering gigantic stage we get our imperative cue and are sprung to sudden labor.

"Double reef that mainsail, and quickly!"

The spectacle is consummate theater, colossal art enlisting a sky, a sea from horizon to horizon, forces incalculable, properties and effects monstrous, awful and dreadfully real.

Two-thirds of our universe are yet unchanged, all monot-

Flying fish weather—A yardarm view of the open decks. Note length of ship and relative narrowness of beam.

onously solid gray. The shores we have skirted and left behind remain sharp, blue cameos.

But see! The West!

From north to south, arched, boiling, oily and solid, is a line squall momentarily higher and closer. Under it sways an impenetrable leaden pall whose fringe tickles and darkens the sea. Its folds sweep over the Horn, hanging it with gauze through which we can see the mountain-cape but vaguely. It is, therefore, less than seven miles away, and coming with hurricane speed. Already catspaws stroke the water and fan coolly on our cheeks.

"Tack lashing all fast!" William yells. "Stretch your sail!" The precision with which everyone works is gratifying.

"Vast heaving! Tie in your reef!" I pass the clew lashing, heaving each turn taut.

A glance shows the storm now very near; the keystone of the arch is in our zenith. The swift interplay and convolutions of its clouds surpass anything I have ever seen. The windward sea shows white teeth. About us fleet ripples scurry away into the east. The air is atremble with the rising, whistling wind.

At this instant I discover the minute tear in the tablings of the clew. It is an insignificant little rip, only an inch in length. Five minutes with needle and thread will mend it.

"Down mainsail! Get her in!" A stitch in time is worth far more here than in pleasanter climes.

We jump fast, hoping to get the loose sail captured before the wind arrives, but the squall strikes first. This wind is more than just wind; it is a solid, palpable bludgeon. Its blow staggers the ship.

The mainsail is all but in when there is a blasting rasp of tearing cloth. This all-pervasive violence has unerringly found the sail's insignificant weakness. Cotton is shredded down-wind and the quick scream of split canvas is in our ears. We cannot even glance at this wound. Other sails must be got in at once, and oil out before we are stricken more vitally.

This is our most furious blow thus far. There is no estimating accurately the wind's force. It is gale piled upon gale, and no matter of miles per hour can convey a sense of the turmoil. We log it at force 10, but we are growing hardened to severe weather and it is quite probable familiarity is breeding not contempt but an objective power of understatement and depreciation which should properly go with wide experience. The wildest sea stories are always told by those who know least of the sea.

Is this gale a "heavy gale"—to use Admiral Beaufort's notation—or a "very great gale, a tempest"? He assigns to them a difference of only fourteen miles an hour. It is quite possibly a hurricane. Between a tempest and a hurricane Beaufort put a

A shark you may have seen starred briefly in the film "Hurricane." Convoyed by his pilot fish (visible just behind the right fin) this visitor broke the harpoon we got in him but was caught by the camera.

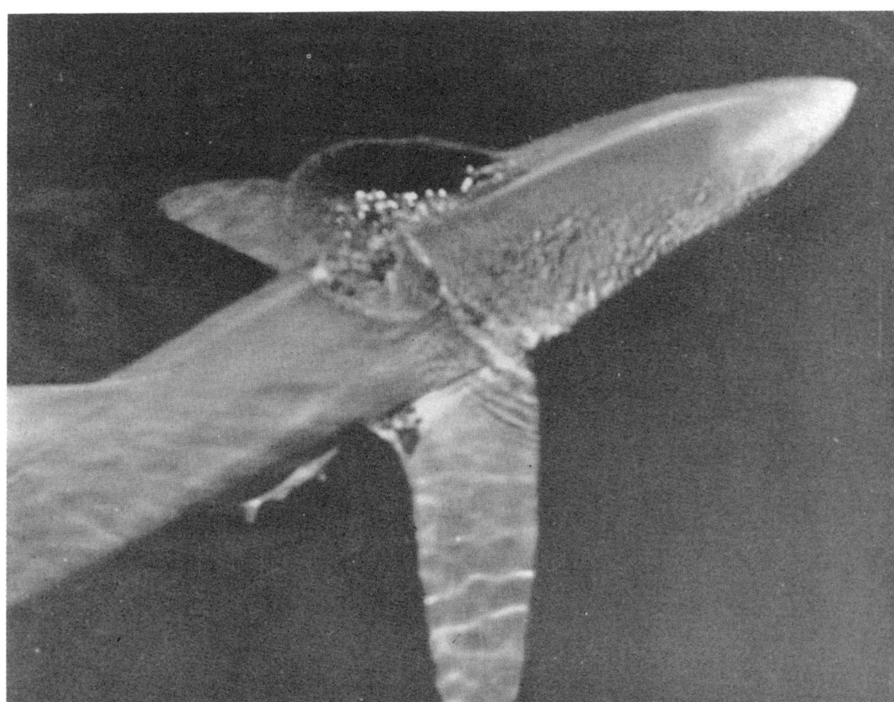

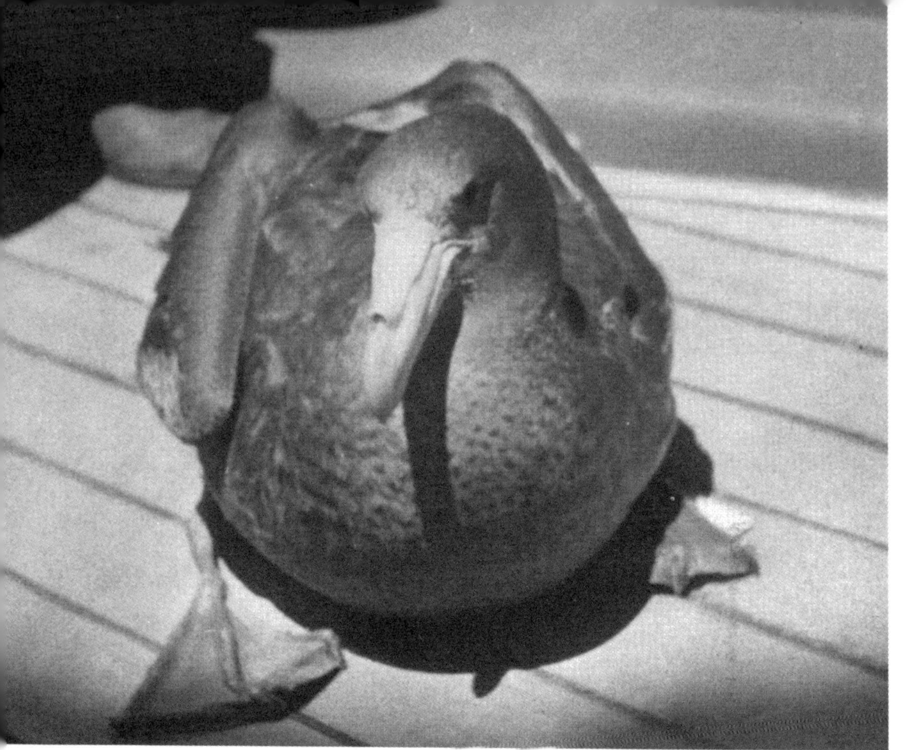

This fellow, a smaller species of albatross, for all his flying skill came to temporary grief when he flew too close and a wing-tip hit a stay. He fell to the deck and could not escape since such sea birds cannot take off from land. After posing for us so graciously we restored him to the water. His down was almost two inches thick.

mere seven miles an hour. I'd like to know more about his arbitrary limitations, the way he measured his velocities, and if he allowed for the anaesthetizing effect of experience.

To bring exactly what I mean closer to the landsman let him consider how fast fifty miles an hour seems on the open road after passing through a town at thirty. How impatiently he trails a truck at the same fifty after an hour spent at sixty or seventy!

It is just so with gales. I have often noted before, as my crew is discovering now, that when one lives incessantly with heavy weather a forty-mile blow can seem relatively mild and pleasant.

After a ship has gone far to leeward, hove-to and beset by foul current, a two-knot crawl under the closest storm sails seems by comparison very fine sailing.

In this kind of weather the mainsail cannot be carried even if it were not damaged, so we are little concerned. The storm trysail is more easily handled and more comfortable. It is no weather to be sewing on deck, and we complacently count on postponing repairs until we are north of Fifty.

Meanwhile it is made very apparent that we are going to have to sail, sail, sail if we want to get to the northwest. Consequently, the first fury of the gale having abated somewhat, we set the jumbo again at 9:30 this morning. Our rig is fantastically short—deeply reefed foresail and the jumbo—but hereafter we shall often count ourselves lucky when we can carry this much canvas. We shall come to congratulate ourselves when we can also set the inner jib, and it will be a joyous occasion when the outer jib is hoisted. Hallelujahs will hail the tiny storm trysail on the mainmast.

Noon Position: 56°—19′ S., 67°—10′ W. (D.R.)
To 50° South in the Pacific: 603 Miles.
Made Good: 8 Miles. Sailed by Log: 68¾ Miles.

The jumbo is set now for less than an hour. The gale rages with new strength again, but the seas are lengthening and treating us less severely. At noon we are almost into the Pacific. Although thirty-three miles from yesterday's position, having sailed nearly seventy, the ship is only eight miles nearer the fiftieth parallel since most of our progress has been to the southward.

It blows all afternoon, but at suppertime we again get moving with the help of the jumbo. At eight o'clock we set the storm trysail.

By midnight it is again calm. What a place!

SUNDAY, November 22.

It is the same old story. Calm at midnight again, but this time the big sea has no intention of smoothing out. That it might, indeed, seems as unlikely as Joshua's halting of the sun itself. These vast rollers near omnipotence. In just such a sea, only a few years ago, the great German barque *Pinnas* rolled her four masts over the side and was abandoned not fifty miles from this spot.

If this sort of thing continues we'll have to repair the mainsail, surely. A calm here does not signify only a cessation of advance. When the wind drops we drift backward at nearly two knots. It is a discouraging thought.

The wind is back again at breakfast, coming fast and from right ahead. At noon we draw scant cheer from calculating we are at last two miles west of the Horn. It was visible early this morning just a half-point west of north, appearing briefly and faintly, probably twenty miles distant, between pallid dawn clouds. We shall not see it again.

Noon Position: 56°—54′ S., 67°—41′ W.
To 50° South in the Pacific: 600 Miles.
Made Good: 3 Miles. Sailed by Log: 48¼ Miles.

West of the Cape we may be, but a day's labors have put us only three miles closer to Fifty, and the next gale may swiftly spew us back into the Atlantic. Horn Island, it is now quite evident, may be but a trifling incident in the passage from Fifty South to Fifty South.

We meet vast swells this afternoon, just such billows as convinced the Dutch explorers they had found a new way into the Great South Sea.

Stout fellows, those! They were Hollanders covetous of a share in the fabulous riches of the Indies, a wealth effectively monopolized by the Dutch East India Company. That enterprising concern had secured a Governmental edict forbidding

While this sailor clears a flag halliard during a calm the camera reveals many points of interest to sailors. Note the fair-leads on the mainmast for peak and throat halliards (on crosstrees and shroud), the main crosstrees on after side of mast to assure the topmast of better staying, the parrals used instead of wooden hoops to hold sails to the masts and the simple wooden yoke holding the square-yard from the mast.

November 21, 1936: The land near Cape Horn shows jumbled and gray under leaden clouds. It was fifty miles away when this picture was made with a telephoto lens.

to Dutch ships, other than Company vessels, the sea-ways around the Cape of Good Hope and through the Straits of Magellan. The fiat was extremely effective, but like other laws it had its loop-holes between the letters. There was nothing in it forbidding a ship from visiting the Indies by another route, if it should find another one. The ships which made the eventful discovery were commanded by William Cornelius Schouten whose expedition was financed by the merchants of Hoorn, Holland, and principally by one Le Maire. Schouten passed between Staten Land and the mainland—Le Maire's son, supercargo, giving the passage his father's name—and beat past Cape Horn in 1615. He generously and modestly christened the Horn for his home town.

The furious and unbelieving agents of the India Company in Batavia, Java, arrested Schouten and his lieutenants when they reached their goal months later. Confirmation of their Horn passage came so slowly that more than one of the first men to round the Cape died in their chains in those tropic jails before the truth of their assertions was proved.

These waters, however, today are called Drake Strait, in honor of that ubiquitous soldier, sailor, pirate and explorer-courtier of Old England. Drake was the first European to sight the Horn, although he issued from the western mouth of Magellan Straits, three hundred miles and more northwestward. There he ran into a long series of foul winds, and before they ceased hammering him he was within sight of the Horn. Doubtless he counted it merely another deadly tooth of the frightful coast, little imagining it to be the monumental marker between Atlantic and Pacific.

Today the waters of Drake Strait are blue, and *Wander Bird*

"Is that Cape Horn, William?" The babes and the Bosun look for the famous corner.

November 19, that is *Cape Horn!* Wander Bird *was set north of the Cape during the night's foreboding calm, and now we see the bleak 1500-foot rock across the intervening low-lying promontory of Cape Deceit. The land dimly seen to Barr's left is not actually south of the Horn, therefore, as it at first appears.*

climbs and slides easily over vast and rounded swells. We are standing off to the southwest. It blows, but not too fresh, and an afternoon free of the customary gale and notable for progress settles one vexing problem.

For several days I have considered a crafty scheme for besting the Horn. It is possible to sail westward back of the Cape, utilizing the smooth reaches of Nassau Bay and leaving the Wollaston and Hermite archipelagoes to the south. This course leads a vessel again into the open sea at False Cape Horn, twenty-five miles west of the real Cape.

There are hampering considerations. It will later be a matter of endless regret if we thus, for the sake of a few days' comfort, avoid the full might of the Cape. Also, possibly a more sensible deterrent, there is risk attendant in navigating narrow channels neither buoyed nor lighted and none too well charted. The end of the passage, too, will put us immediately to windward of the Horn, and it does not make a pleasant lee shore.

Captain Edwin Horace Herriman, of Belfast, Maine, once sailed these channels. He was coaxed from comfortable and affluent retirement to put half his wealth in the smart ship *Paul R. Hazeltine* and to sail her to San Francisco. He took his wife with him for company and his son for second mate. Down here by the Horn he ran into hard February weather. He stood far south, as we are doing, and came back, still to leeward of the Horn. He again went south and again came back to find the Cape still to windward.

Just as with us the winds showed no sign of ever leaving the northwest. Herriman, still hoping for a fast passage, succumbed to the lure of the Horn's back door. He was making eight knots through it, probably feeling very pleased with himself, when the ship sliced her bows away on a sunken rock. She slid clear and went down in twenty minutes. Herriman and his wife, with some hands, got away in one boat (the water being smooth), the first mate took the yawl, and Herriman's boy with the rest of the crew were in the third boat. Food, water and clothing were most inadequate. Herriman's boat and that of the mate were picked up off Staten Land, but the boy and his men were not rescued until much later and news of the lad's salvation did not reach the old man for a long time.

Herriman went to Buenos Aires and put all the rest of his hard-earned money into buying and fitting a schooner. In her he returned to the scene of the wreck and endeavored to salvage it. The end of his story, a sorry tale of the failure to be anticipated—the Horn does not readily surrender that which it takes—came not long afterward in the Hospital for the Insane of the State of Maine.

No, come what may, we'll hold to the open sea.

The day is almost peaceful. No gale comes. For a few moments bright afternoon sun lights the desolation and glints on wheeling Antarctic terns cutting dizzy acrobatics about the ponderous albatrosses and skittering erratically among the comfortably pudgy Cape pigeons. The breathing spell is exceedingly pleasant. We wonder if tomorrow may not let us dry the mainsail and consider repairs.

We are not trying to sail the ship very close to the wind. Under the circumstances (short storm sails, big seas, strong current) we keep the sheets slightly eased and the ship moving through the water.

MONDAY, November 23.

We are reaching deep into the south, and the cold is more bitter. This chill is penetrating and damp, but it is mild compared to the sub-zero days and nights we have known off Cape Cod in December and January. Contrary to the general impression, freezing weather is a rarity at the Horn, even in winter, a season almost identical with that which the calendar indicates as summer. Tales of heavily-iced ships issue from unfortunate vessels driven far south. The water temperature at the Cape is 44 degrees today, and it varies little from season to season. There is so much water and so little adjacent land the climate is perforce equable, if vile.

We have started repairs on the mainsail. Inspection reveals the bolt rope has been ripped clear for more than thirty feet, and in its destructive moment the wind frayed out two inches of canvas along the entire length of the leech.

Calm at Cape Horn—The Old Man, distrustful of this unwonted and uneasy peace, questions the sphinx-like pile which is Cape Horn (small point of land nearest his head) and takes warning from the cloud streamers above.

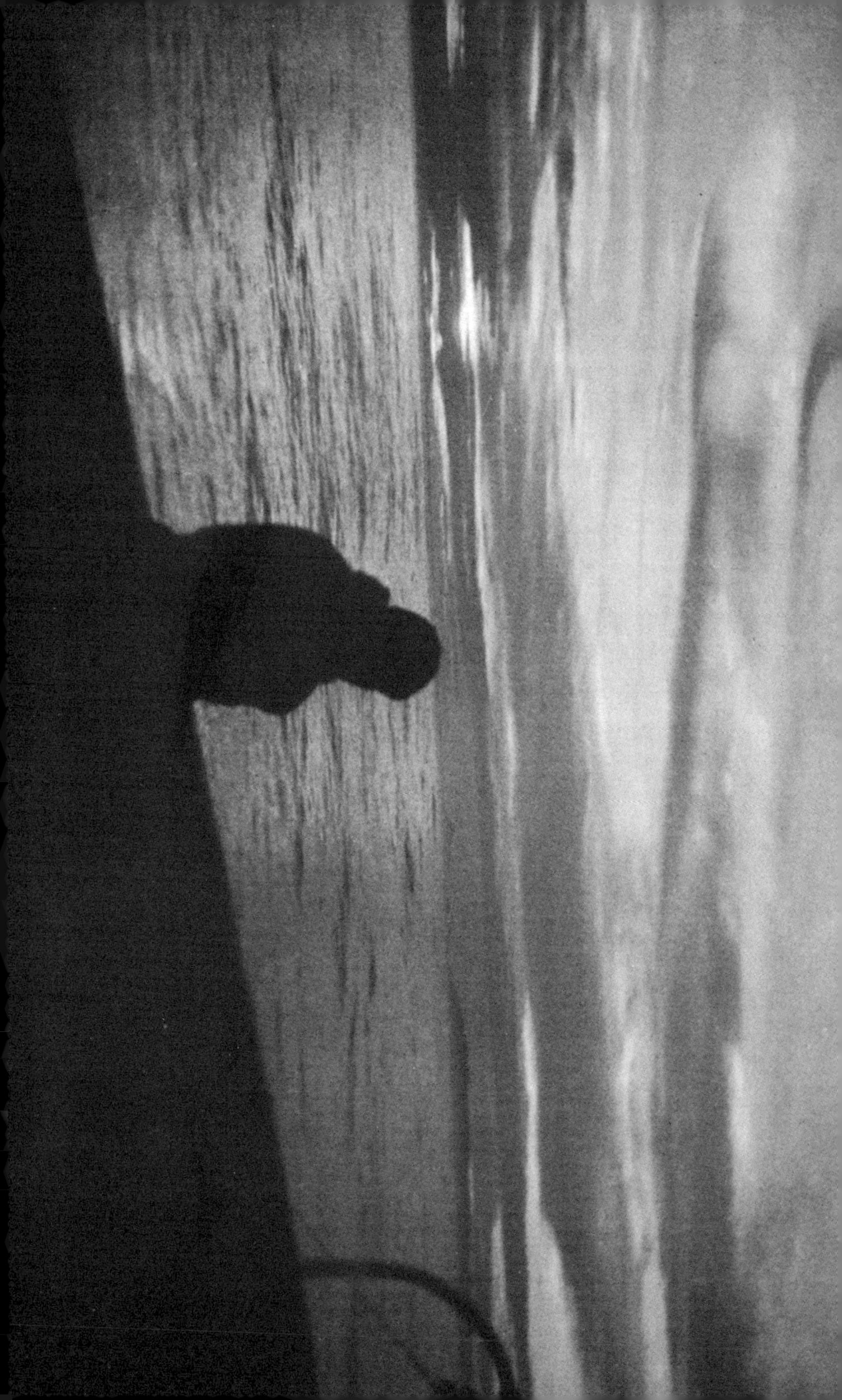

Noon Position: 58°—19′ S. (D.R.), 70°—08′ W.
To 50° South in the Pacific: 583 Miles.
Made Good: 17 Miles. Sailed by Log: 113 Miles.

What's worth doing at all is worth doing well. The proverb is doubly true down here, although doing a thing at all is usually difficult indeed. We shall have to replace the missing cloth. This entails flat-seaming a doubled five-inch strip of number two cotton duck on both sides of the sail. With this done we shall have a stout edge to which we can sew the bolt rope.

William and the Old Man sew doggedly all afternoon and far into the lingering twilight. The sail is heavy with salt, shrunk tight with wet and stiff as only cold, soaked canvas can be. Until ten o'clock they can place, push and pull the needles. When they finally rise, stiff, cold and tired, their task is barely started.

The ship labors through the afternoon. She is undercanvased for this breeze and hobbled by the sloppy sea. Her frequent

Lashed helm—The ship lies hove-to in a Horn gale while the weak Antarctic sun turns spray to snow and patterns the bulwarks with racing shadows.

deep rolls send the sailmakers and their gear sliding helplessly a dozen times. The tumbling seas frequently drop dollops aboard to soak still further the canvas and the men working on it.

The vessel heads back toward the land on the port tack when the night wind shows faint indications of going southwest.

TUESDAY, November 24.

The stars are fading at twelve-thirty this morning. It is light in another hour and the Skipper resumes work on the mainsail. He is interrupted two hours later by changing weather.

It is dirty again in the west; the wind is going to the northward and it is the part of wisdom to get back on the starboard tack, making westing and southing.

Noon Position: 58°—10′ S., 71°—00′ W.
To 50° South in the Pacific: 563 Miles.
Made Good: 20 Miles. Sailed by Log: 70¾ Miles.

There is no more sewing this day. The weather grows steadily worse and there is a gale by noon when computation puts us only twenty miles nearer Fifty than we were yesterday. Current has cost us fifty miles in the last twenty-four hours.

There is sleet in the squalls. We are shortening down again at suppertime, but with only reefed foresail, jumbo and inner jib the ship sails into the night at five knots. Our course is southwest, but what she makes good, with current and sea on the weather bow, is extremely problematical.

The storm trysail is set at midnight when the weather, as usual, moderates.

WEDNESDAY, November 25.

This wind! It teases, bedevils and taunts us until we rage impotently. We are headed on every tack. Throughout the midwatch we jump up and down in a sickening sea, the sails

6.30 a.m. Nov. 21. Breaking of the Horn's strange calm. Under a swiftly approaching line-squall cat's-paws darken the glass-like sea.

slatting and banging until it is a wonder they hold together. Through renewed rain, sleet and piercing cold we stagger on until eight o'clock when another strong gale imperiously directs us back to the southwest.

Such a day! Every prospect is gloomy. The wind remains fixed in the northwest, shifting only enough now and again to trick us into a hopeful gybe to the winning tack. It lightens and freshens in moody tantrums, and we are kept handling the recalcitrant canvas. We cannot even work on the mainsail.

Noon Position: 58°—50′ S., 71°—37′ W.
To 50° South in the Pacific: 585 Miles.
Made Good: Minus 23 Miles. Sailed by Log: 116 Miles.

6.40 a.m. The air is filled with the swiftly rising whistle and scream of wind. The boiling clouds of the squall shut out the light and the guano-covered Barnevelt Isle (right) seems to cower as the wind reaches it.

At noon it is again blowing a hard gale. These last twenty-four hours we have sailed 116 miles. We are twenty-three miles farther from Fifty than we were yesterday.

In a brief evening clear observations of several stars show us well south of 59°. The current has cost us 48 miles these last thirty-six hours.

We gybe north and sail on.

THURSDAY, November 26.

The day comes in with the usual filth, rain, hail and dashes of snow. The thermometer is down to 39 degrees. The sea, even in the experienced eyes of whoever wrote up the log at four A.M., is "Rotten, steep, sharp." The next toneless entry is elo-

6.45 a.m. The squall drops lower and is appreciably blacker.

quent of the outlook: "Continued squalls and hail. Today is Thanksgiving."

Harrison does his noble best to give us something for which we can be thankful. His dinner is a splendid effort. Few sailormen have ever eaten so well hereabouts. When the mess bell rings the ship is sailing herself and we can all be together below.

The main cabin is gay and snug, and the quiet of the strong and marvelous ship is a benediction. The long swinging table is polished to shining rich brown. Gwen and the babes have produced vivid crepe-paper streamers and festive place-cards.

The table, forever leveling against the roll of the ship, is burdened with good things. Two chickens, bursting with dressing, lie flanked by fluffy mashed potatoes, onions swimming in cream sauce, golden carrots, rolls so fluffy they threaten flight,

6.50 a.m. White-caps spring up with amazing speed. The ship heels to the impact of wind, even though already nearly stripped of canvas by a crew desperately at work.

6.55 a.m. Cape Horn stands out briefly against the sweeping skirts of the squall which almost immediately obliterated it and swished on to rip 30 feet of bolt rope from the mainsail. This squall marked the beginning of the long series of northwesterly gales.

emerald pickles, red-hearted olives and quivering, gleaming jellies. Mince and pumpkin pies, fruitcake, raisins, salted nuts, candies, and even cranberry sauce are ready to hand.

We dine amidst a wilderness, fed by a miraculous and astonishing world. These chickens fattened on the corn of Poland and under Polish skies, died there abruptly and were juicily coffined in Polish tin, found their devious way to Boston and thence to Rio and now are joyously resurrected here off Cape Horn! These ruby cranberries, red-blooded, tartly bitter-sweet as natives of Cape Cod should be, grew with bog neighbors who today may be delighting lonely Yankees in China, Persia or Paris!

Walnuts of California wrinkle their faces jostling against fat Brazil nuts from Rio, but there is nothing new in an international convention of nuts, surely! Mother's own dark fruitcake was cooked by the electricity of the High Sierras in her Berkeley oven and then flown to us by plane to be relished by sea appetites here at the remote bottom of the world. The age of miracles is still with us.

Noon Position: 58°—04′ S., 71°—38′ W.
To 50° South in the Pacific: 532 Miles.
Made Good: 31 Miles. Sailed by Log: 91¾ Miles.

Harrison presides, all splendid in white, and it would indeed be a surly sailorman not cheered by this feast. Laughter soon testifies yet again to the vast importance of the ship's cook. Possibly nothing is more miraculous than that this could all have been wrought in the bows of the pitching ship, in pots ingeniously lashed to a gymnastic stove.

The logbook records a sharp rise in spirits. The querulous morning entries give way to a more cheerful tone. The flat noon entry states "practically nothing gained" but Harrison's genius alters the face of a dismal world.

One P.M. Repairing mainsail.

Two P.M. Everything working fine.

Fickle and slightly shifting wind raises and again dashes our hopes this afternoon and then deserts us. The ship is again a plaything for the current. At midnight the mercury stands at 38 degrees and it is "raining like pooches and felines" (i.e., cats and dogs) as Charlie records with a cheerfulness which surmounts the rain and the nasty job of setting the outer jib in the black of such a midnight. Stout fella!

FRIDAY, November 27.

These midnight calms are persistent thieves, filching from us our hard-won miles. For an hour or so this early morning we have gained handsomely with a wind unbelievably east of north, but it proves, of course, a monstrous joke. At three we are back on the starboard tack, creeping at a bare two knots into the west-south-west through a soupy dawn of fog and rain.

Then the wind does shift, abruptly, and comes at last from the south. Our huzzas find their way into the log and we go away merrily at six knots, making our course for the first time—or so it seems—in memory. The fisherman staysail is set at midday in the general jubilation over an astonishing gain of 67 miles. It seems a far more memorable day's run than the time in the Atlantic when we once ripped off 246 miles between noonday suns.

Noon Position: 57°—11′ S., 73°—20′ W.
To 50° South in the Pacific: 465 Miles.
Made Good: 67 Miles. Sailed by Log: 88 Miles.

But this fine, this beautiful, this unutterably lovely fair wind is too good to last for long, and it succumbs slowly but steadily to the returning northwester as we work on the mainsail through the afternoon.

The big job is nearing its end. For days the torn sail has

Weight of command—The Old Man plotting the course through the ever-varying maze of winds, seas and currents. Salt-drip stains the chart. Sailing directions, light lists and mathematical tables sway in unison on the shelves, and under the glass (bottom lower right) unconcerned chronometers tick off Greenwich Time.

haunted us. We have been eternally at it whenever it was humanly possible to work on deck. Asleep we have dreamed of it and of the balls of twine we've sewn. Our hands are scarred and cracked, burning and smarting as minute salt crystals work into the crevices of the skin.

The tablings of the sail, where two, three and sometimes four thicknesses of cloth are superimposed, have often defied even the heaviest needles. We have got through them only with the help of one of John's creations, a Yankee push-drill, drilling each hole and then swiftly replacing the drill with the needle before the contracting wet cotton closes the opening.

We've broken many needles, but fortunately we are well supplied with spares. Our chilled and insensitive hands often fail to push the steels straight. When the eye of a needle snaps the jagged end frequently escapes the iron of the palm and lodges deep in the meaty heel of the hand. The needles also slide very reluctantly through the wet cloth. Consequently the plucking vise of index finger and thumb slips frequently over the smooth metal to be deeply scored by the triangular and razor-sharp points. These minor but painful wounds have left telltale scarlet splashes the length of the job.

But blisters, cuts and the tired forearm muscles are discounted, for the task is nearly done, and well done, too. In a few hours we shall set the mainsail and flaunt it, bloodstained, as a symbol of a renewed challenge to the Horn.

Push, jerk, and heave taut! Push, jerk, heave! In even rhythm the heavy roping needles flash now through cloth and bolt rope. Barr and Charlie, squatting by the sewers, pull the needles through the resistant cloth with pliers. William is shoulder-to-shoulder with the Old Man. The job is virtually complete.

"GOD DAMN!" This is the Old Man's solitary oath, but this time it explodes with a fervency alarming to ears tuned to the significance of his varying accents. "Just look at that sail!"

We should have known better! In our eagerness we have stupidly failed to allow properly for the disproportionate shrinkage of wet cotton and wet manila. Here we are, with three feet of canvas left to be sewn to only one foot of rope. In our laps the leech lies inanely grinning, the sagging canvas jeering beneath its taut rope upper lip.

For five minutes we are stunned by the egregious oversight, appalled by the thought of sewing another painful inch. Dangerous subterfuges occur in a flood.

"Splice in a length of new rope!"

"Take a tuck in the cloth!"

"Sew the bloody thing up as it is, maybe it will hold!"

Then good common sense prevails.

"No, rip the bolt rope off again, all of it." The Old Man calculates hastily, steel tape belatedly in hand. "We will resew it. Thirteen inches of canvas to twelve inches of rope will bring it out right. We started to do this job right, let's finish it that way."

It is doubtless silly to personify the elements and the inert features of Nature. Winds, seas and the barrier headlands do not actually and maliciously hinder men and complicate their peewee struggles, but happily men are so constituted that they imagine this is the case. In this last misfortune we find renewed strength and determination in surging rage against Cape Horn, its winds and its seas. "Damn you, damn you, Cape Horn!" Our jibes blow down-wind. "We'll show you! You can't lick us!"

The supper bell this evening rings to deaf ears. The needles flash on and on. Twilight and clouds darken the sky and lights are rigged so that we can toil in fine frenzy. We sew furiously, hands, cramped backs, aching muscles all forgotten. At eight o'clock the full mainsail is swayed aloft triumphantly. We glance at our handiwork with understandable pride. The great sail sets with scarcely perceptible wrinkles. The new canvas lies snug along the bolt rope. The ship is again whole.

Through the calm midnight hours (if these recurring midnight calms are the regular thing, why hasn't some earlier observer noted them? Can they be merely coincidental?) we sail slowly west, carrying the full mainsail and the fisherman.

SATURDAY, November 28.

This day is unremarkable. We were shortening down at four this morning under windy skies. It blew fresh in puffs and we first reefed and then stowed the mainsail before lunch. It is not so cold, but it rains or sleets intermittently.

Noon Position: 56°—25′ S., 73°—50′ W. (D.R.)
To 50° South in the Pacific: 420 Miles.
Made Good: 45 Miles. Sailed by Log: 105 Miles.

We are heartened by a fairly good day's gain of 45 miles, and in mid-afternoon set the double-reefed mainsail. In the evening the wind goes to the west and so we tack ship for a try to the north. The ship sails now five points from the wind, helped vastly by the mainsail in both pointing and footing despite the bad cross sea.

It is a nasty night.

SUNDAY, November 29.

Today is alternately filthy and fine. A violent cross sea runs during the inevitable midnight calm. The ocean apparently has at last cast aside all thought of obedience to the wind and is at frantic cross-purposes with itself. There is a hard little gale which we drive through, lugging the close-reefed mainsail until daylight brings more rain and new windy squalls. Shorter sail is imperative and the mainsail is in at 9:40.

Whereupon it perversely clears and the deck dries for the

Hurricane at Cape Horn. This sea broke just ahead of Wander Bird. Its tumbling crest appeared to be fully seven feet high and was indubitably very solid and heavy. It left behind—

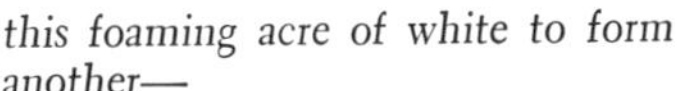

this foaming acre of white to form another—

Cape Horn Graybeard streaked with hair-like strands combed straight by the furious wind. As it lifts the ship we see beyond it the distant steep ridge of another sea which—

now looms high beyond the intervening trough into which we are about to fall and from which we look up at—

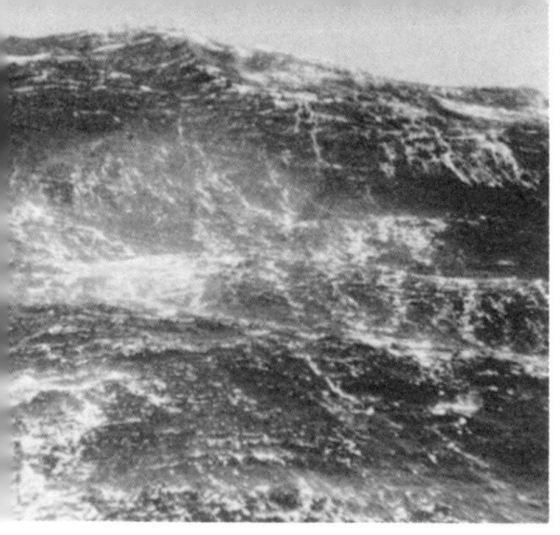

the threatening crest just beginning to curl white and—

ever more steep while—

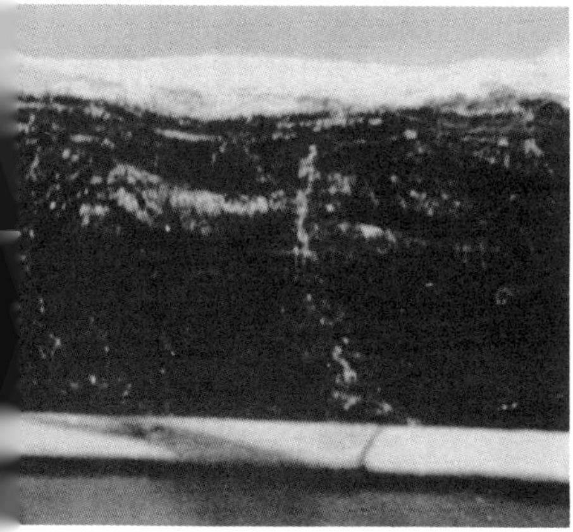

the ship raises its guard to parry the imminent thrust of—

this wall of charging water whose—

bursting crest—

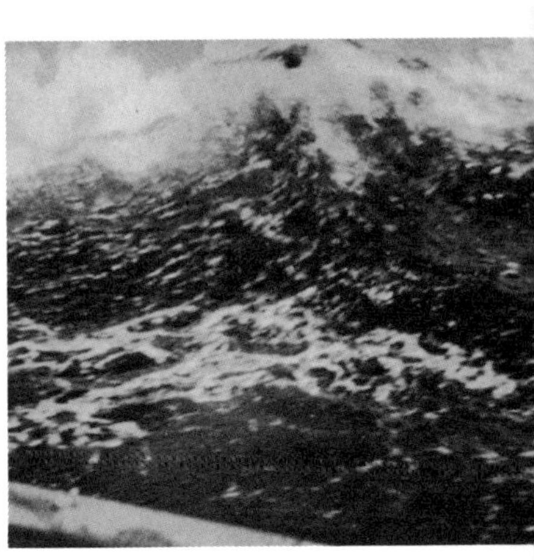

curls in thunder to pass in futile rage—

beneath the stout ship.

The sea's white mane.

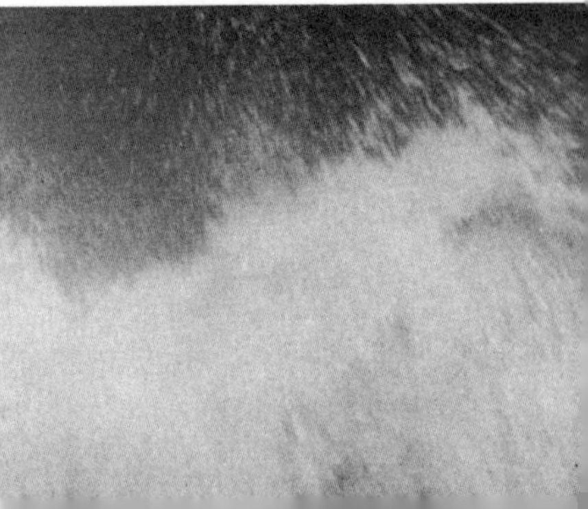

first time in a week. The sun shines and it lures Gwen from below. Julian, with his gift for apt (if not always gallant) phrase, dubs her "ground-hog Gussie" when she takes the wheel and happily discovers she again has a shadow.

Noon Position: 56°—25′ S., 75°—30′ W.
To 50° South in the Pacific: 345 Miles.
Made Good: 75 Miles. Sailed by Log: 86 Miles.

At noon we are almost due south of New York City (a place of complete unreality to us) and—what is much more important—a trifle north (at last!) and all of 250 miles west of Cape Horn. The reefed mainsail is set again this late afternoon. Through heavy seas and patches of moonlight we keep going on to the north through the night.

MONDAY, November 30

This day is memorable, bringing two events of consequence.

Nature assaults us with a new weapon, having failed to halt our advance with an arsenal of gales, rain, sleet and cold.

And the Old Man emerges from a study of his pilot charts with a new tactical policy which shall be followed henceforth.

The new tool is supplementary to the gales; it is the squall, the squall in uniform viciousness armed with speed, striking stinging hail-tipped blows, filled with destructive blasts of wind, reared in awesome pillars all gloomy and dark.

Heretofore we have gained in the relatively calm intervals between gales, lying hove-to and retreating only during their dominance. Today squalls march in close order, filling those opportune gaps between the big winds.

At noon we have gained forty miles of northing but have also been swept east and must again consider the threatening land. As I have done so many times before I study the pilot charts of Matthew Fontaine Maury.

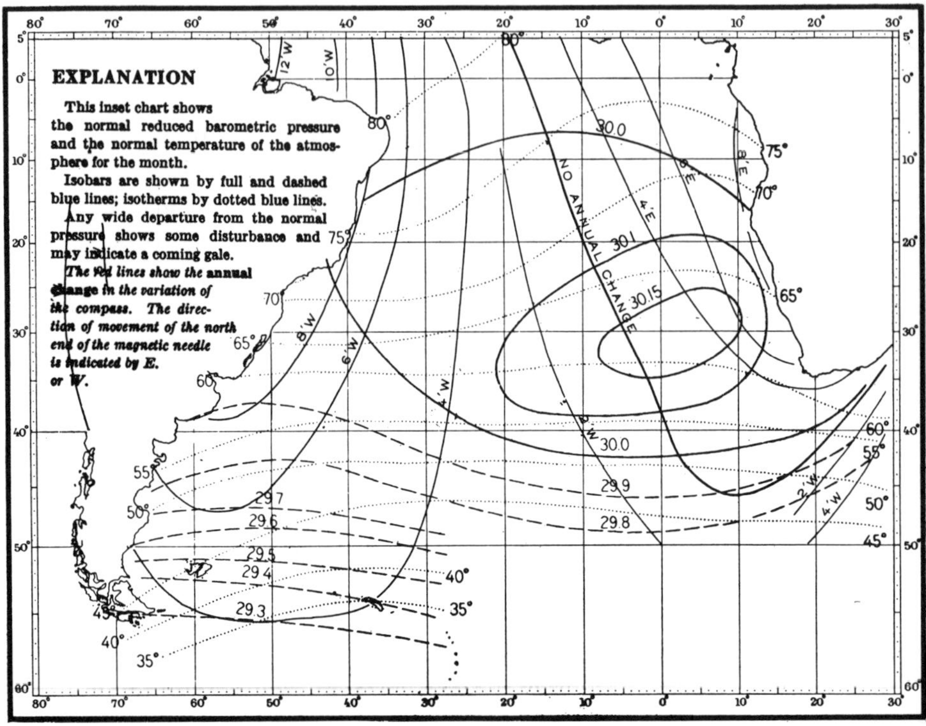
EXPLANATION
This inset chart shows the normal reduced barometric pressure and the normal temperature of the atmosphere for the month.
Isobars are shown by full and dashed blue lines; isotherms by dotted blue lines.
Any wide departure from the normal pressure shows some disturbance and may indicate a coming gale.
The red lines show the annual change in the variation of the compass. The direction of movement of the north end of the magnetic needle is indicated by E. or W.
NO ANNUAL CHANGE
30.0
30.1
30.15
29.9
29.8
29.7
29.6
29.5
29.4
29.3
80°
75°
70°
65°
60°
55°
50°
45°
40°
35°
12°W
10°W
8°W
6°W
4°W
2°W
2°E
4°E
6°E
8°E

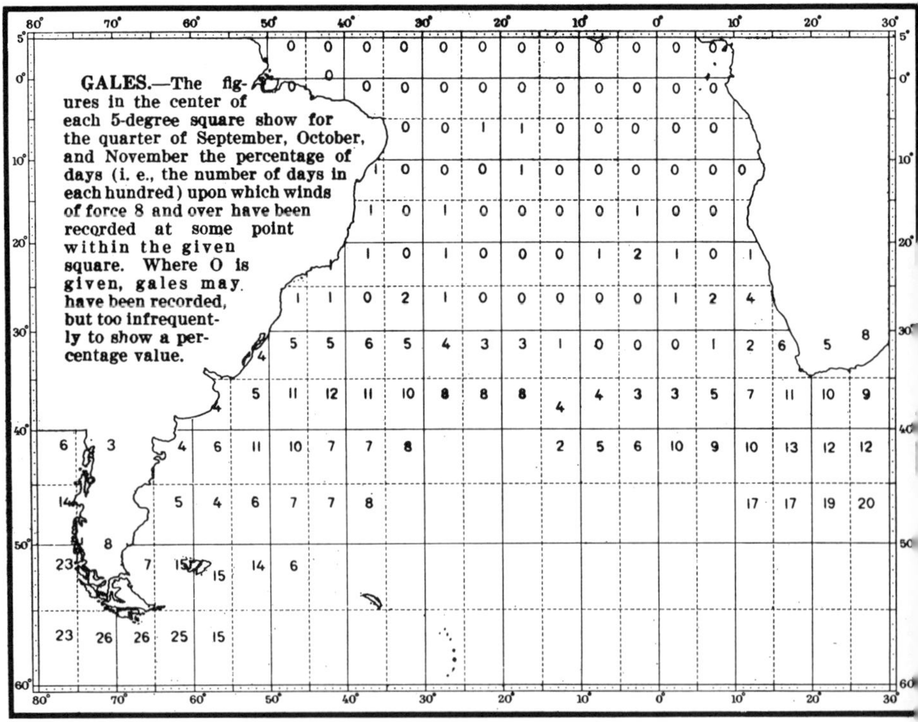
GALES.—The figures in the center of each 5-degree square show for the quarter of September, October, and November the percentage of days (i. e., the number of days in each hundred) upon which winds of force 8 and over have been recorded at some point within the given square. Where O is given, gales may have been recorded, but too infrequently to show a percentage value.

Modern adaptations of Maury's charts.

Maury was a brilliant lieutenant of the American Navy a hundred years ago. His wind and pilot charts are a memorial which will outlive even the navy he served. There is not a seaman alive who has not given thanks, wittingly or not, to Maury.

Such stories as even this simple tale of a little sailing vessel had vital value in Maury's day. Barring a few crazy tinkerers no one seriously believed sailing ships would ever be superseded by vessels utterly independent of the winds.

Sailing ship design was nearing its apogee, but a world which had tasted exhilarating speed was demanding more of it, and to make possible faster, surer voyages Maury commenced his magnificent study of the sea and its weather. He analyzed thousands of logbooks, itemizing each separate report of weather with reference to season and region, making allowance for the skill of observers and the accuracy of their instruments. He maintained a vast correspondence with foreign admiralties and sailormen. Out of these sources he formulated the first pilot charts, building so well and so wisely that the charts of today remain almost exactly as he made them.

He defined the limits of the trade winds, and plotted the sweep of the ocean currents. He proved that in this particular spot in such a season one would find less wind than in the same latitude but a few miles east or west, a few seemingly unimportant miles. Having learned such things he laid down sailing tracks which cut days and weeks from voyages. Cape Horn was, quite naturally, a focal point of his work, for the Canal dream was as phantasmal as the vision of steam.

Noon Position: 54°—40′ S., 75°—15′ W. (D.R.)
To 50° South in the Pacific: 305 Miles.
Made Good: 40 Miles. Sailed by Log: 90½ Miles.

Wander Bird is hove-to this noonday, and I read the chart filled with the bitter knowledge we are again blowing back to the Horn.

Maury forecasts for the Horn winds of gale force (OR OVER) twenty-six days out of a hundred. This is one of the highest gale percentages of any place in the world. The northwesters blow here, he indicates, 35 per cent of the time with an average strength of Force 7, which Beaufort forthrightly terms "strong wind." Westerly winds can be expected 28 per cent of the time, southwesters 18 per cent and southerlies 8 per cent. Between these winds calms may total 3 per cent.

These last eleven days the northwest wind has raged fully 95 per cent of the hours, and the gale percentage has certainly been up to par. Meanwhile, barring the one brief interval with the wind out of the southwest, we've had nothing else but short calms.

The law of averages, therefore, argues strongly for an imminent shift of weather. After these last ten or eleven days the probability of a fairing wind is better with every hour.

We are now due south of the jagged Patagonian coast. Hereafter, even though it brings us closer than is ideal to the land, we shall make northing whenever we can, tacking west only when it is mandatory. Escape is to the north; the port tack is our winning tack. Sometime, somewhere, and very probably soon, these hard winds must go to the southwest.

From this day on our track will show how we pursue this policy. The plan, though it eventually will lead us into dangerous proximity to the shore, I shall always regard as fundamentally justifiable and sound considering the circumstances. Stay-at-home critics will find it easy to criticize storm-harried judgment subsequently. They were not there at the time, wearied by the incessant whistle of wind, plagued by unending motion, raw-handed from swollen lines, weighted with command. Their omniscience will stem from hindsight; I can only estimate and guess at what the untapped future holds.

Cape Horn lookout—Wind NW Force 12

In the early evening all hands rally again and we dress the ship and stream the log for renewed struggle. The log entries succinctly tell the story:

8 P.M. Does not look very good.
9 P.M. Old story, cloudy, great seas, head wind.
10 P.M. Painful progress.
11 P.M. Short squalls. One minute strong wind, next none. Another tough day ends as the ship slogs ahead at three knots, pointing a scant half-point west of north.

TUESDAY, December 1.

The conditions grow more impossible, and the wind is firmly nailed in the northwest. At noon we gybe and stand to the westward, for the land is close aboard although hidden in rain. An observation gratifyingly places us a couple of miles north of our reckoning. We must keep the craven, down-tucked tail of South America from under our lee. It is the cruelest of all coasts, a frontier filed razor-sharp by wind and sea. We must anticipate every eventuality. We are sure our gear is strong, but—who knows?—we may conceivably be stripped of our canvas. Masts have gone by the board before this. If either should befall God Almighty couldn't save us if we had not first insured a clear lee.

Noon Position: 53°—20′ S., 75°—03′ W.
To 50° South in the Pacific: 234 Miles.
Made Good: 76 Miles. Sailed by Log: 71 Miles.

Just beyond the eastern horizon lies the Milky Way, that acreage of rocks awash or nearly so, where these marching seas are forever crashing, the milk of their shattering lying creamy on the reefs.

We gybe and stab at the west.

Night comes on, unalterably foul, with a new gale.

WEDNESDAY, December 2.

Only calloused habitude can explain the crew's uncomplaining acceptance of these monstrous conditions. It is blowing a hard gale at midnight—for a startling change—and the jibs have been torn adrift by seas wrenching at the bowsprit. Charlie and Barr work nearly an hour securing them. Often they have been arm-pit deep, sometimes buried, in freezing water, yet their only comment upon returning inboard is that "it is pretty wet" out there!

The gale is logged Force 10 by breakfast, and doubtless it is blowing at least that hard. The mainsail has been in since yesterday afternoon, but the ship is still sailing, logging three knots under inner jib and foresail. Blow this ice-armored wind down Long Island Sound and generations will recall the fierce-

Off Patagonia Wander Bird *meets the assault of a big sea which comes from very nearly dead ahead. As she did for so many stormy hours the ship is here sailing herself slowly to windward under storm sails and with lashed helm.*

There is enough motion (and to spare!) for most, but these sailors rig a swing out of mainsail reef-points to speed laggard time while the ship is hove-to.

ness of the hurricane! We take it in our stride, setting the jumbo before lunch.

Noon Position: 53°—52′ S., 77°—02′ W.
To 50° South in the Pacific: 235 Miles.
Made Good: Minus 1 Mile. Sailed by Log: 72 Miles

We have gained a good offing and won westing and sea room. The Fiftieth Parallel is a mile more remote than it was yesterday, and Talcahuano (our Chilean port of call) 87 miles more distant. It is depressing.

Back we go to the port tack this afternoon, making northing. For a few hours we sail east of north, hoping the jiggling wind will ultimately let us up, as it does a niggardly point or two. When the Old Man turns in just before midnight the ship is pointing west of north again. Her course made good is probably something east of the meridian, but the wind shift must certainly be near and it is permissible to lose a few miles of sea room gambling on the shift.

THURSDAY, December 3.

The squalls are growing more vicious hourly. Hitherto they have bothered us but little at night and we have been able to luff through them. Early this morning they are doubly strong, and breakfast is delayed while we scandalize the mainsail, dropping its peak, to ease the vessel through a buster. It is a cute trick and one which Bermuda-rig sailors must envy when they are caught overcanvased. The scandalizing of a gaff-headed sail cuts its area instantly and easily in half, spilling the wind from the upper part, and leaves drawing only a triangular sail bound by the luff, foot and the hypotenuse from clew to throat.

When swinging palls an ingenious sled is devised for an 18-foot toboggan slide across the canted deck.

The ship is forty miles off the coast. Our true north course will take her clear, and with the wind for six hours between west and west-northwest we let her go at seven knots.

Noon Position: 52°—14′ S., 76°—14′ W.
To 50° South in the Pacific: 135 Miles.
Made Good: 100 Miles. Sailed by Log: 100 Miles.

At noon we have again found evil weather and the wind is slipping back into its familiar northwesterly groove. We are forced inshore. At three we are steering north-northeast and can hold on no longer. We take the losing starboard tack with a gybe.

The mainsail is in at four o'clock and the ship steers herself into the clear. Having headed us inshore the wind now swings west again to drive us south. In high wind and drizzling rain we tack north once more this evening, making a bad course, with easting in it, but moving so slowly through the water it

School keeps at sea, too. Gwen, Ann, and "Commodore" wrestle with a correspondence course in the after-cabin while forward—

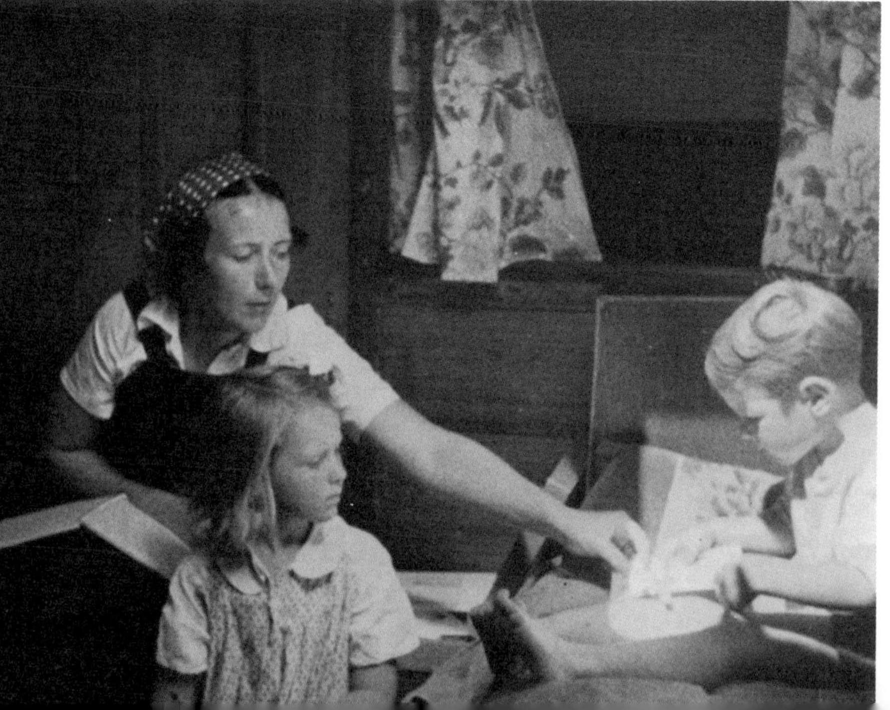

older student-sailors work as intently on navigation under the Old Man's tutelage.

doesn't seem a matter of vast importance. Where, O Lord, where is your southwesterly wind?

FRIDAY, December 4.

We are beaten nearly to a standstill. At noon we are in yet another severe gale and standing offshore. For all our labor we have gained but a pitiful thirteen miles. However, even that is a gain and if we can continue to do as well it is less than ten days to Fifty. Imagine our plight when we reckon spending ten days to make 122 miles! This same laboring vessel has run that between noon and the succeeding midnight, but that was in a dimly-remembered ocean where winds sometimes favored and sheets could be eased.

Noon Position: 52°—02′ S., 76°—40′ W. (D.R.)
To 50° South in the Pacific: 122 Miles.
Made Good: 13 Miles. Sailed by Log: 59 Miles.

At noon we are hove-to, on the offshore tack, in a violent gale.

The children alone retain gaiety and mirth. This morning they have been sliding across the sharply-heeled deck on a sled of their own devising. When that palled they devised a swing from a couple of the mainsail's reef-points. We envy their boundless energy. The rest of us are growing deadly weary, and it is hard to be cheerful and smiling at our work.

We have almost ceased hoping for a fairing wind and are grimly resigned to this struggle of our own seeking. Fools that we are! Think of your Philadelphia home, John! What price now the crackling fireplace, the bedroom slippers, the amber Scotch, the neglected trout flies and guns wanting your polishing hand? Why are you here?

And you, Charlie! What madness is this, leaving a girl, a sleek car and the lights of your loved Chicago for a world you have just summarized aptly in the log as "Rain, hail, sleet, HELL!" You, too, are here of your own desire; no wonder your face is dark and you do not speak hour on long hour!

Gwen is teaching school in the after cabin. It is the height of incongruity to hear her voice above the sounds of the gale as she leads the babes through the old, simple words. C-A-T, D-O-G. The ship bows to a furious squall, and Ann's lodged desk is set adrift. It and she fetch up with a crash to leeward in the midst of a sum. When the scattered pencils and paper are salvaged the little student unconcernedly sets about the problem of THREE PLUS FOUR EQUALS WHAT? Baltimore's famous Calvert School has sent its correspondence lessons to many outlandish places, but never to a wilder school-

Harrison rarely puts more than one foot on deck. Here, an industrious mole sniffing fresh air from his tunnel, he peels spuds at the galley hatch ready to jump below to simmering pots or to duck a spray.

room than this cabin dancing and diving around in the hell of Patagonia's cross sea.

We go back on the port tack this evening, having made a bit of westing. If we are to make our thirteen miles we must work north.

It is blowing very hard at midnight.

SATURDAY, December 5.

Within the jailing confines of the northwest quadrant the wind riots. Twist and turn as we will to its momentary whims, we can hold neither tack profitably. When we seek to make westing we are hounded south. When we come about, hoping for a safe northerly course, the gale at once blows our bow in toward the land.

Black squalls ride us down in the darkest hours, and the sea is frenzied. The long parade of gales, the aggravating internal dissension of currents crowded on the curving shore, and now these pile-driver squalls have maddened it. The plumed ridges lock in shocking internecine war, rearing tripartite and pyramidal, clashing their crests.

Noon Position: 51°—27′ S., 76°—12′ W.
To 50° South in the Pacific: 87 Miles.
Made Good: 35 Miles. Sailed by Log: 78½ Miles.

At noon land is sighted to leeward, dim, blue and far. We again head west, having set the reefed mainsail.

Between the seas we glimpse the first ship we've seen in nearly a month. She shows only a frantically pitching spar and a wraith of smoke; some unfortunate vessel from out Magellan Straits, doubtless.

Throughout the afternoon all hands are on deck, continually scandalizing and resetting the mainsail. Often we can luff through the squalls, but about twice an hour we are fronted by one extorting deeper obeisance.

We have rigged a snatch-block at the main rigging and led the peak halliard through it to the powerful mainsheet winch. It is a vast help in quickly resetting the mainsail when the weight is out of the squalls. At five o'clock the weather is worse, and we must abandon the mainsail altogether. In a blast of sleet it is frapped to the boom.

The wind swings tantalizingly west and we gybe to lunge into the fabled north where the weather is said to be fine. It is so silly. We are clinging most irrationally to the idea we shall find, immediately north of Fifty, smooth seas, fair winds and clear skies. Well, let us have this hope, else despair must needs be close! Let us get free of the Horn!

A terrific sea strikes long after dark. John says its solid and curving head broke right across the furled main gaff, filled the deck and half-drowned him on his lookout tour.

At midnight we gybe and once more claw offshore.

SUNDAY, December 6.

The Old Man is called from uneasy rest at four when the wind again tempts, promising us a mile or two of northing. Once again the horizon is looking brighter, seeming an earnest of a change in the weather. (Bright, unrelinquishable hope!) The weight of responsibility is vast, and the Old Man envies these others who have only to obey, who can sleep forgetful in their watches below and put their trust in another's judgment, letting him work out the salvation of all.

He has brought his ship too close to the famished shore, but he cannot see that he could have reasonably done otherwise. With every passing northwesterly hour it is mathematically more certain the wind must soon fair. In the face of this knowledge it seems impossible to make a long hitch to the west, losing miles, exposing the weather bow to the sweeping current. This way, with our head doggedly north, *Wander Bird* at least stems the running water, and possibly beats it a little. It is something. Her position contains serious possibilities, yes, but it is not desperate.

The coast is full of loop-holes where a smart vessel can get through to sheltered waters. If the worst should come to the worst the *'Bird* can dart through them to precarious safety. (It is a breath-taking thought!) Kelp buoys these deserted channels. The old pilot books assert the brown, floating fronds are more reliable than artificial buoys. Where no kelp shows there is no danger. Before accepting this alternative there is still the possibility of running due south or southwest. The soliloquy ends when the wind drives the ship's head yet deeper south. She is put about but can do no better than north-by-east at one knot. She'd be making six were it not for the sea.

Noon Position: 51°—10′ S., 76°—09′ W.
To 50° South in the Pacific: 70 Miles.
Made Good: 17 Miles. Sailed by Log: 55¾ Miles.

At midday we record a gain of seventeen miles. The afternoon is slightly more moderate and the close-reefed mainsail is carried until five o'clock when another gale punishes the ship.

So, at dark, we gybe and let the ship work away to the west in a deluge of rain. The seas seem to us "mountain high." We look out on the wildest of nights and go below to the comforting realization that things might be far, far worse.

The galley and cabin stoves are red. The blankets, fuzzy, bright and dry, color the inviting bunks. Our wet clothes swing in stiff-jointed unison as they dry saltily on the lines. Untouched stores of boots and rubber garments, woolen underwear, socks, shirts and trousers crowd the shelves.

Ample light makes the scene bright and cheerful. There have been few days so consistently vile we haven't been able at some time to charge the batteries.

Harrison, checking his stores, reveals lockers still brimming with richly diversified treasures ample for months.

Julian, Charlie and John are at a three-handed game of cards. William relaxes in swirling clouds of pungent Prince Albert, dreaming with half-shut eyes of balmy Jamaica. Barr is snug in his meticulously neat bunk and very professorial in spectacles and an erudite volume. The babes, cuddlesome in woolly pyjamas, are intent on the fantastic adventures of the Yongy-Bongy-Bo.

Aloft lights glimmer against the wet gale.

Giant albatross—These greatest of all sea birds sometimes reach a wing-spread of 17 feet and a weight of 35 pounds. Their feathers are often three inches thick. They are gluttons and, when opportunity allows, eat so much they cannot fly. Ordinary storms do not seem to bother them in the least but a hurricane will generally find them riding saucily on the water, spreading their wings only enough to surmount the dangerous crests which at times threaten them.

While we sleep, read and play the ship shelters us, meeting with staunch bow and flanks the night's rage, anticipating the thrust of each sea and parrying it as gracefully as a fencer. From her comes no faintest murmur or complaint.

The lookout on his rounds finds the gear all safe, each strand, fiber, atom and splinter working as ordained.

From contemplation of this think for a moment of other ships which have passed this way! Think of the square-riggers with flooded forecastles and heartbreaking work on dizzy yards. Consider their ill-clad, ill-fed men driven by masters blind to suffering and exhaustion. See how these seas brim with mischief! Others no different have shifted many a cargo and doomed many a ship to lingering death on her beam-ends. These squalls in no wise differ from those old ones so adept at catching square sails aback and uprooting, in an eye's wink, the entire vital forest of masts and yards. Hereabouts many an anguished seam has opened under unendurable stress, and many a pump has clogged and broken in unequal struggle with the ocean.

Verily, we are lapped in luxury. Let the log read:

11 P.M. Darkest night ever seen. Wind howling.
12 midnight. No let up. Blowing like the devil.

Still we sail in incongruous comfort. The ship is glorious.

MONDAY, December 7.

Noon Position: 50°—55′ S., 76°—25′ W.
To 50° South in the Pacific: 55 Miles.
Made Good: 15 Miles. Sailed by Log: 47¾ Miles.

There is nothing to report. Yesterday afternoon we got closer to Fifty than we are this noon, but we've been losing northing ever since we later stood offshore under the reefed foresail and a single straining jib. We have gained fifteen miles, no more, but we are thankful for that.

There are no longer any intervals of relative calm or any signs of clearing. The seas are tremendous. It is blowing with hurricane violence at midnight and we run off before wind and sea to muzzle the jib. The last oil bags are working to windward. We must sew up some more tomorrow.

TUESDAY, December 8.

Last night's gale has set us back fifty-four miles, all we've won in the past four days. We have lost westing as well as northing, but are in no more hazardous a position than before, thanks to the curve of the coast.

The squalls average three an hour today. They are careering through a wind already blowing gale force and outstrip it with ease. Some we can avoid, not many. Their cumulus heads are miles high, pompadoured and silvery. They look disarmingly soft and fluffy up there but underneath they show metallic, gun-metal blue, flat and hard. Each is a pillar of hail, a mile and more in diameter. They sweep over the western edge, envelop us with sleet and screaming wind and are gone so quickly it seems not unreasonable to believe they are making sixty knots.

The entire morning watch we sail northeast-by-north, then gybe to the west until nine. We once more swing to north-by-east as a gale makes up at noon.

Noon Position: 51°—49′ S., 76°—12′ W.
To 50° South in the Pacific: 109 Miles.
Made Good: Minus 54 Miles. Sailed by Log: Log scarcely carried at all this day.

The patch on the foresail clew cringle has started to rip and we have lowered the sail. Everyone is sewing on either oil bags or the foresail.

The sea is something phenomenal, its wildest excesses of all the yesterdays having at last been surpassed. We are assaulted now simultaneously on both sides, from dead ahead and from astern. How such a thing can be defies comprehension, but it is so. There is a savage swell from the north and an equally big one from the west. From the northwest, whence come these gales, the biggest and main sea runs high. Cutting in, sprung from no one knows what, there is now and then a foaming bastard out of the south. Piling and heaping together, these superimposed giants tumble backward and forward and sideways in tumultuous rough-and-tumble.

A new "button hole" patch is fitted about the foresail reef-cringle and sewn hard to both sides of the wet sail. By late afternoon this most vital of all our canvas is again reefed and reset. (How simple it all sounds! What tedious, hard work it is to do!) Four new oil bags are also ready for the next violent gale.

Conditions are worse. Progress seems utterly impossible even though the sluggishly-turning log records a couple of knots. We are exhausting our strength and patience scandalizing and re-setting the mainsail in squalls of sleet and wind.

This course is bad, too. We are closing with the land again. *Wander Bird's* usual slow and easy motion now is jerky, erratic and entirely unpredictable in this anarchist sea. Why she is not rent plank from plank is a mystery.

The angling seas run to form deep hollows, only immediately to fill them brimming with their tumbling crests. The ship bravely fronts each hazard, balances briefly astride each lifting ridge and then falls a-crash into another sheer crater. Her jib-boom and its furled sails plunge into solid water which thunders over the depressed bows to jet white against each obstruction.

Sunshine and shadow, with the wake lying like a mantle of lace on the sea's shoulders. The ship flies from the Horn with a double reef in the main-sail. Streaky cirrus clouds foretell a change of weather.

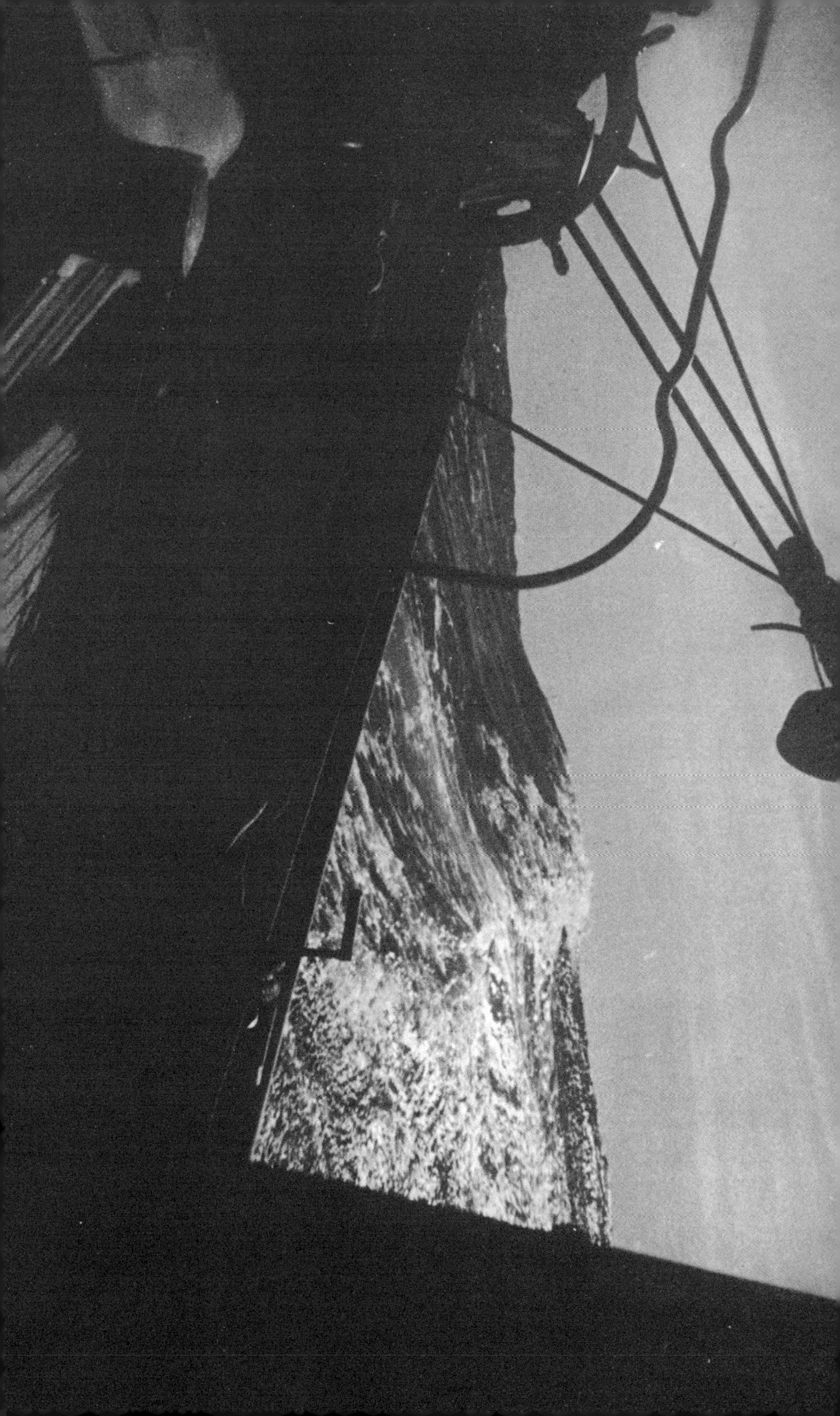

But even this cannot subdue this ship, this living and fighting miracle of beauty, strength and courage. She rises afresh to every assault and tilts anew at the sullen sky with her lancing jibboom.

This sort of thing ultimately rips the outer jib adrift. It was well stowed, double-lashed with new three-quarter-inch line, but the stout rope has snapped and frayed, crying eloquently of the violence of those clutching seas and the fury of the ship's struggle.

We have stowed the mainsail; now we run forward to save the jib, accepting with what fortitude we can muster the cold duckings which go these days with work on the jibboom.

Having clubbed us into submission the weather now perversely moderates almost at once, leaving us too weary and discouraged to set another rag. Undercanvased for this rampaging ocean the schooner bashes ahead, painful mile after mile, long hour after hour.

Night comes and we hold the winning port tack. A year hence I shall possibly agree with critics that it would have been more prudent to have sailed offshore this night. Tonight I want nothing but to get away. God! Can't you understand how we all want to get away?

It is clearing in the northwest; stars are showing for the first time in a week. The wind fluctuates, blowing sometimes, briefly, from west-northwest or a bit more west. Its shifts are torments, each one posing the problem: What tack now?

With the wind at west-northwest we sail north. It is a course which (if leeway, current and sea are not too greedy) will take us narrowly clear. On it every mile sailed is a mile gained. Even allowing for the worst sort of a set to leeward it will be daylight long before we are within sight of the high coast; meanwhile we shall have gained *something* and maybe encountered the expected shift of wind. Now and again, for five or ten minutes, we sail a point west of north. That course is safe; if we make it often enough we will surely go clear.

But if we tack offshore, as chiding prudence suggests, we shall sail back into the deep southwest, losing very nearly a mile for every one sailed!

The Old Man, gored by this dilemma, still clings with touching faith to Maury's forecasts. "It is a thousand to one this weather is clearing right now. Look at that sky!" he tells the tired crew. "We'll hold to the north. Keep a sharp lookout to leeward."

At midnight it seems he may at last have called the turn. The ship is sailing a better course, the stars are serene and brilliant in a clear sky, and hope apparently has been rewarded for its long vigil.

WEDNESDAY, December 9.

In the graveyard watch we buried our midnight hopes. The logbook was scarcely closed on the final entry yesterday when a squall blotted the night and the wind again headed. It was a dirty dawn, but there was no sign of the expected land at four. Possibly we are farther offshore than our cautious reckoning indicates.

Lookout John, alarmed, calls the Skipper hurriedly only a half-hour later. The land *is* there. Making all due allowance for its height it is uncomfortably close. Though visibility is bad it is apparent the ship is headed into Concepción Straits; land is dim on the port bow.

The wind is steady at west-by-north. Had it but settled there yesterday the ship would have sailed clear during the night. The Old Man's gamble has lost, by only a dozen hours or less.

Two courses are open.

Concepción Strait is a tortuous inland waterway leading for three hundred miles north between cramping islands and opening again on the Pacific far beyond Fifty. It is badly charted and flushed by currents and tides of unpredictable strength. If we enter it we sentence ourselves to worry, unceasing toil and all the grave risks of sheltered waters.

Or we can throw away this dearly-bought northing, although heart's blood itself seems scarcely less precious, and run back to the south. With current under us and the coast soon curving away southeast we can clear our lee.

Whatever choice is made it will be better for prompt decision. There will be no reconsideration.

Right now we are being set so fast athwart the entry to the Strait that access to it is problematical. It is unquestionably more prudent to seek safety past that out-thrust shoulder of land dimly seen to the south and east. We can neither hesitate nor equivocate.

Many would reckon our situation desperate. It is scarcely that, but if we fail to clear the land we shall surely have to run the kelp gantlet into God-knows-what nightmare of boiling shoals and rocks. A shipmaster who brings his vessel to such a pass savors a bitterness beyond the comprehension of those who do not know command. It is the Old Man's bitter portion now as he ups the helm in full retreat, abandoning the miles won so laboriously.

The gybe, accentuated by a sudden and inopportune squall, is hard. John, coming aft, discovers it has torn the foresail again at the cringle.

This makes it an even thing, whether or not we can sail clear of that shoulder. We must at all costs repair the foresail, and while we do it the ship will sail badly with the trysail on the foremast. In the face of these shrieking squalls we cannot contemplate setting even a corner of the mainsail.

Without saying much but working surely, spurred by a fear of which none need be ashamed, we get in the foresail. The needles are at it as the trysail is swayed aloft.

The crippled *'Bird* does her best, but can point no better than seven points from the wind nor make more than a couple of knots. The peaks slide past, clearer in full daylight, and their march tells of the current's potency. We are being set south by it, but it angles across our bow, and is putting us onshore, too.

Not until seven o'clock this morning can anyone draw a free breath, but at that hour we emerge from blinding sleet and shout with delight at finding the land at last abaft our leeward beam. The hooked continental tail cringes away. We are safe again.

Noon Position: 51°—44′ S., 75°—40′ W.
To 50° South in the Pacific: 103 Miles.
Made Good: 6 Miles. Sailed by Log: 66 Miles.

All day we stand to the south-south-west, heedless of lost miles in the glowing realization that our ship is safe and the shore ever more remote.

We open the last tank of water. It holds 400 gallons but everyone understands why the Old Man announces that hereafter water will be strictly (if generously) rationed. Each man will be allowed two quarts per day, half of that going to Harrison for cooking, tea and coffee. Ships of the past have fought the Horn for three and four months. We begin to realize how interminable our struggle may be, and precious water becomes our chiefest treasure. Down here rain is usually so fouled with spray there is little chance of ever catching a potable supply.

This evening we are not more than thirty miles from the

mouth of Magellan Straits, and again the Old Man is wrestling with the demons of temptation.

Off there, five hours' sail and just within the Straits, is Port Mercy, all bright with allure. "One of the best anchorages—" say the pilot books and the corroboratory charts, "very conveniently placed for anchoring while waiting for a favorable opportunity—there is no danger in entering, the depth is moderate, the ship will be well sheltered—wood, water and fish abound—"

What sweet poet ever sang more entrancingly?

Against these blessings what has this unendurable sea to promise us? More gales, more sleet, more rain? Is it not the better part of wisdom to forsake all these for the port's mercy?

Why, even the name invites and soothes! Port Mercy! There are not many such soft words to be found hereabouts; most are eloquent only of death, defeat and misery: Cape Deceit, False Cape, Anxious Pass, Desolate Bay, Port Famine, Disappointment Bay, Last Hope Inlet, Non-entry Bay, Wreck Island, Grave Cove. Syllables of heartbreak and despair.

The Evangelista Light we know is winking guidance just beyond the eastern edge. "Go on in!" the persistent inner voice argues convincingly. "Fill the tanks with snow water, catch fish, evade this abrading wind, sleep your fill!" Such voices they were which sang to Ulysses, and he wisely stopped his ears to the siren songs of snug leeward ports. He, too, had a voyage to make.

We shall keep the sea, and though the choice is hard it is right. This is no place for idling at anchor. Keep the sea! Sail the ship! Leave Cape Horn!

The foresail is repaired, reefed and aloft again at eight

o'clock; the ship sails better, pointing higher and footing faster. A sharp lookout is maintained all night but not even the soft loom of the Evangelistas is seen.

There are squalls tonight and they flicker with the first lightning we've seen down here. Possibly this is a good sign, at any rate it is something new.

THURSDAY, December 10.

Possibly we are deluding ourselves, but it seems as though the early hours today are decidedly less violent than usual. Perhaps it is only by comparison with yesterday's dawning that this one seems almost fine. Though there are still squalls about, their punch seems largely gone, and the sea is going down very fast. All hands welcome cessation of the tiring motion which we realize now has been fearfully wearing. The wind (THAT'S why things are so amazingly different!) has ceased its whistling whine! Certainly this is a portent!

Yesterday's retreat has cost us 76 miles. Here is a dismally interesting statistic: Since passing Horn Island we have sailed 1395 miles in twenty days and have gained just 385 miles. Our average speed through the water has been 2.7 knots; average speed made good over the bottom 0.85 knots!

Noon Position: 52°—38′ S., 76°—13′ W.
To 50° South in the Pacific: 179 Miles.
Made Good: Minus 76 Miles. Sailed by Log: log readings incomplete.

The Mexican tamales Harrison discovers today are indubitably tasty, but scarcely the thing to serve sailormen on a water ration!

No one says anything about it, but at one o'clock this afternoon the wind is actually south of west and the ship is actually making four knots on the desired course! We carry the fisherman, yes, but the reefs are left in the working canvas. No one expects this to last and we refuse to let hope rise.

The squalls now are not too bad, and the weather generally is almost fair. For the first time in a fortnight we carry all lowers (reefed, of course!) into the night.

At midnight we reckon we have logged fifty-six miles since the wind came, and although we are still close-hauled we are sailing northwest-by-north. It is all too wonderful. It can't be true!

FRIDAY, December 11.

Noon Position: 50°—39′ S., 77°—47′ W.
To 50° South in the Pacific: 39 Miles.
Made Good: 140 Miles. Sailed by Log: 122 Miles.

Give thanks to whatever gods there be that we eschewed Port Mercy! It is noon, and in a magnificent day we have regained all the miles we won and lost this last week. The log allows us 122 miles, but it is either dirty or worn, for we've outstripped it by almost twenty miles.

The *'Bird* flies with eased sheets, her motion all one smooth-flowing swoop. Her wake is a lacy shawl on the soft shoulders of a gentle sea. The lee rail stoops low to listen to the singing bubbles streaking by and water roars again under the forefoot.

At four the happiest crew afloat shakes out the mainsail reefs. The sail sighs its relief as the wind and stretching halliards iron out the deep, old wrinkles. What a huge sail it is! We have forgotten.

Now it is seven o'clock, the second dog watch. The ship slides on, and never for us shall the speed of plane, skis or plunging eagle compare with these seven knots!

"All hands! Shake out foresail reef! Jump, you bullies!" This

Twenty-eight days after crossing Fifty South in the Atlantic, having sailed 2300 miles to make good a thousand against wind, sea and current, Wander Bird finds a southwesterly and is driven hard with lee rail often rolling a-wash.

is the joyous and awaited signal. By unspoken but tacit agreement we have known all along that the foresail reef would remain tied in so long as the Cape remained unconquered. For nearly a month we have flown it at half-mast, symbol of a challenge which might have failed.

But it is now seven o'clock and the ship is carrying a gleaming bone in her teeth as she snarls across Fifty. The tall foresail is swayed aloft, all the way, and crowned with the bulging fisherman staysail.

"Tonight even the porpoises have to hump to keep up," reads the log at eleven o'clock. Between that happy hour and eight bells we race 9½ knots, and only those who were aboard will ever reply with suitable emphasis to the logged query

"AIN'T THAT SOMETHIN'!!"

IV. FINALE

NORTH of Fifty we found halcyon days and smooth seas. The ship sailed to meet midsummer and her progress had the glide and sweetness of an old song. Each watch took over with bated breath lest this dream of an ordered ocean and fair wind should prove to be only that and we be roused soon to new struggle with other gales.

Fifty-two days out of Rio we entered Talcahuano, the sprawling port for Concepción some three hundred miles south of Valparaiso. Our visit was brief and filled with bustle for we wanted to be on our way home.

Gwen took ashore a doryful of laundry. Since she was wise in the destructive ways of port laundrymen she spent a morning instructing some obviously puzzled but polite Chileans in the art of washing woolens—lukewarm water for washing and rinsing, etc., etc.—quite failing to appreciate that in this country everyone wears woolens and that while our sheets, shirts and handkerchiefs might return leaving something to be desired our heavy-weather clothing would be done to the Queen's own taste.

There was Christmas shopping to be done. It cost me two days and five dollars to find and acquire for Ann just such a washable rubber doll as I can buy anywhere at home for a

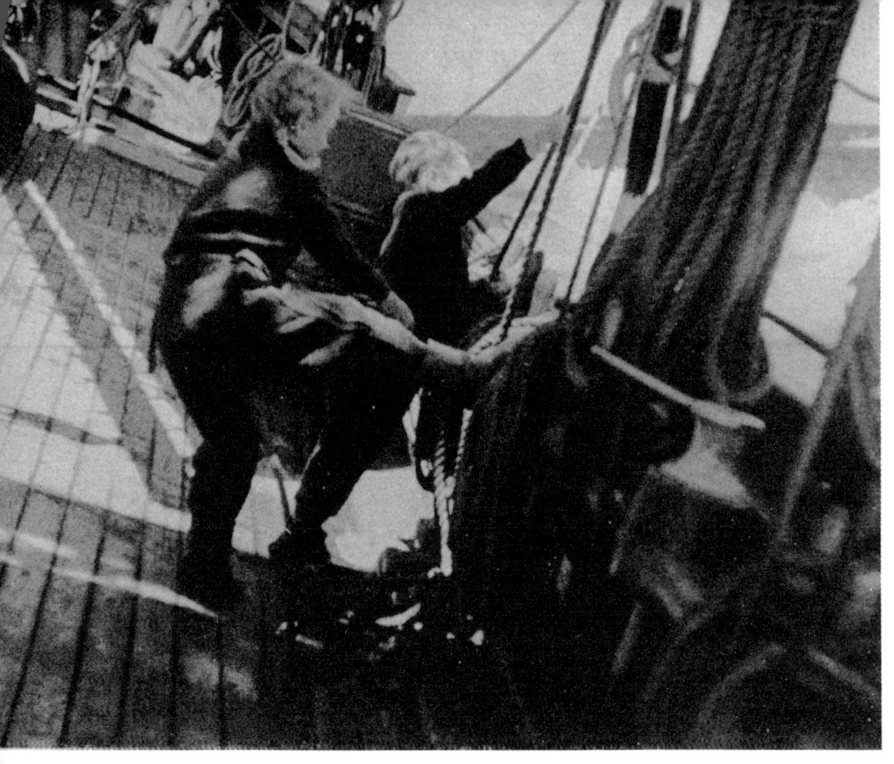

Once more the sea-going babes sway aloft the maintopsail and—

quarter. The steep, forested hill overlooking the anchorage had to yield us a tree for Christmas.

We did not meet many Chileans, but news of our arrival spread rapidly and everywhere we were met with smiles and courteous interest. It was a pleasant contrast to the Brazilian attitude which was strikingly typified by a bald newspaper statement which stated the *Wander Bird* was not at all worthy of comparison with the 1500-ton steam yacht in which an Italian munitions profiteer had recently visited Brazil.

The different outlook is directly traceable, I believe, to the fact that much of Chile's virility springs from the sailors who, having rounded Cape Horn, have jumped ship and settled for life along that narrow sloping ribbon which is South America's west coast. Danes, Swedes, Norwegians, Germans, Hollanders,

Americans, English and Irish sailormen were the forebears of many stalwart blue-eyed Chileans of the present, and their descendants have an instinctive feeling for the sea and the sea's people.

We had much mail to read, and the burden of most opening paragraphs was the concern and alarm felt for our safety by those at home, "safe at home" was the usual unconsciously humorous way the writers referred to themselves. It was funny because, as you have read herein, we came around the Horn without stubbing a toe or mashing a finger, but our Talcahuano mail was filled with complaints of scarlet fever, influenza, auto smash-ups, ski mishaps, laryngitis and colds. One of our landed friends had got himself thoroughly kicked by a pet Missouri mule and wrote of his great concern for us from his hospital bed. Safe at home, indeed!

Christmas found us three days out of Talcahuano. The tree stood in the main cabin bright in decorations and banked with

hoist the ship's international call a few days later as she nears Talcahuano, Chile.

beribboned packages. Its glittering branches rose and fell in rhythm with the ship's ceaseless if easy motion until the poor little fir was exhausted. It folded up in droopy defeat, the most pathetic and weary sapling I've ever seen.

For three solid weeks we held the port tack through the southeast trades, the world's steadiest and finest winds. We averaged 180 miles a day into the northwest, and almost literally touched neither sheet nor halliard.

The kites bulged aloft. Warm, fluid tropic air swept through open skylights and hatches, ruffling freshly starched bunk curtains and tossing candle flames as we supped in soft light.

We black-varnished the rigging and replaced worn ratlines, scrubbed the topsides and painted the bulwarks. It took a week of work to clean the Horn patina from the brass.

I dragged out clean new charts, and mused once again over the grimy faces and zigzag tracks pricked on the old ones. If there was a flaw in the voyage it was there, down off Patagonia, when I got too close to the beach. Some will doubtless feel justified in taking me to task for that, but their criticisms shan't make me lose sleep. I wouldn't go in there again, true, but at the time I acted to the best of my knowledge and was rather the victim of peculiarly vicious circumstances than of an egregious error in judgment.

Again there is that hard sea law—credit must be distributed equably to all, blame is the unchallenged possession of the Master alone.

We followed the sailing track laid down by Maury, crossing the Line for the second time in 114—30W. Out there the Pacific doldrums are very narrow; sometimes the opposed trades meet at a line sharp and plain on the ocean. So it happened the day we exchanged one trade for the other. From running free we came hard on the wind without the ship losing her stride.

West Coast calm—The ship lost her jibboom in the Pacific's NE Trades and came home under jury rig. Here she is shown slatting in the glassy calms and huge swells 600 miles from Los Angeles.

The northeast trades were sullen and squally under a low and leaden sky. For the next two weeks we scarcely saw the sun.

As we neared the California coast our eagerness to get home caused me to drive the ship harder and harder. We were luffing through black rain squalls one night when the jibboom let go, jibtopsail and outer jib having proved too much for it. That night and the following day we had a hard job clearing the wreckage because a nasty head sea was running and the ship was wet forward. Sailing gear looks lacy and delicate when standing in place, but it is awkward, heavy and ponderous when broken all adrift. Ultimately we cleared the mess, rigging the foretopmast stay through a snatchblock at the bowsprit end to steady the topmast. Again we set the jibtopsail. We proceeded then almost as before, though looking very snub-nosed indeed.

Eventually the trades spewed us into the notorious Horse Latitudes off California. These regions, in both Atlantic and Pacific, get their name from the fact that old-timers often had to throw their cattle overboard hereabouts to save drinking water.

From ninety miles at sea we saw the loom of Southern California's astounding electrical illumination and below it was the flash and dull boom of big guns as the battle fleet engaged in night gunnery.

Forty-five days out of Talcahuano we slipped unnoticed into Los Angeles harbor in a cloudburst. Our arrival coincided with the ending of the great maritime strike, the "unusual" weather and the public kissing of a U. S. Senator by Jean Harlow, so *Wander Bird* was lucky to get mentioned in the Marine Intelligence columns of the press.

We were eight and a half days battling up the California coast against hard northwesters and current.

On February 20, 1937, through smoky-gray night mist, over the Bay's oily ebb, *Wander Bird* slipped through the Golden

Power!—An intimate glimpse of the mainmast which is eloquent of Wander Bird's strength and massive construction.

Note the half-oval galvanized iron strips taking the chafe of the boom jaws and the strength of the original mast-winch. The wire paralleling the mast is the radio aerial. Under the boom is a bronze snap-shackle intended for a Cup Defender but used on the boom pennant of Wander Bird instead.

Gate. Commodore and Ann, up scandalously beyond their bedtime, conned the ship from a perch on the square-yard. They were concerned lest the tall homecoming spars foul the flat golden arch of the Bridge.

Two Coast Guard boats purred as they pushed us gently into the Marina where a handful of night prowlers stared at the white ship.

Flung heaving lines and shouts, "All fast forward!", "All fast aft!", were requiem of the voyage.

For all the great joy and triumph of that moment we turned with sadness to the land.

Wander Bird facing new voyages with improved head-rig. Carrying now a single jib set on a longer bowsprit.

V. TRANSCRIPTION OF *WANDER BIRD'S* ROUGH LOG FOR THE DAYS SPENT AT THE HORN

IN the preceding story Miles Made Good each day will be found not to agree with those set down in this copy of the log. The explanation is simple. Under the stress of the Horn conditions the navigator did not reckon each day the distance to Fifty in the Pacific, and generally put down as Made Good simply the distance sailed from noon to noon.

Barring these unimportant inaccuracies this log, written equally by all of the crew, fully substantiates the tale already spun. It is regrettable the original log is so faded, stained and illegible it could not be photographically reproduced in our various handwritings. It has lost personality in its reincarnation in type.

The rough log is bright with red seals indicative of days of heavy gales; sometimes the entries mention "seals" meaning these markers and again the swimming kind we saw so frequently about us. The exigencies of bookmaking forbid reproducing gale markers in red; those days are starred in black.

The "Garbo" mentioned at times refers to Gwen who reminded the gallant John of the screen lady.

Bearings, courses steered and similar directions in the log are MAGNETIC. In the story they were converted to TRUE for sweet simplicity's sake.

JOURNAL *from Rio de Janeiro* TO *Talcahuano, Chile*

H.	K.	COURSES	WINDS	REMARKS, FRI. 13TH DAY OF NOV. 1936
1				Wind jumped to SW at 00^h Down jib-topsail
2	1941	SSE	SW7-8	Mainsail furled. Glass rising again—Damn!
3	1946¼	S		Wheel lashed—She's rolling along
4	1951¼	S		Colder
5	1956½	S	SWxW	Wind about the same—Sea calmer
6				
7	1967¾	S½W	SWxW	Wind just the same—Blowing hard ★
8				
9		SSE		
10	1983¾	SSE		Both jibs down—quite a breeze
11	1987	SSE	SW9	Hard gale—
12	1990¾		SW9-10	South of 50! Starting around ye Horn.
1	↑			
2				
3				
4		Hove-to on port tack, Very heavy gale with enormous seas.		
5		Under double-reefed foresail. Snugged down with 3 oil bags		
6	↓	smoothing things out.		
7	↑			
8		Wind SW10		
9				
10		Blowing so hard the barograph has reversed!		
11		Honest to Gawd! Wind SW-10		
12	↓	ALL'S Well—Breeze holds—Heading W.		

—NOON POSITION—

Made good 126 miles. Noon Lat. by Ob. 50-05S. Lon. by Ob. 62-14W.

H.	K.	COURSES	WINDS	REMARKS, SAT. 14TH DAY OF NOV 1936
1	↑			
2	│	ALL'S Well—Breeze Lighter—Seas Moderated		
3	│	Heading NW—		
4	│			
5	│	Barometer again carrying ball in right direction		
6	↓	Underway—All plain sail & jibtops'l—Fine Day		
7	1998	SSW	W-2	Pumped dry, 4 minutes
8	2000¼			
9	2004½	SSW	W4-5	Freshening. Battening down skylights
10	2011¼	"	"	Snowy-looking and feeling—
11	2018½	"	"	Passed north-bound steamer—
12	2025½	"	WxN5	Seas more regular—Lost 51 miles due
1	2033½	SSW	"	to current & leeway while hove-to
2	2042	SSW		Took in jib top
3	2050¼			All's well
4	2058¾	SSW	WxN4-5	Cold sky looming ahead—All's well.
5	2066	SSW	WxN	Getting a wee bit chilly—49° F
6	2073	"	W4	Lighter airs but still going nicely
7	2080	SSW		Light rain
8	2086	"		Many seals about—Grand sunset
9	2092	SxW	WSW	Wind Heading. Clear and fine
10	2098	SxW	"	Wind Lighter " " "
11	2100½	WxS	SSW2-3	Wind ahead—Tacked to Westward. Clear, Cool
12	2102¾	WxS	SWxS2	Beautiful night. Very light airs

—NOON POSITION—

Made good MINUS 20 miles. Lat. by Ob. 49-45S. Lon. by Ob. 62-13W.

H.	K.	COURSES	WINDS	REMARKS, SUN. 15TH DAY OF NOV 1936
1	2104	WxS	Phewy!	Probably plenty of leeway!
2				Finally got about—2:30
3	2107	S½E		
4	2110½	W		Came about 3:30 Headed Westward!
5	2115	W½N	S	Sun rises at 4.20 Wind getting fresher.
6	2119½	W½N	S	Wind trying to head us.
7	2123½	S½E	SW	Tack ship 6:30 Clear but cold
8	2129	S½E	SW	
9	2133	S	WSW	Reef in mainsail—good going
10	2138¼	S½E	SWxW7	Blowing harder—Clear & fine
11	2145¼	SxE	SWxW7	
12	2151½	SxE	"	Wonderful day and sailing. 310 miles To Cape Horn
1				Dropped foresail—Repaired and now putting reef in it.
2	2164	S'	WSW6	
3	2168¾	S		Topsail furled—
4	2173	S		
5	2181	S¾E	SWxW	Large seas—going O.K
6	2185¾	S½E		Set reefed foresail. Short calm spell
7	2191¼	S	WSW6-7	Wind back again—Sky overcast.
8	2198	S	WSW	'twas a dark and stormy night - - - - !
9	2205	S	" 7	Radiantly glorious sunset. Breezing up again.
10	2213	S	W	Making time with snug rig.
11	2213	"	W8-9	Garish phosphorescence—Overcast - - - Light ahead
12	2220¾	"	W7-8	In the clear again—Brite stars

—NOON POSITION—

Made good 89 Miles. Lat. by Ob. 51-11S. Lon. by Ob. 63-55W.

H.	K.	COURSES	WINDS	REMARKS, MON. 16TH DAY OF NOV 1936
1	2228½	S		
2			W9-10	Very heavy gale. Took in mains'l & jibs
3				
4		SSE		Cold—strong winds
5		SSE		Colder— 43° F
6	2247½	SSE		Took in forestays'l—Hove-to; Oil Out
7	Log In	ESE	S8-9	Wind and seas high
8				Glass going straight up.
9				Headed about SE. Wind from S.
10				Clear— Strong wind.
11			★	
12				
1				
2				
3				
4		SxE½E	WSW	Underway again at 4 P.M.
5	2250½	SSE	WSW	Beautiful day—Gale in the offing.
6	2252½	SSE		O.K. Greased steering gear.
7	↑			Slatting and banging—Lumpy old seas.
8	↓	WxS½S	SSW0-1	Gybed at 7.30 & tried to make a little Westing
9	2253	SSE	——	Gybed back to Southward at 8. All's well
10				
11	NO BREEZE ON OCEAN.			ALL'S WELL
12				

—NOON POSITION—

Made good 83 miles. Lat. by Ob. 52-40S. Lon. by Ob. 63-37W.

H.	K.	COURSES	WINDS	REMARKS, TUES. 17TH DAY OF NOV. 1936
1	2253	SxW		Did you get a breeze?
2	"	"		No!
3	2254¾	SxW	WxS	Yes! Wind getting fresher.
4	2257½	SxW	WxS	Wind coming up all the time—Clear
5	2261¼	SxW	"	Clear sunrise 3.55. Temp. 43° F
6	2265	"	" 3	Overcast
7	2268¾	"	"	Choppy sea. Wind Light
8	2272½	"	"	Hint of Rain.
9	2275½	"	"	
10	2278½	"	"	Big Charles Reports All is well
11	2279½	"		All's Well
12	2280¼	"	W0-1	Calm—of all things.
1		"		Fisherman Up at 12.40
2	2287	"		Working on electric pump.
3	2292	SxW	W	Pump OK.—Nice going.
4	2295	SxW	W	Wind drops again—Slow going.
5	2299	"	"	A Little Breeze helping us Along
6	2302½	SxW½W	"	Breeze Gone Light
7	2306	SxW½W	" 1-2	Breezing Up and Glass Falling Like A Stone
8	2312	"	WxN2-3	
9	2316¾	"	"	Freshening—and glass levelling again.
10	2321¼	SxW½W	WxN1	Wind dropped off—Glass Rising—All's Well
11	2323¼	"	WxN1-0	Rain—Squall to South—Lone star.
12	2324			No wind—Julian may get a breeze?

—NOON POSITION—

Made good 36 miles. Lat. by Ob. 53-16S. Lon. by Ob. 63-38W.

H.	K.	COURSES	WINDS	REMARKS, WED 18TH DAY OF NOV 1936
1	2324½	SxW½W		Did you get a breeze?
2	2326½	SxW½W	WNW	Yes—We got going again and fine going, too.
3	2331½	SxW½W	"	Nice going—Lots of seals—Not Red!
4	2337	SxW½W	W	LANDFALL — Staten Island 4^15 Up fisherman. S½W
5	2342½	SxW	WxS	Clear as crystal—Cool—Nice sunrise
6	2346¾	SxW	"	Snow-clad mountains of Terra de
7	2347	"	↑	Fuego & Staten Is. shining in distance—Calm.
8	2348¼	"	│	Calm—Shook out Reefs in mainsail
9			│	
10			↓	10^45 Set ballooner.
11	2349	SxW	NW-2-3	A balmy day—90° F in Sun; 59° in shade
12	2351	SxW	NW0-1	Becalmed.
1		Becalmed—Ballooner in as we tack twice to fickle zephyrs		
2		from SE and N.W.		
3				
4	2354	SxW½W		Fisherman Up again
5	2356	SxW½W		
6	2359	SxW		Fine evening, but very little wind
7	2360¾	"	NNE1-2	Very light airs—Fog over Staten Is. lowlands
8	2363	"	" "	20 miles to entrance Strait of Le Maire.
9	2365¾	S½W		Cool and Damp—Barograph 30.15
10	2367¼	S½W	NNE	No breeze—Clear Nite—Cape San Diego Light WSW
11	2368¾	S½W	"	Raised Staten Island Light 11.30
12	2370	SxW	NNE	Wake Skipper when log reads 80 Cape San Diego WSW 9 miles

—NOON POSITION—

Made good 63 miles. Lat. by Ob. 54-10S. Lon. by Ob. 64-28W.

H.	K.	COURSES	WINDS	REMARKS, THURS. 19TH DAY OF NOV. 1936
1	2372¼	SxW	ENE 1-2	Dawn coming since 0030. Sliding thru Strait.
2	2374½	S	NxE 1-2	
3	2379	SxE	NNE	Very strong current running
4	2385	SxE	NNE	Sun rises—3:50 A.M. Gybed for C. Horn at 4.
5	2391¾	SWxS	NNE4	Grand going. Horn 89 miles ahead
6	2398¼	"	N3	
7				Sprinkle of rain, but grand going nonetheless
8	2408	SWxS	NW3	Sliding smoothly on course
9	2413	"	" 3	Lite rain—Pumped dry 5 minutes—Set balloon jib $8^{\underline{25}}$
10	2413½	"	"	Rain cleared—Breeze backs again—Good going.
11	2418½	SWxS	NNW4-5	Freshening—Slight sleet & snow squall—All's well.
12	2425½	"	"	Fine going—What luck this is!!
1	2433	SWxS	N	Raining—Temp. 45° F
2	2441	"	N3	Clearing—Rain over—Wollaston Islands showing
3	2447¾	SWxS		Sighted C. Horn SWxW at 2.15—
4	2554¾	SW½S	N	Altered course to SW½S at 2.45. Find ship 11 miles behind reckoning
5	2560¼	SW½S		No Wind—Clear
6	2565¾			Dropped fisherman & stopped bal-
7	——			looner. Rainbow opposite fine sunset
8	2566			No wind–Sheeted In–Beautiful sunset
9	↓			" " " " Sun set at 8.20
10	↓	No sign of a breeze by 10.00 All's Well		
11		No Breeze as yet. The "Sea Serpent" apparently had		
12		plenty!		

—NOON POSITION—

Made good 105 miles. Lat. by Ob. 55-37S. Lon. by Ob. 66-07W.

H.	K.	COURSES	WINDS	REMARKS, FRI. 20TH DAY OF NOV 1936
1				★
2				
3				
4		Flat calm all night—Sun Rises at 3:50		
5				
6			N-o-1	Barnevelt Isles SW¾S 8 miles. Fine Day—Set fisherman
7	2567	SxW½W	NNW	Very light airs
8	2568	..	..	.. .. ..
9	2569	..		Fine sun—Peaks 50 miles away clear as crystal
10	2570¼	SSE	SW1-2	Freshening.—Raising the Horn again.
11	2573¾	SE	SW	Going along.
12	2576¼	W¼S		Freshening—Passing Barnevelts off Port bow
1				Port tack—Standing in for Barnevelts
2		SxE	SW7-8	Squall—Fisherman Down—Mainsail down—
3	2586	S½E	SWxW	Both jibs in—Double reefs—Blowing again
4	2589	S½E		C. Horn SW¾W 19 miles
5			..	Strong wind.
6			SW10-11	Wind gets stronger—Took in mainsail. Hove-to—
7	2594½	S		Out 3 oil bags—Rotten breaking seas.
8	2596	S½W		Jumbo set again at 6.15. Gale moderating.
9	2599¾	S½W		Still very strong wind—Cold—Temp 42—Wheel lashed.
10	2598¾	SxW½W		Very fresh Beautiful sunset sky—Land lost—
11	2599½	SxW½W		Wind making to westward. Barometer Rising.
12		SxW	WSW4-5	Strong Puffs from WSW & Lumpy sea —A good sailing Breeze: Set jibs and double-reefed mainsail.

—NOON POSITION—

Made good 13 miles. Lat. by Ob. 55-49S. Lon. by Ob. 66-29W.

H.	K.	COURSES	WINDS	REMARKS, SAT. 21ST DAY OF NOV. 1936
1	2600	S½W		Flat calm
2				
3	2601	SW	WNW	Going again
4	2605¼	SW	WNW	Shook reefs out of mainsail; 4 A.M.
5	2613	SWxW½W	NNW	Such a grand break! Hope to pass Horn during our watch.
6	2621	"	"	Deceit Island on starboard beam.
7				Cape Horn bears WxN¾N, 7 miles—Squall—Thick—
8	2633¼	SxW½W	W8-9	Mainsail down — Torn — C. Horn NW¼W—Jibs down.
9		SxW		Hove-to: Blowing severe gale—Oil out
10				Jumbo up at 9.30. Course SxW
11	2643½	SxW	W10	Jumbo in 10:30. Hard blow. Seas building & lengthening
12	2645¼	S	W10	Very big seas—Ship going nicely—Almost in Pacific!!
1	2646½	SxW	W10	Hove-to 12:55. Strong wind and sea
2	Log In	SSW	W	Wind and sea about same.
3				No change—Wind blowing Hell-o-Boy!
4			★	Wind and sea just the same—Ship swinging from SW to S
5				
6	2647	SWxS	W8-9	Still blowing hard but with more regular Seas
7	2648¼	SxW		Underway 6:10—jumbo; storm trisail on deck.
8	2650	SxW	W6	Moderating—Set storm trisail $8^{\underline{00}}$
9				
10	2653¼	SxW		Slogging—Light airs and big seas.
11	2654	SxW	W1	Breeze gone—Slatting—All's well
12	2654½	SxW		Shift of wind—NW—Steering WSW at midnite

—NOON POSITION—

Made good 33 miles. Lat. by Ob. 56-19S. Lon. 67-10 D.R.

H.	K.	COURSES	WINDS	REMARKS, SUN 22ND DAY OF NOV. 1936
1		WxS	WSW	No wind—Standing still—Inner jib up
2		WxS		Flat calm.
3	2656¼	WxS½S		Trying to stear a course in flat calm
4	2657	"		Breeze trying to come up—Outer jib up
5				
6				Rain—42° F—Cape Horn NNW from us
7	2661	SWxS	WxN	
8	2667	SSW	W6-7	Overcast—Blowing up
9	2674	SSW	W6-7	
10	2680¼	SSW	W	Reckon we are at last 2 miles west of C. Horn
11	2686¾	"	"	Clearer—In huge Pacific rollers now —Sailing nicely
12	2693½	"	"	Foggy spell—Many kinds of birds about—Good sailing
1	2700¾	SSW	"	Now well west of C. Horn
2	2706¾	SSW	"	Doing fine — Weather looking good as yet.
3	2712½	SSW	W	Ann's first day as mess cook—a fine job
4	2719	SSW	W	Nice going—Wind a little fresher
5	2724	SWxS	WxN6	
6	2729	"		Wind letting us up—Brite sunshine for a few minutes.
7	2234	"		Clear—Cool—Perfect
8	2739	"	WxN5	Dry cloud squalls passing over and killing wind.
9	2743¾	SWxS	WxN4-5	Still sliding on to the west
10	2749	"	"	Going along nicely—Numerous squalls
11	2753½	SWxS	WxN3-4	Clearing some "Nicht neues". Eased somc
12	2757¾	SW	WxN4-5	Cloudy night—Wind frees a bit—Making SW½W—All's well

—NOON POSITION—

Lat. by Ob. 56-54. Lon. by Ob. 67-41W.

H.	K.	COURSES	WINDS	REMARKS, MON. 23RD DAY OF NOV. 1936
1	2760¼	SW¼W	WNW5	Cold as a etc. - - - -
2	2763¼	SWxW	WNW5	Wind drop light. Heavy Seas running & cold
3	2766¾	SW¾W	WNW6	What? No sun!
4	2771	SWxW	WNW6	Nice going
5	2776	SWxW	WNW6	Clearing somewhat and a little windier
6	2781½	SW½S	WxN	Wind headed us but clear & fine going
7	2786¼	SWxS	WxN	Squall—Sleet—Clear again.
8	2791¾	SWxS	W	Heading wind
9	2796¼	SWxS	W3-4	Beautiful day, all's well.
10	2798¾	SWxS½S		Slow slogging.
11	2802	SWxS	W	
★12	2906½	SSW	WxS3-4	Wind heading
1	2909	SSW	W	Gybed—Sewing mainsail
2	2910	NNW	WxN	Heavy swells
3		NxW½W	WxN	
4	2913	NNW	WxN	Slow going.
5	2914½	NNW	WxN	Still slower going—All's well
6	2915¾	NNW	WxN	Repairing mainsail—All's well
7	2917	NW½N		Wind favoring us in its own good time
8	2917¾	NW½N	WxN	Head sea—
9	2919¼	NWxN	W	
10	2921¼	NWxN	W	Clear evening—Sewing. Cold
11	2923	NWxN	W	No "poosh"
12	2925	NW½N	W½S	Still no poosh

—NOON POSITION—

Lat. by Ob. 58-19S. Lon. by Ob. 70-08W.

H.	K.	COURSES	WINDS	REMARKS, TUES. 24TH DAY OF NOV 1936
1				Dawn at 12.30—Day light 1:30
2	2930	NNW	W3-4	Sea slowing us—Wind tending to head us off
3	2932¾	NNW	WxN	Able to read log at 2.a.m. by daylight —Repairing mainsail
4	2935¾	NxW½W	WxN	Gybed at 4
5	2939	SSW	WxS	Looks like a blow coming
6	2943	SWxS½S	WxS	Just a breeze—Getting nowhere fast
7	2947½	S½W		Breeze working around to free us now
8	2952½	SW½W	WxN	
9	2957¾	SW½W	WxN½N	Breeze fresher
10	2963½	SW½W	"	Wind heading slowly—fresher—
11	2970½	SSW	W	
12	2977¼	SSW	W7-8	Blowing fresh today—Sleety—Rotten.
1	2983¾	SWxS½S	W7	
2	2989	SWxS½S		Good day to be below by fire with a wee nip (Not so wee)
3	2995	"	"	Cold and wet
4	3000¼	"	"	" " " Temp 42°
5	3006½	SWxS¼S	"	★ Big sea gave us a bath
6	3013¼	SWxS	W7-8	Nice weather for ducks—All's well
7	3019½	SW½S	"	Wet up forward—and aft
8	3027¼	SSW	"	Outer jib in—freshening
9	3032	SSW	"	Still blowing fresh
10	3038¾	SSW	"	Hard blow and cold
11				Took in storm trisail 10.45. Blowing
12	3048	SSW		Gybed ship 12 midnite—Storm trisail set again—Weather clear up a bit.

—NOON POSITION—

Made good 30. Lat. D.R. by 58-10S. Lon. by Ob. 71-00W.

H.	K.	COURSES	WINDS	REMARKS, WED. 25TH DAY OF NOV. 1936
1		NW½W	WxN3-4	Filthy night—Rain—Cold
2				Rain—Cold—Sloppy, big seas and relatively little wind
3		NxW½W		
4	3058	NxW½W	WxN	Rain—sleet—cold. Temp. 40°—Heading wind.
5	3060½	NNW	WxN	Still cold—Rain, etc. All's well
6	3062½			
7	3067¼	N½W	WxN	Will gybe after breakfast
8	3071	N	WNW8	Confused seas
9	3075½	SW½S	" "	★ Gybed at $8^{\underline{35}}$ Heading SW½S
10	3081	SW½S	" 8	Rotten weather—Rain—Cold—Heavy Sea
11	3087¼	"	" 8	Beautiful day—Grrrr!
12	3093¼	"	" 8	
1	3098¼	SW½S	WxN	Long seas—Not much water coming over
2	3102¼	SWxS	W3-4	Trying to clear & wind heading. Go south, honey!
3	3105¾	SSW	WxN	
4	3108	SWxS	WxN	Cold and raw. Temp. 40°
5	3113	SW½S		Seems to be trying hard to clear.
6	Gybe ship—		WxN	Sights show current has set us 48 miles East in 36 hours
7	3119¾	NWxN	"	One may use a red seal before long.
8	3121¾	NW½N	W	I doubt it.↑Kallammittee Houllur! !
9	3123	NWxN	W½S	Not much headway
10	3127	NW½N		Nice going for a change
11	3129½	NW½N		Wind cold but not wet tonight
12	3132¾	NW¾N	W	Breezing up a bit

—NOON POSITION—

Lat. by D.R. 58-50S. Lon. by Ob. 71-37W.

H.	K.	COURSES	WINDS	REMARKS, THURS. 26TH DAY OF NOV 1936
1	3135¼	NWxN	WxS5-6	Oh! for a real southerly! Could read log at 1. a.m. by daylight
2	3139¼	NWxN½N	"	Clouds that look hopeful for change pass astern.
3	3143	"	"	Big clouds in S.W. but wind hangs West still
4	3148¼	NWxN	WxS7-8	39° F. Breezing up—Rotten, steep, sharp seas
5	3152	NW½N	WxS6-7	Continued squalls and Hail. Today is Thanksgiving.
6	3156¼	"	"	Clearing—and plenty cold.
7	3160	NW½N	WxS	Wind heading a bit—Pumped ship—Captured jib
8	3163¼	"	WxS	Clear and cold
9	3168	NNW		Still clear and cold—Wind heading again.
10	3173	NNW	W	Nice Day
11	3177¾	NNW	W	
12	3182	NxW		Not so cold at present—Practically nothing gained
1	3186¾	NxW	WxN	Repairing mainsail.
2	3190¾	NxW½W	"	Everything working fine.
3	3195	NxW	"	
4	3199¼	NxW	"	Gybed ship at 4 P.M.
5	3200	SW½S	"	Slow—Little wind—Overcast
6	3201	SW½W	NW	Hardly holding own against the current.
7	3201½	SW¾W	WNW	Maybe this will be a shift of wind?
8			"	
9	3203¾	W	NWxN	Wind shifting—Wheee! !
10	3206¼	WNW	N	Raining like pooches and felines.
11	3208¾	WNW	NxE	Snow—cold—Brr! 38°—Rain.
12	3212¾	"	"	Same—outer jib up.

—NOON POSITION—

Lat. by Ob. 58-04S. Lon. by Ob. 71-38W.

H.	K.	COURSES	WINDS	REMARKS, FRI. 27TH DAY OF NOV 1936
1		WNW	NNE3	Wind gone at 12^{50}. Slatting.
2	3221	W½S		Rain and light wind heading.
3	3225	SWxW	NW3	Hard on wind again. Glass falling fast
4	3227	SW½W		Practically no wind—Half fog and rain.
5	3227¾	SW	Gybe ship	Gybed ship—Steering NNW. Very light breeze.
★6	3229½	WNW	(((S)))	We are off—Huzza and Huzza! ! ! ! !
7	3235½	WNW	(S)	And <u>we</u> are the guys who <u>lose</u> the wind!
8	3242¾	WNW	SxW6-7	Feels like an honest wind.
9	3250	WNW	SSW	Sun out—Nice going
10	3258	WNW	SSW	Seas still heavy
11	3264¼	WNW	SSW	Wind and sea a little lighter
12	3270	WNW	SW5-4	Doing well. Set fisherman 11.30
1	3275½	NWxW	"	Wind heading
2	3281	NWxW½W.	WSW4	Grand and glorious going—Wonderful afternoon
3	3286¼	NWxW	"	Wind tending to head — Repairing mainsail
4	3290¾	NW½W	"	Wind tending to head and lighter.
5	3294½	NW	WSW4-5	" " " " And Lighter
6	3299½	NW		Sometime Light—Sometimes strong—All's Well
7	3303½	NW		Clouding up—Much cooler
8				Set full mainsail—Cleared decks
9				
10	3312¾	NW½W	WSW	Mainsail set—Calm night
11	3314½	NW½N	W	Breeze heading—So far fine night. All's well
12	3316	NxW	WxN	Came about 12.15 All snugged down. All's well

—NOON POSITION—

Made good 76 miles. Lat. by D.R. 57-11S. Lon. by Ob. 73-20W.

H.	K.	COURSES	WINDS	REMARKS, SAT. 28TH DAY OF NOV 1936
1	3319	WxS½S	NW2-3	Tacked at 00h—Smooth sea—pleasant going.
2	3324	WxS½S	NW	Bright full moon and dawn—Good steady breeze
3	3329¼	WxS½S	NW	Freshening—Windy-looking skies
4	3334	WSW	NWxW	Fisherman stowed—Wind heading a bit
5	3338	WxS	"	Not so cold this morning
6	3342¼	WSW	NNW	Cloudy and not looking so well
7	3347	WxS¼S		Fresh in the puffs.
8	3353	W		Doing fine
9	3358½	W	NWxN	Very puffy—Seas making up—All's well
10	3365	WxS		Mainsail down after reefing.
11	3370	WxS	"	Bad seas—Rain.
12	3375	WSW	NW	Rain and sleet
1	3379¼	"	"	Wind greatly moderated. Weather changing
2		WSW	"	
3	3386½	WSW	"	Put up single-reefed mainsail at 2.50
4	3391¼	WSW	"	Rain and sleet. Cold, but making good westing.
5	3395¾	WxS½S	"	★ Freeing us a bit.
6	3399¾	WxS½S	"	Rain.
7	3402¾	WSW	"	Tacked ship—7.30. NWxN½N
8	3405¼	NNW	WxN	Rain—Head seas—Lousy night. All's well.
9	3409	NNW	WxN	Rain—Heavy head sea—Blow up quite a bit.
10	3412½	NxW½W	WxN	Very unsettled—Rain stopped
11	3415¾	NxW½W		Clearing up very well—Moon out for once
12	3418	NxW½W		Very heavy seas running. Slow going

—NOON POSITION—

Made good 77 miles. To go 1150 miles. Lat. by D.R. 56-25S. D.R. Lon. 73-50W.

H.	K.	COURSES	WINDS	REMARKS, SUN. 29TH DAY OF NOV 1936
1				Violent cross seas
2	3424	N½W	NWxW9	42°F. Almost impossible to go ahead in these conditions.
3	3427	W¼W	" 9-10	Seas are mountains—Much headway impossible
4	3429½	NxW	★	Wind moderating some
5	3433½	NxW	NWxW9	Heavy head sea. Sun trying to get through.
6	3436¾	N½W		Breeze lighter. Seas eased—Cold rain
7	3441	NxW	NWxW	Bad squalls—Choppy sea—All go to make a fine day.
8	3445	NxW½W		Bad squalls—Choppy sea!!!!
9	3448¾	NNW		Blowing hard with rain squalls
10	3453¼	NNW	NWxW	Mainsail down 9.40
11	3456½	WNW	"	First clear day for a week and dry deck
12	3461			
1	3461¾	NNW		Beautiful afternoon—great swells—Wind favoring us
2	3463¾	NNW		
3	3465½	NNW		Garbo at wheel. All's well
4	3467¾	NNW		
5	3472¼	NWxN½N	SW	Set reefed mainsail 4.30
6	3477½	NW½N	WSW4	Sea more moderate — Wind heading again
7	3483½	NW½N	WSW4	Still going—Squalls to windward
8	3487¾	NW½N		Looks squally—and getting fresher
9	3493¼	NWxN	WxS	Getting black and wind freshen up
10	3498¾	NWxN½N	W	Seas still heavy—Moon rise 10.00
11	3503¼	NWxN		Squalls pass over all the time but we keep going
12	3508¼	NWxN	W	All's well—Hope the midwatch fares as well.

—NOON POSITION—

Made good 46. 1104 to go. Lat. by Ob. 56-25S. Lon. by Ob. 75-30W

H.	K.	COURSES	WINDS	REMARKS, MON. 30TH DAY OF NOV 1936
1			W3-6	Fluky airs—Squalls and seas killing our way
2	3517	NNW		
3	3521	NxW	WNW3-7	Windy dawn—Squalls and calms. Wind heading
4	3527	NxW	"	40° F. Raw and mean.
5	3532½	N½W		Rawer and meaner—Lots of squalls
6	3538¼	N	WNW	Breezing up a bit—All's well
7		WSW		Gybed ship 6^{20} Down mainsail. Big seas
8	3548			Blowing!
9	3551½			Hove-to 8^{30}
10		Gale		Blowing hard—Took in all headsails. Hove-to.
11				Raining with heavy sea. Lots of little birds.
12		SW		Hard blow—Hove to. Took in log
1				
2				
3			★	
4				
5				
6				Underway 6.40—Jibs, mainsail.
7	3553	NWxN	W5	Set forestays'l—Weather looks better
8	3555½	NWxN	W	Does not look very good.
9	3559¼	NNW	W5	Old story—cloudy—great seas—head wind.
10	3562¼	NNW	W5	Painful progress
11	3566	NNW	W	Short squalls—One minute strong wind, next none
12	3569¼	"	W	Trying to clear

—NOON POSITION—

Made good 60 miles. 1050 miles to go. Lat. by D.R. 54-40S. DR. Long 75-15W

H.	K.	COURSES	WINDS	REMARKS, TUES. 1ST DAY OF DEC 1936
1	3572¾	NWxN½N	WNW3-4	Rotten—trimmed jibs with handy billy
2	3576¼	NWxN½N	WNW3-4	Slogging along. Dawn starting to break
3	3579	"		Cold—Seas moderating—Same rain.
4	3582½	NWxN½N	WNW3-4	WAKE SKIPPER! ! Lousy cold rain. All's well
5	3585	NWxN½N		Stop raining for a while
6	3588	NWxN½N	W½N	Heavy swells killing speed.
7	3591	NWxN½N	WxN	Not much speed last hour. Sun trying to shine
8	3593½	NxW½W	WxN	Seas getting a little better.
9	3596½	NxW½W	WNW	Gloomy—Seas still bad.
10	3600¾	NxW½W	"	Rain—Sleet squalls—The hell hole of creation.
11	3604	NxW½W	WNW5-6	Tough going. Wind nailed in this NW quarter
12	3607	NxW½W	"	Pleasantly north of DR—Gybed to get offshore
1	3610½	SWxW	WNW	Breeze fresher.
2	3613½	SW½W	WNW4-5	There we go to Talco—all's well
3	3616½	SWxW		Seas building up—Confused.
4	3620¼	SWxW½W	NWxW	Breeze eased a bit—All's well
5	3628½	SWxW	NWxW8	Blowing hard—Mainsail in again
6	3631	SWxW	"	Heavy sea running—Stearing herself
7	3634	SWxW	NWxW9	Dropped inner jib 6[35] Hard wind—Rain
8	3636¼	SWxW	NWxW	★ Getting colder—Wind still blowing hard
9	3639	SWxW¼W		Little warmer—Rotten seas from every direction.
10	3642	SWxW		Blowing harder and light rain.
11	3645	SWxW¼W		Same.
12	3647	WSW		Still blowing hard gale—Very large seas—
12[35]				Blowing very hard—Rain—Cold—All's well.

—NOON POSITION—

Made good 80 miles. 970 miles to go. Lat. by Ob. 53-20S. Lon. by Ob. 75-03

H.	K.	COURSES	WINDS	REMARKS, WED. 2ND DAY OF DEC 1936
1	3650½	WxS½S	NWxW	Outer jib lashings being replaced
2	3654¾	WxS	NWxW	Jib restowed—It's very wet out there
3	3657¾	WxS½S	NWxW	Weather seems to be moderating a bit. All's well
4	3661¼	WxS¼S	NWxW9-10	All's well—Breezing up.
5	3665	"	"	Rain—Still hard blow.
6	3668½	"	"	★ Still hard—
7	3671½	"	"	Jumbo down
8	3673½	SWxW	NWxW10	Blowing harder if any change.
9	3675	"		Moderating very slightly—Cold rain.
10	3676½	"		Trying to clear.
11	3677½	"		Gybed—Sun out—Gybed at 11.—Put up jumbo
12	3680	NxE		
1		"		
2	3682½	N	WNW	Squall coming out of the West. May pass over?
3				Set outer jib and mainsail
4	3685¼	NxW½W	NWxW	Pie bald porpoises and moderating sea Make fine day.
5	3687¼	N½W	WNW	Mainsail up
6	3689½	NxW	"	
7	3691½	N½W	"	Squalls all around
8	3694½	"	"	" " "
9	3697½	NxW	WNW2-7	Sleet bad seas as usual
10	3700	NxW	"	Squalls and calms
11	3705	NNW	W2-7	Clearing—Eased sheets. Sea still lumpy.
12	3710	NNW	WxS7	Blowing pretty hard—Seas cutting speed. Very clear

—NOON POSITION—

Made good Minus 87 miles. 1055 to go. Lat. by Ob. 53-52. Lon. by Ob. 77-02

H.	K.	COURSES	WINDS	REMARKS, THURS. 3RD DAY OF DEC 1936
1	3716¼	NNW	WxS	Moon out—Also a few squalls
2	3722¼	NxW¾W	WxS	Going ahead a bit—Bad squalls—All's well
3	3726¼	NxW	NWxW4	Bad squall—and shift of wind—Colder—Glass upping
4	3730	NNW	WxN	The breeze was teasing us—All's well
5	3735¼	NNW	W	O.K. slacked sheet
6	3742	"	"	Squalls coming
7	3748¼	"	"	Main peak scandalized.
8	3755¼	"	WxS	Going fine—Fair wind
9	3762¾	"	WSW7	Boy! What a wonderful day and thrill to be tearing along on our course!
10	3769¾	"	"	
11	3776¼	"	WxS6	
12				
1	3786½	NxW	NWxW	Wind going ahead—All's well
2	3790¼	NxW		Warmer—Looks squally again.
3	3795	N	NW	Wind steadily going ahead
4		NxE	NWxN	Gybed 3 50. Rain—Thick—Hard wind.
5	3803¼	SWxS	W9	Mainsail down 4 10 Gale wind.
6	3806¾	SW¾S	W9	Outer jib down—Another gale
7	3809¼	SW¼S	W	Weather just the same. 'Bird stearing herself
8	3812	N½W		Gybed to North at 7 45 Moderating.
9	3814	N½W	★	Cloudy—Still blowing hard.
10	3815	N½E		
11	3816	N		Very dark—Light rain—Wind about same
12	3817½	N½E		Wind little stronger

—NOON POSITION—

Made good 105. 950 miles to go. Lat. by D.R. 52-14S. Lon. by Ob. 76-14W

H.	K.	COURSES	WINDS	REMARKS, FRI. 4TH DAY OF DEC 1936
1	3819	NxW	WNW8	Gybed—Standing offshore—Blowing hard.
2	3821½	SWxW¾W	WNW6	Hard puffs, Wicked Sea—All's well
3	3824	WSW		Rotten seas—Hard wind and Rain.
4	3826¾	WSW		Fresher—Wicked seas.
5	3830	WSW	WNW7	Sea still rotten—Blowing harder. Jumbo down.
6	3831¼	WSW		Blowing this morning.
7	3832¼	WSW		Blowing—Squalls—Raining. Heavy sea
8	3834	WSW	WNW9	About the same.
9	3835½	WSW	WNW10-11	Blowing harder—Tremendous seas.
10	3837¼	WxS½S	NW10-11	Schuckie!
11	3838½	"	"	
12			NW11	★ SEVERE GALE
1	3842¼	WSW	NW10	
2	3843	WSW	NW10	Beautiful, vicious seas
3	3845¾	"		Hail and driving rain. Filthy day
4	3846¾	WxS¼S		Rain—Hail—Sleet—Hell! ! !
5	3848¼	SW	WNW	Calmer
6	3849¾	"	"	Gybed ship 6.20. All's well.
7	3850	NxW	WNW	Set storm trisail & jumbo
8	3851½	NxW	"	Very big seas running. Weather not looking too bad.
9	3858½	NxW	WNW8-9	Very bad squall with sleet. Wind heading.
10	3863¼	NxE	NW8-9	Still hard squalls, but wind favoring us.
11	3867½	N	NWxW7	Clearer, fewer squalls
12	3872¼	N½W	WxN8-9	Breezing up—Blowing really hard

—NOON POSITION—

Lat. by DR. 52-02S. DR. Lon. 76-40W

H.	K.	COURSES	WINDS	REMARKS, SAT. 5TH DAY OF DEC 1936
1	3877¾	N¼W	NW	Wind changes all the time. Black squalls coming
2	3881¼	N½W	NWxW	Very nice comfortable mountains come aboard unanounced.
3	3884—	NxW¼W	WNW	Wind lighter—World's very worst seas —clearing—we hope!
4	3887¼	NxW	WNW	Bad squall to port—It didn't blow, though.
5	3891	N½W	WNW	Going O.K. Light squalls—Sleet.
6	3894½	N		Squalls all the time. Not much change
7	3896¾	N	WNW	Clearing up—Wind and sea calmer
8	3899	NxW	WNW	Clear up a lot this last hour.
9	3902	N½W	" 7-8	★ Big seas—Clear
10	3905¼	N¼W	"	Squalls and clear. Clear and squalls
11	3907¼	N¼W	"	Put up single-reefed mainsail at 10.50
12	3909¾	N¼W		Land sighted far to starboard 11[20] Gybed ship 11.45.
1	3913	SWxW½W	WNW9	Steamer sighted—Heading North
2	3916¼	SWxW	"	Breezing up a bit—Squall passing ahead.
3	3919¼	SWxW½W	WNW10	That squall hit us plenty—and more are coming
4	3922¼	SWxW	"	More squalls—Scandalized peaks
5	3926			Dropped mainsail—Heavy sleet
6		NxW	WNW	Tacked as wind shifts to WNW in blinding squall
7	3932¼	NNW	WxN8	Looking dirty at present. Squalls
8	3935¾	NWxN½N	WxS8-9	
9	3939¼	NNW	W	Wind apparently favoring us for once
10	3942¼	NNW	W	Clearer—Wind heading again
11	3946	NNW	W	Still blowing hard—Great sea hit sending solid water over boom and mainsail.
12	3950	NxW	WxN	Gybed to stand offshore as wind tends to head.

—NOON POSITION—

Lat. by Ob. 51-27S. Lon. by D.R. 76-12W.

H.	K.	COURSES	WINDS	REMARKS, SUN 6TH DAY OF DEC 1936
1	3951¼	SSW	WxS	Cloudy—Seas moderating
2	3952½	SW	WNW	Hail—Rain—2 Squalls in sight
3	3955	SWxS	WNW	The dawn awards us with a better horizon! !
4	3955¼	SW		★ GIVE SKIPPER WEATHER & HEADING REPORT
5	3956	N	WxN	Gybed at 4. Gale—Rain—Cold
6	3957	N	WNW	Clearer
7	3957¼	NxW	WxN	About the same
8				
9	3960½	NxW		Sun out—Still strong wind
10	3961½	NxW¾W		Clouds—but fine day
11	3962¾	NNW		Rain squall just passed—Chili in sight in distance
12	3965¼	NNW		Set mainsail—Squalls—Not as bad as yesterday
1	3968¼	NxW½W	WxN	Slogging along.
2	3971½	N½W		Rain—slow going indeed.
3	3975	N¼W	NW	★Wind going ahead—Bad hail & rain squalls
4	3979	N¼E		RAIN.
5	3983½	NxW	NWxW	Rain—Sea gets much smoother
6	3987¼	N½W	NNW8	Mainsail down 5<u>45</u>. Gybed offshore, log 86¼. Rain
7	3989	WxS½S	NWxW	Blowing hard—Seas mountain high this eve
8	3991¼	WxS½S	NWxW	Bad night—Card and chess games in progress
9	3994	WSW	NW9	Hard gale—Snug below
10	3995¼	WSW	NW9	Raining—Blowing hard
11	3997½	WSW	NW	Darkest night ever seen—Wind howling.
12	3999¼	WSW		No let up—Blowing like the devil.

—NOON POSITION—

863 Miles to go. Lat. by Ob. 51-10S. Lon. by Ob. 76-09W

H.	K.	COURSES	WINDS	REMARKS, MON. 7TH DAY OF DEC 1936
1	4001½	WSW	NW9-10	Blowing hard—Blowing itself out
2	4003	WSW	NW9	Jumbo down. CALL SKIPPER 2:50. ALL'S WELL
3	4004¼	WxS½S	NW9	Rain clouds coming up
4	4005¼	WxS	NW9	Ditto
5	4006¼	WSW	NW ★	Blowing just the same. Sea going down.
6	4007½	WxS	NW	Clear with rain—Blowing same
7	4008½	WxS	"	Raining again Wind just the same
8	4009½	WxS	NW	No change in the weather. Still blowing.
9	4010½	WSW		" " " " " " "
10	4011½	WSW		" " " " " " "
11	4012½	WxS		Trying hard to clear. Tremendous seas
12	4013½	WxS½S		We took a REAL SEA that time!
1	4014¾	WxS	NW	AND HOW! Alls well
2	4015¾	WxS		MORE of the SAME
3	4017¼	W½S	NNW	Still MORE of the SAME
4	4018¼	W	NNW10-11	Still a whole gale
5	4019¼	W½N	NNW10-11	SAME and MORE of it
6	4021	W	NNW11	VERY HARD GALE
7	4022¼	W½N	"	Water heavy white sheets like heavy snow storm
8	Hove-to OIL BAGS OUT			Blowing Like HELL
9		WxN	NxW11	
10				
11	Log inboard		NxW11	BAD squalls Make the storm Agreeable
12		WxS	NNW11-12	Black Night—Wind at times hurricane violence

—NOON POSITION—

Lat. by D.R. 50-55. Lon. by Ob. 76-25W

H.	K.	COURSES	WINDS	REMARKS, TUES 8TH DAY OF DEC 1936
1		SW	WNW	A Little calmer. Stars out
2		SSW	WxN	Same—Moon out
3		N	WxN	Gybed 2.00—Looks good
4		NxE	WNW	Large swells—Wind calmer
5		NxE	WNW	Great seas. Still strong gale of wind.
6		NxE	"	Heavy squall passed over with wind and slight rain.
7		NxE	"	Looks like more dirt coming from West. Yes—wind, sleet & snow
8		NxE	"	Squalls continue to come up over horizon
9	4023	WSW	NW8	Sleet and rain—Gybed—Set jib and jumbo
10		NxE	NW	Looks like another westerly gale coming up.
11				Sewing-bee—Making new oil bags—Set mainsail
12	4028	NxE	★	Discovered rip at foresail reef cringle. Sail down for repairs
1				
2	4032½	NxW	WNW	Foresail nearly ready to set. 4 oil bags ready
3			"	
4	4038½	NxW	"	Set foresail—Looks bad in N.W
5	4042½	NxW	Scandalized mainsail—Stowed outer jib—Heavy sleet squall	
6	4045	NxW	Squall after squall. Impossible to make progress.	
7	4048	NxW	WNW8	Blowing hard squalls—Mainsail down
8	4050	NxW	"	Clearing—Looks like a break in the weather
9	4053	NxW½W	WxN	Breeze trying to free us — Going fine.
10	4055¾	NNW	W	Breeze steady. Slight head sea. All's well.
11	4058	NxW½W		Trying to clear in the N.W.
12	4060	NWxN½N		Nicest night yet—still clearing—Bright stars.

—NOON POSITION—

Lat. by Ob. 51-49. Lon. by Ob. 76-12W

H.	K.	COURSES	WINDS	REMARKS, WED. 9TH DAY OF DEC 1936
1	4062¾	NWxN½N	WNW	Squall—Get black and thick again
2	4065	NNW	WNW	Blowing hard this hour—Clear up a lot
3	4067¼	NWxN		Dirty-looking Daybrake—Squall.
4	4070	NWxN	Heavy seas running—All's well—No land in sight	
5				Gybed $4^{\underline{30}}$ Land bearing ExN
6				Tore foresail again gybing—Down foresail. Set trisail on fore
7	4077½	S	WxS	Clawing south & offshore—Heavy sleet storm.
8	4081½	S	WxS	Sleet again—Clawing off nicely—Rationing water.
9	4085	S½W		
10	4084½	S½W		Repairing foresail—Heavy squalls
11	4091¾	S½W	WxS	Leaving the land in good shape
12	4094½	S½W	WxS	Calms and heavy squalls, followed by squalls and wind.
1			WxS	
2	4099½	S½W		Squalls getting lighter
3	4101	S½W		O. K.
4	4104	SxW¼W	★	Call Skipper at 25 to 5
5	4106	SSW		Trying to get offshore with head wind.
6	4109	SxW		Heavy squalls & calm—Bad seas—Tough
7	4111			
8	4113	SxW	WxS	Set repaired foresail—A good job.
9	4115¼	SxW½W		No sign of Evangelistas Light as yet. All quiet
10	4117½	SxW¾W		Trying to let us off to Westward. No sign of Light yet.
11	4119¾	SSW	W	Evang. Lite not visible—No boats in site. All's well
12	4122	SSW	W	Light not visible—Squalls with lightning. All's well

—NOON POSITION—

Lat. by Ob. 51-44. Lon. by Ob. 75-40W

H.	K.	COURSES	WINDS	REMARKS, THURS 10TH DAY OF DEC 1936
1	4124¼	SSW	WxN	Nothing in sight—Squall ahead
2	4126¼	SWxS½S	WxN	Fresher breeze—No light
3	4128	SSW	WxN	Looks good
4	4130¼	SxW½S	WxN	About same
5	4132¼	SSW	WxN	Nothing special except squall after squall
6	4134¼	SWxS½S	WxN½N	Looking somewhat better.
7	4136	SSW	WxN	Headed high as SW and low as S during hour
8				Set mainsail—Wind SW for 20 min. Set outer jib & fisherman
9				Wind heading and very light. No squalls for a while—
10				Cleared broken signal halliards. Calm this hour. Sea going down
11				
12	4144½	NW	SWxW2	Have sailed 1395 miles to get 385 miles from Cape Horn
1	4148½	NW	WSW2-3	
2	4154	NWxW	SWxW	Going fine this evening. Hope we are able to keep it.
3	4160	NW	WSW	Fine going
4	4165¼	NW	WSW	Fisherman down
5	4170½	NW½N	"	Wind tending to head us.
6	4175½	NW	"	Temperature 42°. Hail in squalls
7	4179¾	NWxN	"	Light wind. Very changeable
8	4184¼	NWxW	"	Sleet squalls. Temp. 42°
9	4187¾	NW½W	"	
10	4192¼	NW¾W	"	Squall. Lotsa breeze.
11	4196½	NWxW	"	Fair weather—A few bad head seas.
12	4200¼	NWxW	"	For the first night in two weeks we carry all lowers—reefed foresail and reefed mainsail. All's well

—NOON POSITION—

Lat. by Ob. 52-38S. Lon. by Ob. 76-13W

H.	K.	COURSES	WINDS	REMARKS, FRI. 11TH DAY OF DEC 1936
1	4204	WNW	SWxS	Going fine. Making good course
2	4209	WNW	SW	Light squalls—Nothing in them.
3	4213½	WNW	SWxS	Making it fine—Squalls, but nothing come out of them.
4	4217¼	WNW	SWxS	Talc. BEFORE XMAS!
5	4223¼	"	SWxS	Good looking Day
6	4228½	NWxW	WSW	Squalls, but nothing evil
7	4234	WNW	SWxS	Wonderful wind — Beautiful day! What a thrill to be on our way! [Poet John!]
8	4240	WNW	SW	Going great guns. All's well!
9	4246	NWxW	SW	Breezing up slightly. All's well
10	4252	NW½W		Squall with hail. Breeze all over the shop.
11	4257½	WNW	SWxS	Squall headed us off to W. A'll's well.
12	4264	NWxN	SW	Log 62½ at 11.45. All's well. [Long hour]
1	4269½	NW	WSW	Fine going.
2	4275½	NW	WSW	Block in Four and Main sheet going good
3	4281	NW	WSW	
4	4286	NW	WxS	Reef out of mainsail
5	4292½	NWxN	"	Looks fine. What a wonderful change!
6	4298½	NWxN	"	Great afternoon. Grand and glorious feelin'! !
7	4205½	NNW	"	Shook out reef in foresail. CROSSED 50° SOUTH
8	4312¾	NNW	"	Set fisherman.
9	4320	NxW½W	WxS	Here we go—We hope it is for keeps.
10	4327¼	NxW¾W	"	Squall making up on port side—All's well.
11	4335¼	NxW¾W	"	Even the porpoises have to hump themselves tonight
12	4344¾	NNW	"	Ain't that something?

—NOON POSITION—

Made good 134. 864 miles to go. Lat. by Ob. 50-39S. Lon. by Ob. 77-47W.

VI. APPENDIX

THE lazarette of a ship is a locker filled with odds and ends of gear which may sometime, somewhere, prove useful. It reeks of leather, canvas, tar, paint and oil, and in it all sorts of dissimilar odd things lie curiously mingled.

So it is with this Appendix. In it I am stowing assorted paragraphs which I hope will prove interesting to others who will hear the old sea call and have to go. Some of the things mentioned seem so fundamental and simple that for these very reasons they have usually escaped discussion, but are yet important. Some of the devices I have worked out for myself, but I claim no originality for them. So many thoughtful men have worked so long over ships that there is doubtless nothing entirely new to be done in them.

It is a pleasant privilege to be able to mention by name some of the manufacturers of gear which experience has demonstrated to be of superior quality. I hope it will expose neither them nor myself to entirely unfounded suspicions of subsidization.

No lazarette has ever yet been big enough. Just so this appendix will be far too small to include everything that might well go into it. But if a man in a lifetime can't learn all there is to know about the sea, how can anyone expect to find very much about it in one small volume?

HORN VOYAGE IN THE *SEA SERPENT.*

In 1821 Captain George Coggeshall, a distinguished sailorman of New York, took a schooner from that city to Lima and his record of his Horn voyage is the only one I have ever been able to find other than those of big ships. The whole story is found in the relatively rare volumes of his *Voyages* but we shall pick him up on January 27, 1822, when—

"As we increased our latitude the weather became daily more rough and boisterous; we encountered storm after storm, and the weather was more cloudy, cold and disagreeable, which kept us reefing and changing almost hourly. On the 27th of January at 5 A.M., daylight, we made the Falkland Islands, bearing from S. to S.E., distant five leagues; the winds being light and the weather moderate, we stood in shore. The wind at this time at W.S.W., we were unable to fetch to westward of the islands, and therefore commenced beating up alongshore to weather the westernmost island. These islands appear at a moderate height and generally rocky and barren. Lat. by obs. this day 51°—18′ S., long. about 61°—06′ W. We continued to beat to the westward all this day and the day following, standing off and on the land, with open, cloudy weather and moderate gales from the S.W. Saw a high rock appearing like a lofty sail, marked on the charts Eddystone Rock.

On *Monday, January 28th,* the land still in sight, at meridian the wind shifted to the N.W., which enabled us to weather the land, and thus we steered on our course to the southward and westward towards Cape Horn; lat. by obs. at noon 50°—58′ S., long. 61°—50′ W. On the afternoon of this day the weather became thick and rainy; passed several tide rips, and saw a number of penguins. The little flock of Cape pigeons before alluded to still followed the schooner—they are our constant companions by day and by night, in sunshine and tempest. The variation of the compass here is from one and three-quarters to two points easterly. The weather was now cold and disagreeable; temperature by Fahrenheit's thermometer 50 degrees above zero.

Tuesday, January 29th. Light winds and variable. This day

the weather appeared to change every hour or two; at times the sun would shine out, and then suddenly disappear and become obscured by a thick fog. This would continue but for a short time, when a strong breeze from the northward would blow all the fog away, and the sky remain pretty clear for a few hours, then the sun would again break out and shine for an hour or two, and perhaps another hour would bring a flight of snow. Sometimes, even when the sun was shining, the decks would be covered for a few minutes with snow, which would soon melt away and be followed by a violent shower of rain and hail. In fine, I find it very difficult to describe the weather in this dreary region; though we were in the midst of summer, we had all the seasons of the year in the course of a day. These continual changes kept us consequently making and taking in sail throughout these twenty-four hours. Lat. by obs. 53°—01′ S., long. 64°—00′ W.

January 30th. These twenty-four hours commenced with a strong gale from the westward, with a high head sea running. At 1 P.M. hove-to under a two-reefed foresail; dark, cloudy, cold weather, with violent squalls of hail and rain. At midnight the gale moderated, when we again made sail, the schooner laboring violently and making much water. [She was very deeply laden and not too sound. Coggeshall previously states that a whaler's pulling boat which came alongside previously had more freeboard than the *Sea Serpent*. Note by W.M.T.] Lat. by obs. 53°—30′ S., long. 64°—00′ W.

January 31st. This day commenced with strong gales from the westward with a high head sea running; weather dark and gloomy. The wind throughout these twenty-four hours continued to blow strong from the westward, and were glad to hold our own without losing ground. During the day we had much thunder and lightning. Lat. by obs., 54°—01′ S., long. 64°—00′ W.

February 1st. Last night the sky was clear for a little while in the zenith, when we saw the Magellan clouds nearly over our heads. This day we had a continuation of strong gales from the westward, and very bad, stormy weather; we, however, continued to ply to the windward under close-reefed sails, but having a strong westerly gale and a lee current against us, we made but little progress. At 6 A.M. made Staten Land; this land, like the Falklands, appeared cold and dreary, and only a fit habitation for seal and wild fowl, which are here very abundant. The sea in this vicinity also abounds in whales of monstrous bulk. At meridian the sun shone out, when we found our latitude to be 55°—31′ S., long. 64°—08′ W.

February 2nd. This day, like the last, was dark and gloomy, with a continuation of westerly winds, but not so strong as to prevent our plying to windward under close-reefed sails. The thermometer fell down to 45 degrees above zero. In consequence of contrary winds and a lee current we gained but little on our course during these twenty-four hours. Lat. by obs. 56°—20′ S., long. 65°—27′ W.

February 3d. On this day, when within about 50 miles of Cape Horn, a terrible gale commenced blowing from the westward. It continued to increase until it blew a perfect hurricane, and soon created a mountainous sea. We got our fore-yard on deck and hove the schooner to, under the head of a new foresail. I then ordered all the bulwarks and waist-boards to be knocked away, that nothing might impede the water from passing over the decks without obstruction; otherwise, so great a quantity would have lodged in the lee waist our little schooner would have been water-logged and swamped with the weight of it. With crowbars and axes the waist-boards were all demolished, and the sea broke over the decks and passed off without injury to our little bark, and she rose like a stormy petrel on the top of the sea, which threatened every moment to swallow us in its abyss. The ocean was lashed into a white foam by the fury of the tempest. The same weather continued with but little intermission for a space of five days. During a great part of this time it was almost impossible to look to windward, so violent were the hail and snow squalls. In the midst of this tempest my officers and men behaved nobly: the most perfect order prevailed; not a whisper of fear or contention was heard during the whole of our perilous situation. To render the men more comfortable I removed them all from the forecastle to the cabin, where they continued to live until we had fairly doubled the Cape and found better weather.

My Italian passenger was terribly alarmed during the tempest and entreated me, in piteous tones, to put away for Rio de Janeiro. He said if I would do so he would instantly sign an agreement to give me all his interest in the vessel and cargo. I resolutely declined his offer, and told him that while we had masts and sails and the vessel would float under us, I would never put back.

This Cape is rendered more dreadful from the fact of its inhospitable position, and being so far removed from any civilized port. It is a cold, cheerless, barbarous coast, where no provision, or supplies of any kind, can be had in case of ship-wreck or disaster, so that the greatest vigilance and perseverance are necessary to bear the many obstacles that present themselves.

February 8th. The gale abated, and we were again enabled to make sail and ply to the westward. Our faithful little pigeons had hovered about during the long tempest and now resumed the journey with us. We got an observation of the sun this day and found ourselves in lat. 57°—33′ S., long. 66°—12′ W.

February 9th. We had, throughout these twenty-four hours, favorable gales from the N.E. and open, cloudy weather. Made all sail and steered to the westward and gained 160 miles distance on a direct course, and everything began to wear a better appearance. We made better progress this day than we had since our arrival in these high southern latitudes. Lat. by observation at noon, 57°—16′ S., long. by chronometer, 71°—04′ W.

February 10th. This day commenced with strong gales from the southward, with dark, squally weather; under reefed sails, standing to the northward and westward, made a distance of 155 miles per log. Towards noon the sun shone out, when we found ourselves, at meridian, in lat. 55°—44′ S., long. 74°—48′ W. We had now fairly doubled Cape Horn, and I hoped in a few days to descend to lower latitudes and find warmer and better weather. It was now fifteen days since we made the Falkland Islands, so that we were from thirteen to fifteen days weathering Cape Horn, which is not an unusual length of time; and had our vessel been a good ship of three or four hundred tons we should have suffered nothing in comparison with what we experienced in a deep-loaded pilot-boat schooner of one hundred and forty tons, leaking badly."

LINES.

Wander Bird's lines are printed herewith for the first time. That they are those of an exceptionally fine vessel has been proved beyond question.

The record shows this is a hull which is fast in any kind of weather, comfortable, dry, close-winded, powerful and easily driven. This is a ship which heaves-to as a vessel should, treats crew and gear with considerate and easy motion and never needs to heave-to with a fair wind. In a word she seems the ideal compromise (all ships are compromises to some extent), a ship which does everything well and many things superbly.

She is similar in many ways to the historic and fast Baltimore clippers. Architects approve of her sweet underwater lines, the flat and smooth buttocks, the slightly hollow waterlines of the entry, the clean run and the fine distribution of her displacement.

The lines are published without copyright strings, and may freely be built-to by anyone wishing such a sea boat.

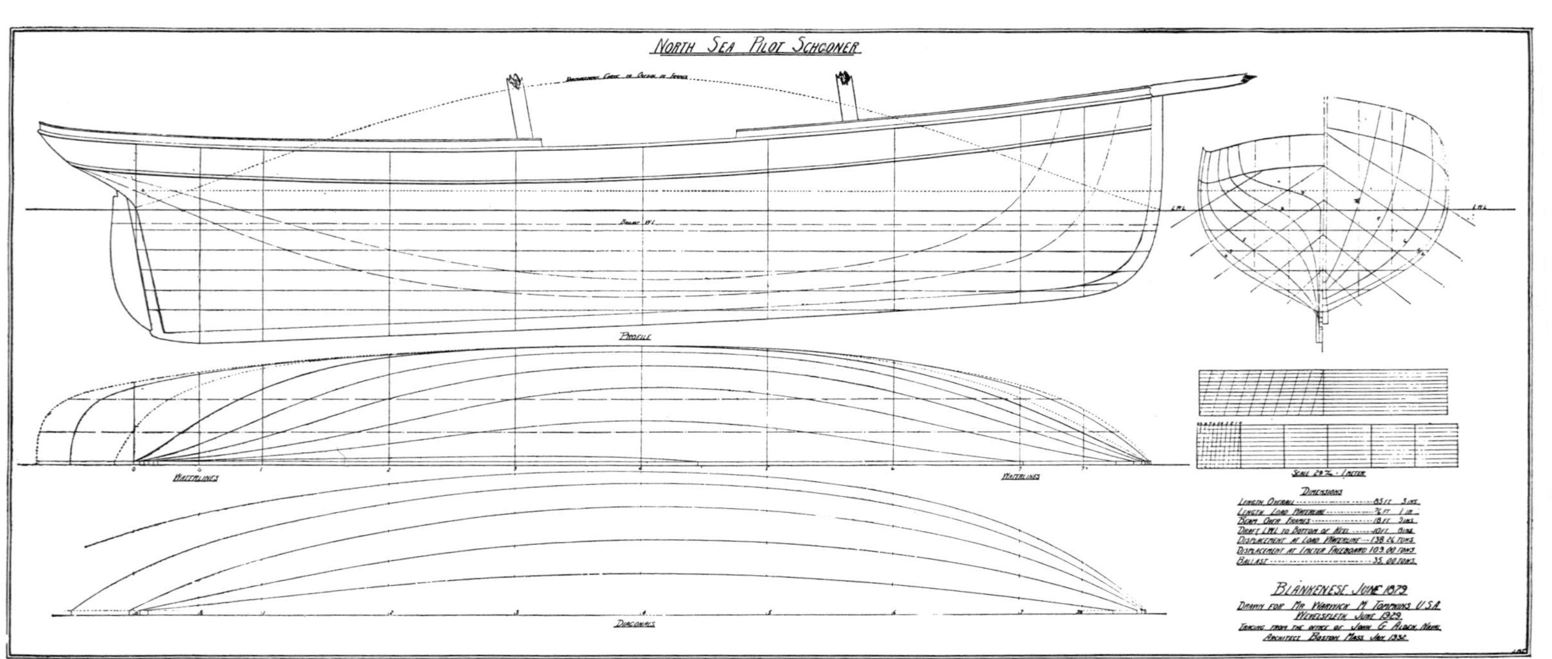
North Sea Pilot Schooner
Ballast W.L.
Profile
Waterlines
Waterlines
Diagonals
L.W.L.
Scale 2 9/16 - 1 Meter
Dimensions
Length Overall .... 85 ft 3 ins
Length Load Waterline .... 76 ft 1 in
Beam Over Frames .... 18 ft 2 ins
Draft LWL to Bottom of Keel .... 10 ft 8 ins
Displacement at Load Waterline .... 138.26 tons
Displacement at 1 Meter Freeboard 109.00 tons
Ballast .... 35.00 tons
Blankenese June 1879
Drawn for Mr Warwick M Tompkins U.S.A.
Wevelsfleth June 1929
Tracing from the office of John G Alden Naval
Architect Boston Mass Jan 1932

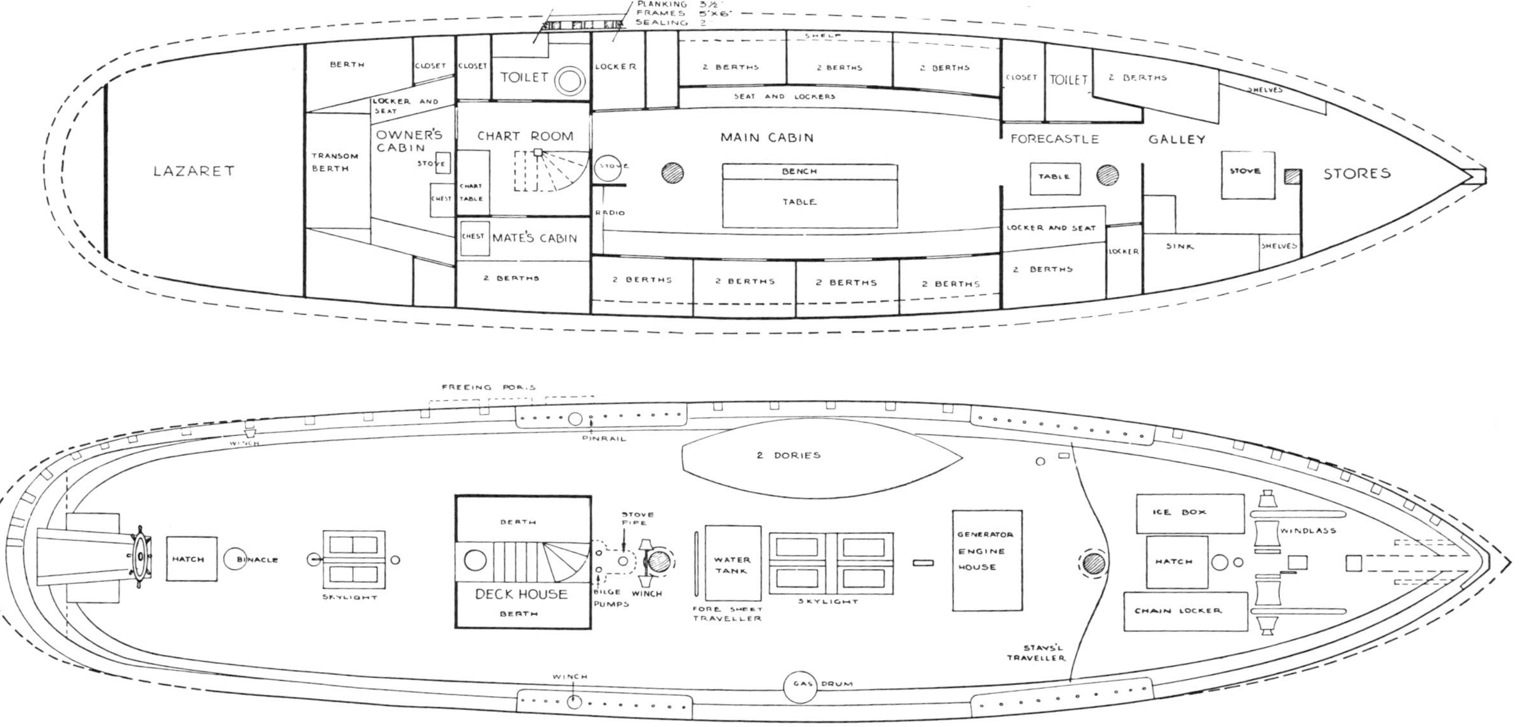

PLANKING 3½"
FRAMES 5"×6"
SEALING 2"
SHELF
LAZARET
BERTH
CLOSET
CLOSET
TOILET
LOCKER
2 BERTHS
2 BERTHS
2 BERTHS
CLOSET
TOILET
2 BERTHS
SHELVES
LOCKER AND SEAT
SEAT AND LOCKERS
TRANSOM BERTH
OWNER'S CABIN
STOVE
CHEST
CHART TABLE
CHART ROOM
STOVE
RADIO
MAIN CABIN
BENCH
TABLE
FORECASTLE
TABLE
GALLEY
STOVE
STORES
CHEST
MATE'S CABIN
LOCKER AND SEAT
LOCKER
SINK
SHELVES
2 BERTHS
2 BERTHS
2 BERTHS
2 BERTHS
2 BERTHS
2 BERTHS
FREEING POR.S
WINCH
PINRAIL
2 DORIES
HATCH
BINACLE
SKYLIGHT
BERTH
DECK HOUSE
BERTH
STOVE PIPE
BILGE PUMPS
WINCH
WATER TANK
FORE SHEET TRAVELLER
SKYLIGHT
GENERATOR ENGINE HOUSE
ICE BOX
HATCH
CHAIN LOCKER
WINDLASS
STAYS'L TRAVELLER
WINCH
GAS DRUM

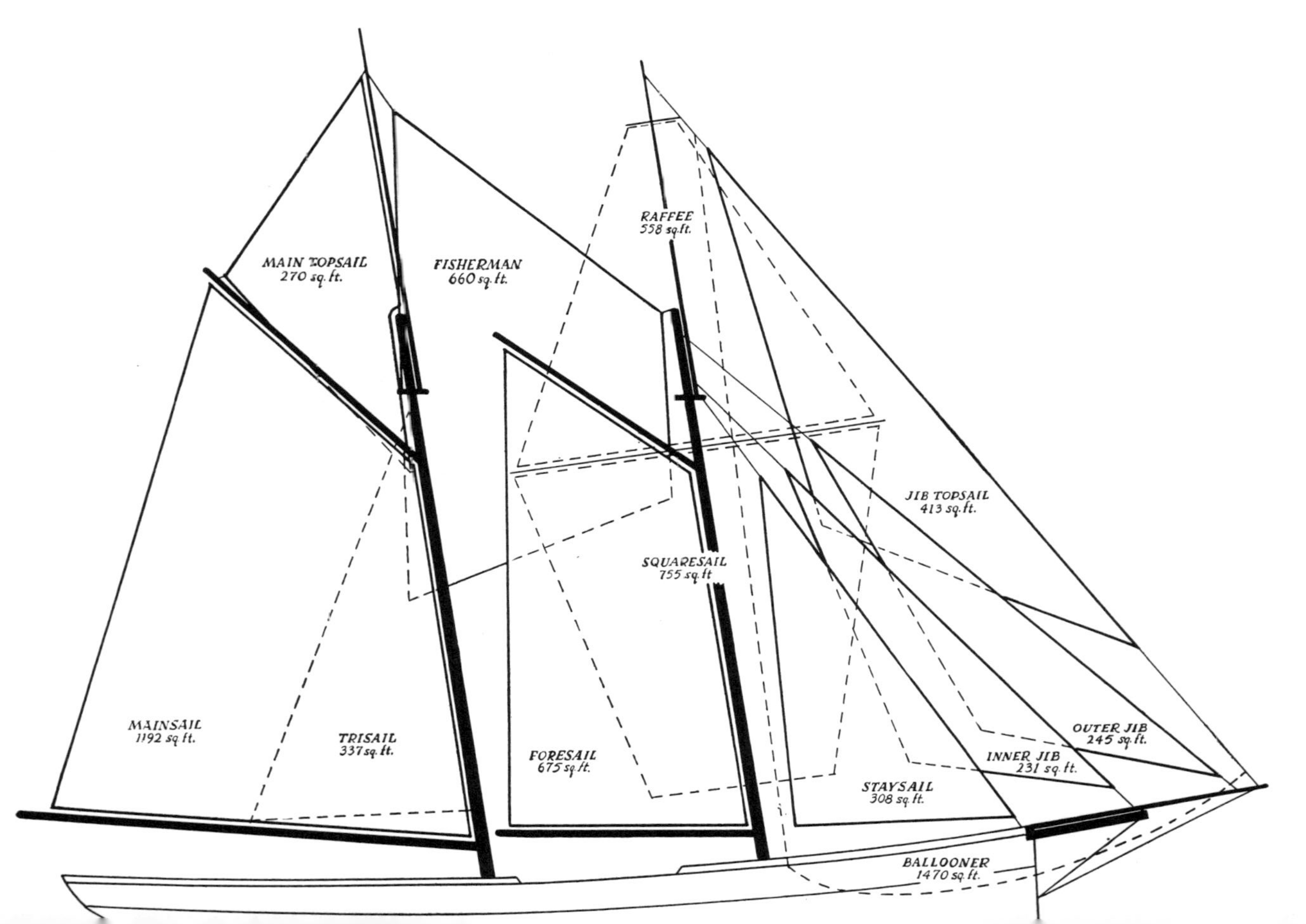
MAIN TOPSAIL
270 sq. ft.
FISHERMAN
660 sq. ft.
RAFFEE
558 sq. ft.
JIB TOPSAIL
413 sq. ft.
SQUARESAIL
755 sq. ft.
MAINSAIL
1192 sq. ft.
TRISAIL
337 sq. ft.
FORESAIL
675 sq. ft.
STAYSAIL
308 sq. ft.
INNER JIB
231 sq. ft.
OUTER JIB
245 sq. ft.
BALLOONER
1470 sq. ft.

TABLE, Showing the FORCE and VELOCITY of the Wind, from Light Airs to Heavy Gales

Pressure in Pounds on Square Foot	VELOCITY		POPULAR DESCRIPTION
	Feet per Second	*Miles per Hour*	
0.002	1	0.68	Gentle airs, unappreciable by gauge.
0.004	1.47	1	BEAUFORT SCALE 1
0.019	3	2	Light airs, just appreciable by gauge, would fill lightest sail of a yacht.
0.032	3.9	2.66	
0.043	4.5	3	BEAUFORT 2
0.065	5.28	3.8	
0.071	5.87	4	
0.090	6.6	4.5	
0.100	6.98	4.75	Light breezes, such as would fill the lightest sails of a large ship.
0.112	7.34	5	
0.130	7.89	5.38	BEAUFORT 3
0.162	8.8	6	
0.228	10.4	7	
0.260	11	7.6	
0.291	11.8	8	
0.364	13.2	9	
0.390	13.6	9.27	Moderate breezes in which ships can carry full sail.
0.452	14.7	10	
0.521	15.8	10.77	BEAUFORT 4
0.551	16.2	11	
0.650	17.66	12	

Pressure in Pounds on Square Foot	VELOCITY		POPULAR DESCRIPTION
	Feet per Second	Miles per Hour	
0.780	19.3	13	Fresh breezes, topgallant sails and royals. BEAUFORT 5
0.830	20	13.6	
0.884	20.6	14	
0.910	20.9	14.25	
1.042	22	15	
1.170	23.6	16	
1.250	24.2	16.5	
1.302	25	17	Fresh winds, reefs. BEAUFORT 6
1.470	26.5	18	
1.563	27.39	18.67	Strong winds. BEAUFORT 7
1.630	28	19	
1.790	29.35	20	
2.084	31.15	21.47	Gales, close-reefed topsails and reefed courses. BEAUFORT 8
2.600	35.32	24	
3.126	38.73	26.40	Strong gales, close-reefed topsails and staysails. BEAUFORT 9
3.647	41.83	28.52	
4.168	44.83	30.56	
4.689	47.44	32.34	
5.200	50	34	Heavy gales and storms. BEAUFORT 10
7.800	61.18	41	
10.400	70.72	48.2	
13.000	79.07	53.91	
20.800	100	68.18	Very heavy gales, great storms, tempests. BEAUFORT 11
26.000	111.74	76.18	
31.200	122.62	83.6	
41.600	141.30	90.34	Tornadoes, cyclones, hurricanes. BEAUFORT 12
52.000	157.98	107.7	
62.400	173.06	120	

CHAFE and CHAFING GEAR.

Chafe must be guarded against unremittingly at sea. The damage it can do in a few brief hours is almost unbelievable.

Chafing gear—baggy-wrinkle or sennit, as it is also called—is made out of short lengths of old rope unlaid into yarns and secured to a doubled length of marline as shown in the drawing. It should be wrapped in a tight, close spiral about any wire against which a sail may rub.

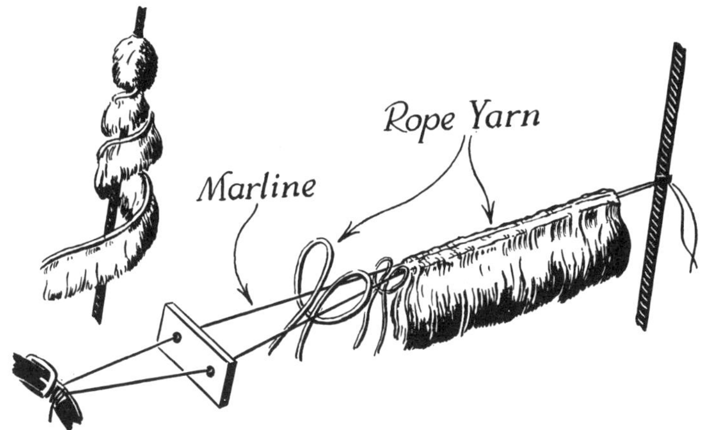

When making this gear work goes faster if a little wooden spreader is kept between the marline, to avoid repetitious separating of the string, and if the loose ends are passed around one's belt so that it will feed out slowly as one backs away from the growing "grass skirt."

Chafing strips sewn on sails where there is unavoidable chafe will save the vital cloth of the sail. Forestaysails often ride on jib pennants, a fisherman's clew on the topmast shrouds and jibs invariably on the forestay. These places must be watched. Leather affords even stouter protection to bolt ropes than canvas.

HALLIARD CHAFE—Halliards chafe on sails, rigging, blocks, crosstrees and themselves and must be watched incessantly.

They cannot be equipped with chafing gear, because that will foul their blocks, but leather, canvas or sections of rubber hose can often be placed under them to eliminate dangerous rubbing. When the end of a halliard is subjected to hard wear and unavoidable friction on the sheave of a block, it is well to splice in a short length of chain of equivalent strength.

Throat and peak halliards often chafe badly. Their hauling parts should be belayed on pin-rails at the side of the ship rather than right on the mast, and fairleads used in the rigging to assure them a clear lead. Only much study and experiment will arrange their parts aloft so that there is absolutely no chafe, but this can be done. Often a halliard which does not chafe in one position, or on one tack, will play merry hell with itself through a change of tack or some other seemingly inconsequential alteration of position.

If blocks are too small, halliards and sheets, especially when wet and swollen, will chafe badly in them as well as jambing so hard as to ruin dispositions. Lines chafe in blocks if the block is not free to swing straight to its load and a corner of the shell is cocked enough to lie athwart a sawing rope. Introduction of another shackle between band and block or, better still, a swivel shackle will ordinarily eliminate this trouble. The use of good, polished bronze sheaves will prevent chafing common with cheap cast-iron sheaves.

MAST CHAFE—Masts must be protected from chafe at all costs. In the normal working of gaffs and booms they are heir to much of it. The outside fibers of a mast are its strongest and when they are destroyed there is no way to renew them. The common way of preventing this chafe is by tacking sheet metal around the mast where gaff and boom jaws ride. This is bad practice. No one can see what goes on behind such metal which all too often catches and holds water and then conceals a rotting mast.

In *Wander Bird* we screwed half-oval strips of galvanized iron two inches wide and five feet long to our masts, and they seem to be perfect for their purpose. The condition of the mast is evident between them—they are an inch apart—and they cannot hold water. Contrary to some predictions they have not scarred gaff or boom jaws in 25,000 miles of sailing. The counter-sunk screws securing them never lose their heads or fall out, as is continually happening to tacks or screws in sheet metal.

Finally, on this subject of chafe, it must be remembered that there is a possibility of chafe wherever there is motion (clothes

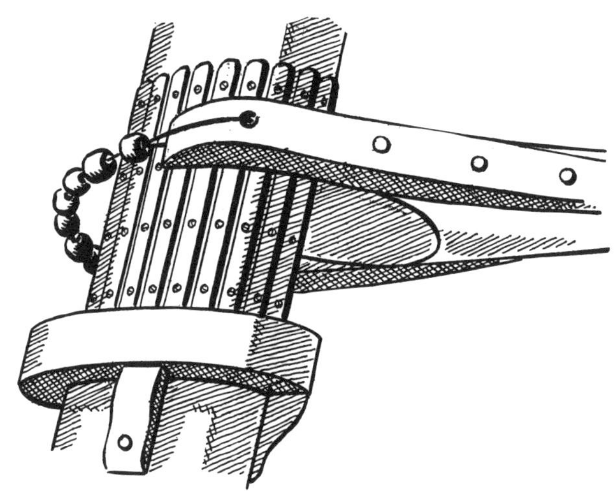

in your lockers, even, unless made fast will wear holes in one another during a voyage!). A sailor is always on the alert for this most destructive enemy of all.

SAIL HANDLING.

HANDLING SAIL IN HEAVY WEATHER—Here is how we handle sail in *Wander Bird* in a gale of wind.

The ship is run off before the wind until the after canvas blankets the jibs. This is work for a good helmsman who can tell instinctively and by "feel" when the ship is near a gybe, an eventuality he must avoid at all cost. Never entrust this job to a green hand; it is properly the Master's.

With the ship running the strength of the apparent wind is greatly lessened, the deck is steadier and more level, there is slight risk of washing anyone off the bowsprit and the blanketed sails come in easily as falling leaves.

A hand slacks the jib halliard, the sail is pulled down by the downhaul while the leeward sheet is slowly eased. A hand on the bowsprit now jumps on the head of the sail until no more slack can be got on the downhaul. Now the jib is furled as tightly as possible because of the beating it will get if the seas start lapping over it and also to reduce windage.

In really hard going we keep the ship before the wind until all outboard work is finished. A lost mile or two is immaterial in a long voyage and is nothing to the remorse which would follow the loss of a shipmate overboard.

JIB GASKETS—Jib gaskets should live on the bowsprit where they are always to hand. No one wants to go looking for loose ones in heavy weather. We favor two lanyards for a jib, and lash the sail to iron jackstays running the length of the bowsprit an inch and a half above the spar.

JUMBO and FORESAIL—The jumbo is a very simple sail to handle, by the same procedure as outlined for the jibs, because all the work is inboard. The foresail of a schooner likewise rarely gives difficulty. It is handled in the same manner as I shall now describe for the mainsail but it is so much smaller the work is light. Also it can be blanketed by the main.

FURLING MAINSAIL—The mainsail cannot be blanketed, of course, but even so we invariably run to take it in. If a ship is headed up into a gale the headsails take a terrific slatting, and beside this consideration those of a lessened wind and a level deck are worth remembering. The next steps are as follows:

1. Set taut the weather topping lift preparatory to slacking the peak halliard.

2. Throw both main halliards on deck and BE CERTAIN they are clear for running.

3. Carry peak downhaul aft to a windward cleat or pin.

4. Slack peak halliard, spilling wind out of upper half of sail.

5. Get the mainsheet in flat.

6. Slack weather topping lift and secure boom in gallows by setting taut on main sheet. If there is any possibility of the boom sliding, rig a small tackle to hold it steady.

7. One man can now readily slack both peak and throat halliards *if* they are properly clear. Let him lower away.

8. All other hands now heave on the peak downhaul or stand by to prevent the sail from blowing overboard as it settles.

9. Capture the gaff to keep it from swinging wildly. When the canvas is wet and the ship rolling heavily it is virtually impossible to stow the sail neatly. It is parbuckled to the boom in the following manner:

A ¾-inch (diameter) line is tied to the boom at its forward end, passed UNDER the sail and thrown to windward across the gaff. Two or three hands now heave on the line while one or two others lift up on the heavy sail. When the sail has been hoisted the line, always keeping it taut, is similarly passed again under the boom and under the sail further aft and once more hove taut, capturing the bight of the sail. Two hands unassisted have been known to furl *Wander Bird's* wet mainsail this way, setting their furling line taut and lifting the sail with a watch tackle.

A good-sized line is recommended; small ones cut hands softened by rain and spray.

PARRALS vs. MAST-HOOPS.

Nothing I have ever tried has given more gratifying results than the parral-loops with which I hold foresail and mainsail to the masts. They differ in no way from the hardwood beads used for years on the jaws of gaffs and booms. Why they did not displace everywhere the scraping, splintering and bothersome wooden mast hoops ordinarily in use remains a mystery to me.

My parrals are strung on manila line. Thimbles are eye-spliced into the ends and the sails shackled to the loop. The life of the parrals is indefinite; the ones I bought in Hamburg are entering their tenth season with virtually no sign of their hard service. They cost twice as much as hoops in the first place, but outlast hoops five to one. These wood balls act like ball bearings on a mast and neither scrape nor mar its varnish. Their shackles obviate the tedious and endless labor of forever relashing sails to wood hoops.

Do not string parrals on wire, which does not stand up nearly so well as manila, and do not try to use them for gaff topsails. The constant swinging of a gaff, with the consequent excessive rotary motion of the sail, is unsuited to them and the ordinary hoops are better.

STOPPING A SAIL.

The breaking out of a properly stopped sail is beautiful and gratifying, and the bending of a stopped sail is much easier than if the sail is all adrift. It is sometimes impossible to set a vital storm sail unless it is stopped; otherwise it clings frantically to everything it touches and blows out of the strongest hands, not to mention slatting dangerously.

To stop a sail spread it out on the deck as flat as possible, fold it so that the boltropes of the leech and the foot (assuming it is a triangular sail as it will be most commonly) lie along the boltrope of the luff or hoist.

Now roll it neatly and tightly from the folded edge toward the boltropes.

Be sure the clew is left protruding beyond the boltropes so the sheet can be bent on when the sail is to be used.

Now put on stops, varying their strength from the head, where a single turn of light twine is usually sufficient, to the bulky part at the clew where the stops must be strong. The stops properly should be placed right at the snap-hooks on the luff of a jib. I don't know which of two possibilities is worse: using weak stops which break out while the sail is going up or stops too strong which necessitate lowering the sail after it is hoisted. Experience with varying sails and wind strengths will be the only sure guide to stops of the right strength.

Be very careful when setting a stopped sail that (1) there are no twists in it, and (2) that the sheet is clear and not led foul somewhere.

CARRYING SAIL.

The "let-em-blow-off" school of sail carriers does excellently for filmed dramas and magazines purveying cheap thrills to the dull, but the tyro who expects to make consistently good passages or races by pursuit of such tactics will be better off ashore.

More accidents happen at sea through over-driving than from all other causes. While experience is the only guide which will indicate when a particular vessel is over-sailed a word or two on the general subject may not be amiss here.

As a broad general rule, applicable to all ships, the following is remarkably accurate:

When the edge of a deck is forced (not rolled) down to the water no gain in speed will be achieved by burying the rail.

A ship will sail fastest (barring, of course, rule-cheating racing machines) on the sharp, sweet lines of her upright hull. When she is so over-pressed she starts dragging assorted boats, ventilators, rigging and cabin trunks through the water she may make a grand picture—wide wake, flung spray and all that —but she isn't doing her best. She will go faster and be far happier to live in with less sail.

It is especially easy to carry on too long when running, because the ship is free, her speed is exhilarating and the danger point stalks upon her gradually for the apparent wind is far less than the true wind. There comes a time, however, when she may be in grave danger of broaching-to, when she may be thrown on her beam ends, rolled over and sunk. Ships have been run too long and sailed right *under* when the bows scooped up a load of water as a following sea lifted the stern high.

To remove such a risk quickly take in after sail and be content with a little less speed. It is after sail which makes a ship hard to steer and increases the broaching tendency. It will be found invariably the ship is safer and more comfortable once she is thus slowed.

TACKING IN HEAVY WEATHER.

It is my thought that a ship should be gybed rather than put about in a bad sea and heavy wind. If tacking seems best, however, these pointers may prove helpful.

1. A ship is very apt to take a couple of swift, hard pitches when brought head to sea. Be sure the backstays are not slacked

until there is no possibility of pitching a topmast over the bows. Strains aloft at such a moment are enormous.

2. Never let the leeward jib sheets fly in heavy wind. They should be eased off slowly, control of the clew being maintained to avoid slatting, as the ship heads into the wind, and hauled over and sheeted home instantly the sail fills on the new tack. Similarly, always keep the leeward sheet moderately taut when setting a jib in heavy wind, slacking it as need be. Otherwise the clew is apt to slat to ribbons.

3. If, as very often happens, seas and wind combine to put the ship in irons, so she hangs indecisive in the wind's eye, she may ordinarily be got about by *reversing* the helm as she gains sternway. The stern will go to the same side as the rudder is put when a vessel goes astern. In doing this the helmsman must ease the wheel over gently and not allow it to spin. The shock of a heavy rudder bringing up hard otherwise may shatter the gear.

REEFING.

When a ship is sailing in regions where reefing may be frequently necessary reefing pennants should be rove permanently through the luff cringles and an outhaul secured to the highest leech cringle. This obviates troublesome searching for suitable line at a busy time and the outhaul assures easy control of the slatting leech which otherwise makes trouble in high winds.

A reef goes in more easily ordinarily if the sail is lowered no more than is necessary to get the desired reef band only a little below the boom. Having done this the reefing ritual is in order, and it is a vital ritual worth memorizing because it must be followed exactly but in reverse order when shaking out the reef.

1. Take a couple of turns around the mast and through the tack cringle with the pennant. Heave taut. This holds the tack *forward* against the stretching strain to come on the outhaul.

2. Pass the same pennant several times *around the boom,* heaving taut on each turn and making the end fast. These turns will take the weight of the boom and hold the tack *down* when the sail is reset.

3. Stretch the sail by the outhaul, using a tackle or a winch to gain power. If you are not using the deepest reef, to whose clew cringle we assume the outhaul is made fast, the outhaul can be shifted at will once the sail is secured safely. The sail should be stretched until the reef band falls into place atop the boom and it has very little curve.

4. When the reef band is taut secure the clew cringle with its pennant. Three or four turns should lead right aft along

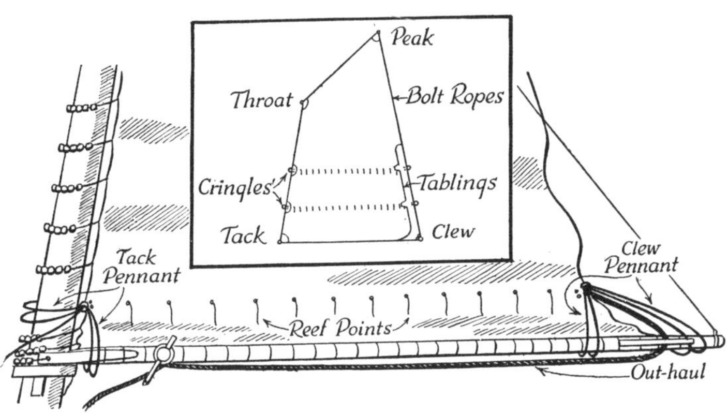

the boom, to keep the sail on the stretch when the outhaul is eventually slacked, and three or four more go 'round and 'round the boom directly under the cringle (and through it, of course) to hold it in place. Now the outhaul can be slacked away if desired, although it makes a useful footrope from which to tie in and shake out reef points if the boom is so high as to be inconveniently placed.

5. Tie in the reef points, using single-bow knots or simple reef knots. Bows are more easily untied later and hold equally well. Guard against GRANNY KNOTS which will either slip or jam.

Be certain no one has tied together reef points from different bands nor adjacent ones together in the same band. Be sure that neither flag halliards, peak downhaul, fisherman sheet, boom pennant nor any other running gear is tied into the reef, and reset the sail.

If the reef is well tucked the sail will set without wrinkles and the reef points will all be carrying a fair share of the burden. Only at the clew, where the thickness of tablings and the boltrope make it unavoidable, is an untidy bulge at all permissible.

When the reef comes out do not forget this rule:

REEF POINTS ARE ALWAYS TIED IN LAST WHEN REEFING AND SHAKEN OUT FIRST WHEN UNREEFING.

Otherwise you'll have a split sail to repair.

Having shaken out the reef points follow on through the reversed procedure of reefing. The clew cringle lashing is cast off next and finally the throat lashings, after which you can hoist away smartly and reset the sail.

SAILS.

Wander Bird's Cape Horn sails, which had seen one year's service previously, were made by *L. Nickerson,* of Boston, and they were excellent. His work was in no way to blame for the difficulties we had with the torn cringles, a trouble attributable probably to faulty clew lashings, to the severe weather and possibly to the fact that rot tends to get in its deadly work in heavy tablings which dry far more slowly than the body of a wet sail.

Our outer jib, ordinarily the first sail to come in, is Number 4 canvas, the inner jib Number 3 and all the other lowers Number 2; hence all are far heavier than would be indicated by yachting practice.

Heavy sails hold their shape better, wear longer, are less easily damaged by chafe and cost but slightly more than lighter ones. Knowledge of their strength is most comforting in heavy weather and compensates for the difficulty of handling them.

Our lighter sails were all ten-ounce duck.

All sails were made of *Olympic Duck,* a product of *Wellington Sears & Co.,* New York. I have found it excellent material, strong, even in texture (an important feature if a sail is to hold its shape) and moderately priced.

Flax sails, used extensively abroad, last longer than American cotton but do not hold their shape nearly so well and I'd rather buy new sails oftener than sail with an ill-fitting suit which is as annoying as a motor missing on one cylinder.

Wander Bird gets about 40,000 miles from a suit of such lowers which costs $1000.00. Loft charges for winter storage and thorough annual overhaulings average about $300.00 a year during the three or four years her sails last. The wind is free all right, but it costs good money to harness it!

Our mainsail and foresail lace to their booms, experience with loose-footed sails indicating conclusively that they are not nearly strong enough for the abuse of long deep-water passages. Loose-footed sails get most of the strain on the tack and clew, and a boom, alternately slatting in a calm and then perhaps tripping badly in deep rolls, puts unbearable strains on them, strains supported far better by a sail laced the length of the spar.

For a time we laced the foot of the jumbo to a boom, but we have reverted to a loose-footed sail and like it much better. It is strong enough, in proportion to its size and strains, so it has never torn.

Jibs get the hardest wear of all sails, and often give out a year before the other lowers.

Our light sails usually give only two years of service, since they get much abuse in calms.

We think our rig of squaresail and raffee far more practical for cruising than a spinnaker. Either is handled easily and neither give any trouble when set from our permanent yard. A spinnaker, on the other hand, is at best a sort of jury rig complicated by troublesome fore and after guys and a boom apt to trip and break.

Hand-sewn sails cost about 15 per cent more than triple-sewn machine-made sails like ours. They are supposed to be greatly superior because:

1. Threads sewn by hand are waxed; machine threads are not.

2. Threads are knotted every few feet instead of running the length of a seam as is the case with a machined seam.

3. Smaller needles are used when sewing by hand than are in machines, and these have less tendency to damage the cloth.

4. No hand-stitches are missed, as sometimes happens if a careless operator allows his speeding machine to slip momentarily from the edge of his cloth.

On the other hand I have no complaint whatever to make of machine-sewn sails. Our canvas actually wears thin and fragile in vital spots before the seams start going. Furthermore the extra cash requisite for hand-sewn sails can be used after a couple of seasons to have an entire machine-made sail resewn, as I thus use it, and a resewn sail is bound to be in good shape as long as the cloth retains its strength.

The argument seems a toss-up to me. Good sails can be had either way.

ROPE AND ITS CARE.

When rigging a small boat endeavor to use not more than two sizes of line for running rigging. This simplifies making replacements and simplifies the problem of buying blocks.

I have used *Whitlock Cordage* for years and have found it excellent in every way. Buying a reputable concern's product is the beginner's best guarantee of getting good rope.

Four-stranded rope is only slightly more expensive than three-stranded, but its greater suppleness makes it pleasanter to handle.

Rope repays good treatment and will last a long time if never over-loaded (a sure sign of over-loading is a marked diminution in size), stowed away wet, allowed to chafe or run over sheaves or corners so sharp as to break fibers.

When a rope has had a half-season's hard wear it is an excellent practice to change it end-for-end so that the old standing part, which has been idle on the pin, is aloft. The former working end will be found to be much smaller than it was originally.

Wire running rigging is not suitable for deep-water work except possibly as a Genoa or ballooner sheet spliced into a manila hauling part. Wire will scar winch heads, cut hands terribly when its strands start to go, and is downright dangerous if it partially breaks and then jams in a block as it is apt to do.

WIRE ROPE and STANDING RIGGING.

When wire rigging is once properly fitted and stretched and when it can be set up by rigging screws a ship should be able to girdle the world without further rigging troubles other than prevention of chafe and an occasional rub-down with hot linseed oil. This being so, few yachtsmen learn to splice wire proficiently and if they do, usually lose the difficult knack swiftly through lack of practice. The increasing use of sockets, which eliminate the need for eye-splices, is another factor making at once for stronger, neater rigging and fewer wire splicers.

Here are a few possibly useful pointers on rigging a ship:

Stainless steel rigging--which is so strenuously advertised today—costs roughly three times as much as galvanized iron rigging. Its faults (which are never mentioned by the publicity experts) are that it will rust like any other steel once any iron or iron filings touch it and that it is subject to the weakness of variability which is the lot of all alloys. It is grand when it is right, but it may look right and yet be brittle and untrustworthy if some slight fault existed in its making.

Galvanized iron rigging, given reasonable care and an annual rub with hot linseed, should last for at least twenty years. It is larger for the same strength than stainless and it stretches amazingly when new, but it remains the favorite of deep-water men.

Manufacturers of wire ropes and the sockets mentioned above will secure wire into sockets and guarantee the union to be as strong as the wire. Splices, which necessarily involve spreading strands and altering the shape of a wire, weaken a rope almost one-eighth even when put in by a master. Sockets are thus not only stronger but there is no need for parceling and serving above them, as there is over every splice. Including the cost of the socket and its installation you can get a stronger, neater and more modern job for no more money than a rigger will charge for a turned splice parceled and served.

Many times it seems necessary to replace an entire stay when only its lower end or a lower nip is damaged. And if the entire stay has to be removed it seems invariably that it is at the bottom of all the others and can be got at only by lifting all the rigging, a costly and bothersome job. To avoid this, shackle the upper ends of shrouds and stays to heavily-served, leather-covered strops with eye-splices in each end. Then taking down any shroud involves nothing more serious than removing a shackle-pin.

It is thought extremely scientific these days to rig boats on the strength of laboratory tests, and to whittle down their gear to the last possible ounce on the basis of slide-rule calculations. Possibly such wire is quite safe for yachting in sight of home, but what the technicians seem to forget often is that even a very slight chafe on a light wire may reduce it very quickly to a tensile strength far below what it should have. Oversize rigging, on the other hand, will often stand all the undiscovered chafe it may possibly get and yet be strong enough to bring the ship home with its spars and people safe.

MASTS and MAST COATS.

Masts rot most frequently at the deck and under the very mast coats designed to keep them dry and safe at this point.

It is difficult indeed to make a mast coat tight in the first place and to be sure thereafter that it is remaining tight.

After losing a mast (not at sea, thank God!) only a couple of years old through a leak in an apparently tight mast coat

I had my new mast turned so a quarter-inch eave was left about a foot above the deck-level, as shown in the illustration. Immediately under this little ledge we placed the usual mast coat, with its upper edge snug up under its protecting eave. The mast drip cannot possibly get into the crevice left between canvas and spar when the coat is tacked, glued or tied in place.

WINCHES and JIGS.

In a busy world where it is often difficult to muster good companions winches make powerful, economical and ready shipmates. *Wander Bird* has five, not counting the big anchor windlass, and they make possible to a great degree the ease with which we handle her.

Three of these are *Merriman* products, the last word in efficiency, beauty and utility. The ship's original crude mainmast winch still functions well. On the mainboom we have a *Pascall-Atkey* band winch with independent ratchet heads for the express purpose of handling the gafftopsail tack and fisherman sheet, lines which are always on opposite sides of the boom.

Many yachtsmen multiply manpower by using double-ended halliards with a small tackle, or jig, on the standing end. These are useful for getting in only the last few feet of a halliard. With a winch the sail can be hoisted all the way if necessary. Much talk is heard about the convenience of changing the nip in a block when a halliard is rigged with jigs, but if the halliard is small and free of chafe and the block is big and properly rigged there is absolutely no need of ever changing the nip. Jigs are expensive and unnecessarily complicate the sufficiently-involved lines leading to every pinrail.

The first cost of a handy little winch is but slightly more than a jig, and it will last a lifetime.

BLOCKS.

Blocks are to a sailing ship what jeweled bearings are to a watch, and, like jewels, cost real money. Even so the best blocks are always most economical in the long run.

Wander Bird sailed from Hamburg with the best available German roller blocks with lignum vitae sheaves. Today only the shells remain. The wood sheaves checked and broke, the pins rusted, the brass rollers wore lop-sided under great strain, jammed and then broke.

Merriman Bros. refitted the shells with their stainless steel pins, bronze sheaves and *Lubrite bushings.* It was costly, but our blocks are now good for life, and if we'd had the same equipment in the first place our bank account would be considerably larger.

Our first stainless pins have gone 60,000 miles in the *'Bird's* service and have yet to show the first signs of stress or wear.

Lubrite bushings are bronze bearings containing many small depressions into which a mixture of beeswax and graphite is pressed. When a bushing warms from friction a microscopic film of graphite is at once deposited on the pin by melting wax. This automatic lubrication will serve our peak halliard blocks (the hardest used of all) for 20,000 miles. Then the bushing is pressed (not hammered) out and replaced by a new one, a job anyone can do with a bench vise, while the old bushing is returned to the makers to be reloaded at insignificant cost.

The friction in a Lubrite bushing is a little more than that in a freshly greased roller bearing. It remains virtually constant, however, while that in a roller bearing increases rapidly as the lubricant is dispersed by weather and wear. When the roller block soon runs hard and complains it must be knocked apart for greasing, and that is very bothersome.

Merriman's bronze sheaves are turned with precision and polished like mirrors. They cost little more than the rough and vastly inferior cast iron sheaves often bought in mistaken effort to economize on gear.

MARINE HARDWARE.

The name of *Merriman* is so well known that the praise of another sailorman doesn't make much difference one way or another, but it is a great pleasure to come back from deep-water voyages and report that their excellent products serve as well there as in less arduous service.

Whatever it is you want in hardware, winches, turnbuckles, snap shackles, blocks, bitts, thimbles, fairleads, cleats, snap-hooks, eyebolts, bales, travelers, or what not, Merriman can supply, and each item will be eloquent of scientifically thorough study, careful manufacture and proud Yankee craftsmanship. The cost will slightly exceed that of competing makers, but Merriman goods I have used have never needed replacements or repairs and have never let me down.

HOLLOW vs. SOLID SPARS.

Wander Bird had hollow gaffs on both masts rounding the Horn. I would not take them on such a voyage again nor on any extended cruise. They are light and extremely agreeable in slatting weather, but I do not believe they have the strength or endurance of a solid stick. Both of mine let go the following summer. Capt. Johnson, of the *Yankee*, also took hollow gaffs on his second world cruise and informs me that his also folded up after some months of tropic heat and moisture. They cost twice as much as a solid spar.

BOOM GALLOWS.

Every sea-going vessel should have a gallows for her main boom. *Wander Bird's* type is inexpensive, very satisfactory,

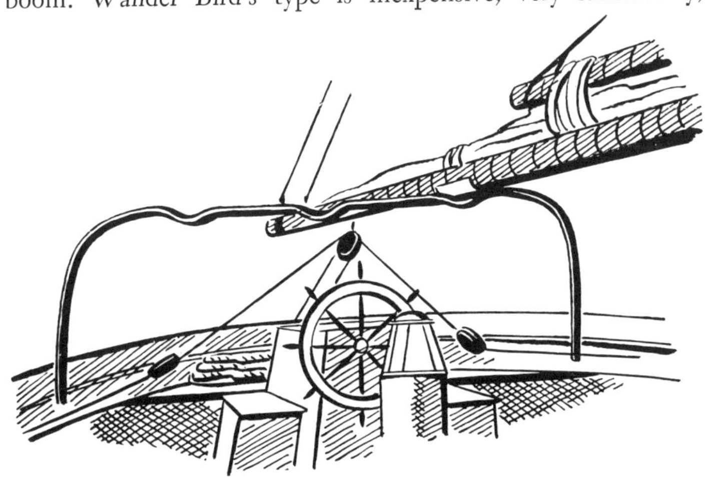

sightly and readily made by any blacksmith. It is a galvanized iron bar 1½ inches in diameter, bent into an inverted block U with three depressions in the cross-bar so the boom will stay to either side or amidships as we may wish. Its ends go through our quarter-timber and are set up hard with big bolts. On a smaller vessel without a quarter-timber a similar gallows would go equally well through the deck and a deck beam.

The boom is protected from chafe by a heavy brass plate screwed to its under side.

COMPASSES AND HOW TO IMPROVE THEM.

Compass bowls are invariably glaring white, proving, it would seem, that no manufacturer ever spent hours at sea staring at his product. Conversely, the lubber line, which should be most easily detected, is traditionally black, the most negative of all shades.

Have a compass-maker paint your bowl black and rig you a brilliant white lubber line. See then how much fresher you feel after a night's wheel trick. A white lubber line shines like a lighthouse against a black bowl and eye fatigue is largely eliminated by the black bowl.

An ideal lubber line can be made out of a fine capillary tube cut to the right length for the bowl, filled with any brilliant white powder and sealed at both ends in a Bunsen flame. Alcohol, in which the card floats, will penetrate any other type of seal, and it will discolor in time any white paint which otherwise might be used on the lubber line, but a glass-enclosed powder will stay brilliant forever.

No small vessel can be steered to degree-accuracy, and therefore it is silly to use a card marked in degrees. Your eyes will appreciate it and your steering will be better if you use the old-fashioned cards marked in points, half-points and quarter-points.

The modern spherical compass seems to me to be a great improvement in design and principle over the older flat-topped type. Doubtless their use is nearly mandatory in many modern yachts characterized by quick motion, but the old-fashioned style does very well in *Wander Bird* with her sea-kindly motion, although I have sought to make improvements which should have occurred to manufacturers long ago.

I have never yet seen a manufacturer's oil binnacle lamp worth a damn. In 1936 I bought a fine new skylight-type binnacle. Its oil lamp not only had no chimney to protect the flame, but that flame was entirely open, and there were no instructions given for lighting the thing or keeping it lighted, feats so utterly impossible in anything except a flat calm that the makers probably knew their lamp was only a decoration.

Every binnacle lighted by oil must have chimneys to protect and steady wick flames, and even so such a light is far inferior to electricity. But electric systems do go wrong at times, and their widespread use does not exempt the manufacturers from the necessity of using common sense in supplying sailors with reserve lamps which will work.

If the binnacle is lighted by electricity, from either below (which is ideal) or from above, it is well to put a rheostat into the wiring so that various eyes and tastes can be pleased with regard to the brilliance of the light.

It seems silly to even mention it but many people forget that iron or steel is taboo near a compass, and just because it is under decks makes no difference, since magnetism scorns all barriers. Look out for tools, motors, etc., which may be placed under the compass. Never allow anyone to stow anything in or near the binnacle, otherwise lads will be found some day leaving knives and spikes in this convenient spot, with disastrous results.

When the ship is ready for sea, with motors, tools, etc., all stowed, have the compass adjusted by a professional adjuster. He will eliminate most of its errors, if any, and thereafter in a wood ship you will probably have no troubles so long as you keep magnetic material six feet or more from the compass and make no major shifts of gear stowed below it. The wiring of the binnacle or other lights will not affect the compass so long as the wiring is twisted so the fields of each wire are neutralized.

If your ship is built of iron you can never be free of compass-worry. Long sailing on one tack or the mere motor vibration may alter the ship's magnetism at any time and without warning and thus vitally affect your compass.

An occasional drop of oil on the gimbals is a help to every compass.

OIL ON TROUBLED WATERS.

In my opinion no ship should ever go outside a harbor without provision for using oil.

Fish oil is best, but *any* oil at all is beneficial in a bad sea and it doesn't matter just how it is got overboard, either. Animal and vegetable oils are more effective than mineral oils, but even kerosene has an appreciable effect which might sometime be well worth invoking.

Oil is used most economically when spread from bags. Those we make in *Wander Bird* are about 12 by 20 inches and are made of heavy canvas roped all around. They are made strong because they take a beating in hard weather. Each has a moderate stuffing of oakum, which retards dispersal of oil, and a canvas spout or neck through which it is filled. The necks should be made big enough to take readily the neck of a bottle, and each should have a piece of twine sewn to it so it can be lashed closed. The bags are liberally jabbed with sail needles to provide slow leaks. In such a bag a quart of oil is good for an eighteen-hour gale, since such a minute quantity is needed. It is estimated that a film only one-millionth of an inch in thickness will give the protection desired.

Oil bags are trailed on lines about five fathoms long and they should be weighted to prevent their being thrown inboard by breaking seas.

Oil is ordinarily used only when hove-to, but when running it can decidedly lessen the menace of a following sea. In this situation the oil bags are hung over both bows so the oil can spread before getting aft.

Oil is also useful to make a smooth in which to gybe or turn safely. In this instance use it lavishly, since a big slick is wanted and quickly.

Oil affords some protection even in a surf, but there it is not nearly so valuable as in the open sea.

Oil should be stowed in quart bottles or small and handy tins. A bulky drum is not a pleasant thing to wrestle with on a storm-swept deck.

If caught without such preparations as mentioned here a five-gallon tin of engine oil can be given a small puncture and then lashed in the leeward scuppers of a vessel lying-to.

PEAK HALLIARD BANDS.

Naval architects state that nine-tenths of the strain on the masthead of a gaff-rigged vessel is that caused by "wringing" or twisting resulting from the great sidewise pull of the gaff which

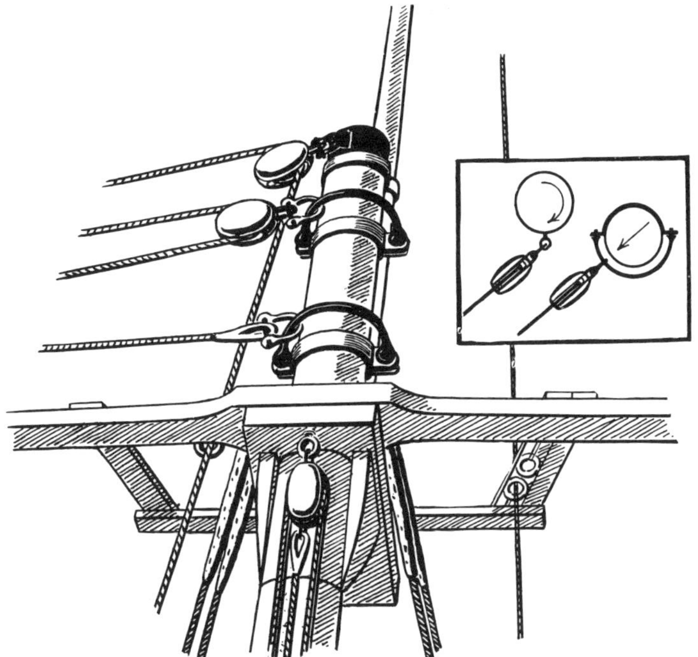

is transmitted to the mast through the tightly-clamped bands supporting the peak halliard blocks.

The sketch shows how I rigged common main-boom bales to the masthead to entirely eliminate this strain. The peak halliard blocks travel beautifully on these bales and the mastheads are good for many years more than the usual span. Incidentally, the bales also make excellent hand- and foot-holds when working aloft.

STOVEPIPES.

Stovepipes do not like the mixture of salt water and heat, and in a ship really at sea they will have to be renewed once a year if made of galvanized iron and almost as frequently if of brass. It is an expensive item I have never yet known a budgeting tyro to figure on.

Stainless steel pipes seem to be the answer, provided their upper and lower ends are fitted with copper or brass "neckbands" to fit to the iron of stove and deck-plate. They will not remain stainless, alas, for they grow dark, but they will give enough trouble-free service and last enough longer to more than justify a first cost twice as high as a galvanized pipe.

STOVEPIPE HEADS.

After having tried a great variety of stovepipe heads (which by their very numbers and varying design testify to the difficulty of getting an efficient one) I have fitted *Wander Bird*

with a device which was designed for Southern Pacific R.R. diners. Richard Danforth, cruising sloop champion in 1937 on San Francisco Bay, took this fine head to sea first and was so pleased with it that he gave me a pair. It is almost perfectly efficient, and is far ahead of the various rotary heads, T-headed affairs, ordinary Liverpool heads, etc.

Unfortunately the design—with its careful consideration of all areas—is not a matter of simple proportion for varying size stovepipes, and it is not possible here to give the many tables of figures and the many drawings which would be required to adequately satisfy both big and little ship owners. Anyone wishing such a head (they are small, exceedingly neat, and have no moving parts whatever) can secure one at shipping and manufacturing cost (about $10.00 for a four-inch pipe) by writing to Richard Danforth, Alco Co., Rialto Building, San Francisco, Cal.

LIGHTS and LIGHTING.

There are now available reliable little electric generators which use so minute a quantity of fuel and take up so little room that electricity is within the possibilities for even the smallest boat. Electric running, binnacle and chart lights are a blessing difficult to appraise properly—if they are installed so that they work!

The expensive plug-in boxes commonly seen on the decks of ships are a constant source of trouble. Water *will* get in them

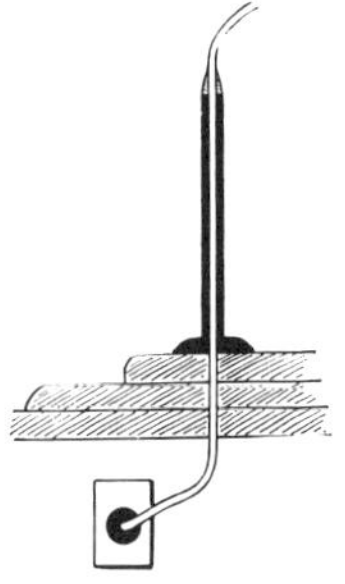

to corrode and destroy and blow fuses. If the best and most heavily insulated wiring is used and it is led through stand-pipe conduits (as illustrated) to connections below decks the problem is almost completely solved. The sockets in the running lights themselves may give trouble after considerable use, and may have to be either cleaned or replaced.

Oil lamps *must* have chimneys if they are to burn at all in heavy going. Take along a supply of spares; there was never yet a lamp-man who couldn't break chimneys in the most amazing numbers.

One of the best purchases we ever made in *Wander Bird* was that of an *Aladdin Lamp,* a kerosene mantle lamp giving about ten times as much light per unit of oil as the best old-fashioned wick lamp. It gives a pleasant amount of heat in a small cabin when weather is chilly or damp, and yet lacks the difficulties and dangers of pressure gasoline lamps. The Aladdin, with its manufacturer's shade, is apt to be rather large for a very small boat, but by replacing this big shade one can be got in much less space.

We use ours at sea constantly, checking its swinging by the simple expedient of a spring fastened to the bottom. This effectively steadies the lamp.

I think that our record of using the same mantle for fifteen months, carrying it meanwhile from Rockland, Maine, to California by way of the Horn, is an unique record.

The Aladdin Lamp is an American invention and information regarding it can be obtained at most sporting goods stores.

GROUND TACKLE.

The old-fashioned and picturesque navy anchor has the approving stamp of the years on it. Beware of new-fangled anchors whose best claims to merits are found in bought advertisements written by the manufacturer.

The finest anchors are of no avail in a jam if they are on bad chain, and nothing is so destructive to peace of mind as doubt about one's chain.

If there is no manufacturer of chain cable in your vicinity arrangement to test your chain can be made at any U. S. Navy Yard for a small cost per fathom. The $25.00 I spent several years ago to have *Wander Bird's* stout stud-link chain subjected to the Navy's searching examination has bought more comfort to me since than could be measured.

SKYLIGHTS AND THEIR LEAKS.

Battening down the top of the ordinary skylight provides a dead-end trap which invites the destructive and penetrating might of every boarding sea. It is no wonder that skylights leak. It is almost a miracle that the sea doesn't more often show disapproval of faulty design and rip the whole rig from the deck. Rubber gaskets, baffle-strips, and all the costly hold-down rigs in the world won't stop leaks half so well as the simple device shown in the drawing.

It consists of nothing more costly or involved than a triangular strip of wood fitted to eliminate the dead-end pocket.

It is a deflector which reroutes driving water and thus stops leaks and removes a real hazard.

Now this is indeed, it seems to me, an obvious and cheap improvement which in no way mars a ship's yachty appearance. Nevertheless a prominent West Coast builder and designer, when I suggested he incorporate it in a new yacht he was building, said he wouldn't do it "because no one else ever used it, and anyway this boat will never get out in heavy weather!"

Every wooden skylight I have ever seen leaks along its ridge, maybe not at anchor in a perpendicular rain, but at sea under sea tests. The only sure way of stopping such a leak (so far as I know) is to cover the hinged edges their entire length with canvas, sheet-rubber or some other material at once flexible and impervious which allows of opening and closing of the tops.

Water-proofed white canvas skylight covers pass an amazing amount of light. We used them, battened into place, at the Horn and not a drip ever got below.

WATER TANKS.

If you can find a cooper who can install wood water tanks when you build your ship do not fail to give him the job. Wood tanks not only preserve water infinitely better than any metallic container but they are cheaper, stronger and less susceptible to chafe and punctures. Their one drawback is that they take up a little more space than metal tanks, but the difference is slight and amounts to only a few gallons of water.

Although its shape may differ widely from that of a barrel, a wooden tank is built on the same principle. Our tanks, fitting the bilge, were made of exceedingly dry and fine cypress planks 2 inches thick by 4 inches wide by 9 feet long, and the edges were planed to fit to a nicety. The tanks were built to have a slight taper, and they are held together by heavy galvanized hoops wedged into place and hammered tight with mauls. When the tanks swelled with moisture the tension was so great the hoops sank into the wood a distance equal to their own thickness. A good tank will not leak a drop after its first day's service. If a tank does leak a trifle it can be caulked with a thread of cotton.

Every tank should have a man-hole in the top so it can be entered for cleaning. This hatch is caulked into place so it can't leak; it won't be opened oftener than every three or four years if ordinary care is used in choosing your water supply. At the bottom of each tank, at its low end, there should be a bung hole—big-end of the bung inside so it can't work loose!—by which the tank can be flushed.

Because of their inherent strength wood tanks do not need baffle-plates such as we cautiously installed. Each of our two tanks holds 450 gallons.

In 1932, for copper tanks of like capacity which would similarly have been assembled below decks, I should have had to pay $1000.00. My wooden tanks (I'd never even heard of such a thing before that lucky time) cost me only $240.00 installed.

Wood sweetens water, absorbing strange tastes and odors which even wholesome waters sometimes have. On long passages we have found our water grows progressively better as the days spin out. None has ever soured. The tanks have never developed either odor or taste and have never leaked.

If the time comes when the tanks need deodorizing it is accomplished by taking a hose from any tugboat boiler and blasting the tank for ten minutes with steam.

Copper is the next best bet if wood tanks can't be had. The copper must be tinned heavily on the inside, and it should be very heavy stuff. Tanks properly go into a vessel before the deck beams, and they should be stout enough to stay there forever. Alterations thereafter are very expensive and troublesome, and parsimony in building is especially unjustifiable in a matter so vital as water tanks. Do the job right the first time.

Galvanized tanks cost nearly as much as copper ones, since labor is the major expense. They cannot be recommended and are found only in jerry-built vessels.

Water pipes should enter tanks from above so that no defective connection or break in the lower end of a pipe can waste water. Lead the pipes down to within an inch of the bottom: from this position they will suck almost none of the sediment which slowly accumulates there and they will also suck dry when there is yet a scant ration of water in the tank, a hard-to-get-at ration which may be wonderfully welcome some day.

Each tank should be controlled by a valve which shuts it off from the others, and it should be an iron-clad rule that no tank ever be opened without permission from the Master.

Deck-fillers and the air vents (don't forget to install them!) are far too small on most ships to take care of the heavy jets thrown by commercial water boats. Results are, at best, annoying geysers spouting from the deck and, commonly and much worse, burst tanks and a bilge full of water. It is cheaper, safer and better to lead filling hoses right to the tanks themselves where a three-inch filling hole will take care of both water and escaping air, however fast the water boat pumps.

WATER RATIONS.

A gallon per day per man is an unnecessarily generous water allowance. If people are only reasonably careful they can shave, wash and drink almost at will and still use less than a gallon.

On two quarts per man per day, the only water ration I have ever imposed, we all got along handsomely at the Horn, although this meant but a quart for drinking. In a hot, dry climate a quart would not have seemed so big, doubtless, but few of us drank even our entire quart (we had tea and coffee besides, it must be remembered) and I think that even in the tropics we could have gotten along without serious discomfort on a quart.

If it is ever your misfortune to be really hard-up for water do not forget that rectal injections of dilute (but quite undrinkable) salt water will sustain life indefinitely, since the salt will be eliminated by the lower end of the intestine and the body will get its necessary moisture. If reduced to this expedient husband what fresh water there is for merely moistening the throat and mouth, since most people are such creatures of habit that they will feel thirst even though the body is satisfied, unless they go through the familiar motions and sensations of drinking. The salt-water solution must be slightly less salt than blood, so osmosis can take place. Straight sea water will not work, being denser than blood.

NEVER WASTE A DROP OF WATER, since at sea one never knows how long it will be before tanks are refilled. And death by thirst is possibly the ultimate in torture.

WATER.

The common fear of dangerous water is almost baseless these days, at least in any ports I have ever visited. I have been sold water (such as at Newport, R. I.) that was nasty to taste and exceedingly hard, but nevertheless no menace to health, but I have never bought or known of a ship being sold dangerous water. The very presence of regular water boats and the fact they supply liners is pretty definite indication of good water. But if there is real doubt all drinking water should be boiled.

In an out-of-the-way spot watering ship is sometimes a problem made easier by conveying water in bulk in a carefully scoured boat rather than in breakers or buckets. It is an old and handy trick of whalers and we have used it often.

Tropic rain squalls, often coming when there is no wind at all, are a useful source of water. They quickly scour all salt from sails and decks, and the scuppers can be plugged and good water scooped from the waterways. A long strip of canvas tied under a boom will gutter water to buckets faster than a crew can empty them. Useful canvas gutters can be carried permanently along the edges of raised cabin trunks. Often at sea it is not practical to get rain water since it is so fouled by spray as to be unusable.

Rain water left to stand in warm weather soon develops a squirming population of animal and vegetable life. Despite this it is quite safe (if not too appetizing-looking) for drinking and is excellent for washing and bathing.

GALLEY HINTS ON FUEL, STOVE AND SINKS.

Because a ship sailing a tack is relatively steady in her angle of heel a thwartships stove is more satisfactory than one placed forward-and-aft.

In temperate climates anthracite coal is hard to beat for fuel if a stove is to go day and night. Such coal, alas, is procurable *only* in the Eastern States and England. Elsewhere seemingly honest dealers will sell soft coal with reiterated assurances it is anthracite, and its soot, smoke and stench are damnable. Gasoline and canned gas are dangerous and costly. The latter is unobtainable except in yachting centers. Diesel oil seems a natural fuel if a ship is driven by a motor using it too. Alcohol is clean and relatively safe, but it is expensive if used for heating as well as cooking.

Many briquets contain chemicals fatal to stove pipes and the best ones are prohibitively expensive for long use. A synthetic fuel called *Presto-Logs,* made of sawdust compressed to log-like hardness, is clean, almost ashless, harmless, smokeless and contains many heat units.

Coal and ordinary iron stoves are bad business in the tropics.

The Swedish *Aga Cooker* is the answer to a sea-cook's prayer either in tropic heat or elsewhere. By clever use of heavy insulation *Aga Cookers* apply all their heat to cooking, thus effecting at once a cool galley and amazing economy in fuel. One will run night and day for a year on only slightly more than ONE TON of coal or coke!

Aga Cookers can be had in the Eastern United States from the *Aga Stove Co.*, 1029 Newark Avenue, Elizabeth, N. J. Their first cost is seemingly high and the company will not sell unless the stove is installed by their own men (cost of which is included with that of the stove, about $350.00) but the stove soon pays for itself while providing unequaled galley comfort and convenience. The *Aga's* chief drawback, as far as small ships are concerned, is its weight of about 1200 pounds, but when it is considered how little fuel need be carried this is a fault more apparent than real.

A galley should have *two* deep sinks side by side. They are invaluable in weather when dishes elsewhere are apt to be tossed about and when a shallow sink sloshes water hither and yon.

Stainless steel or Monel metal is unbeatable for making a galley neat and snappy and encouraging the cook to keep it that way.

FOOD.

With or without refrigeration sailors can now have at sea virtually anything they'd find ashore (consider our Thanksgiving menu off the Horn!) and anyone contemplating living long afloat should plan on carrying as wide a variety of high quality food as he'd have at home. Good food is the traditional preventive of ill-health, discontent and unhappiness at sea.

After having experienced years of victualing vicissitudes at the hands of the various great chain stores in America and ship-chandlers abroad we got our 1936-37 supplies from the old house of *S. S. Pierce*, in Boston. Our happy conclusions are enlightening and should prove of vast interest to anyone planning a long voyage.

Contrary to common belief, Pierce prices exceed those of

their most reliable competitors by not more than 2 per cent. Consider for a moment what this negligible price difference brought.

The Pierce expert who took our order (which totaled something over $2000.00) answered off-hand definitely, accurately and truthfully every question we put about quality, size of containers and brands, questions which usually hopelessly confuse and bewilder the local managers of chain stores.

The supplies were delivered punctually when promised, they were packed with a care and thoughtfulness quite novel to us, and nothing had been overlooked.

At sea our fine impression of Pierce service was continued by discovery that our foods were tastier, and packed tighter in cans than any we'd had before.

In other years we had always lost some hams or sides of bacon through mildew or dampness. Pierce hams and bacon came mummified in linen wrappings covered by damp-proof seamless pitch sheathings a third-of-an-inch thick. When opened eighteen months after delivery those meats are as appetizingly fresh and savory as any lying in refrigerated state on gleaming slabs in the store. Not one ham even started to spoil.

Other perishables, such as crackers, dry cereals, flour and sugar, came solidly sealed in convenient-sized tins and we lost none at all.

In many ports where one would naturally expect to get fruit it is often impossible to do so, due to seasons, blights or other causes, so I included cases of oranges, lemons and grapefruit in the big order of Horn sea stores which were to meet us at Rio. I asked the Pierce order-man to send us unripe fruit, and the efficiency with which he carried out a request which had often before proved beyond the care or patience of other chandlers, deserves special mention.

We arrived in Rio a day before schedule, but the stores came the next day, October 15, the date set four months previous in far-away Boston. Brazilians laughed at us for shipping expensive American fruit to their country and we felt a bit sheepish about it ourselves, since Brazil is a great citrus country. Our goods spent a week in a hot customs-house warehouse, too, and although the fruit seemed in good shape when we eventually got it we took along a liberal supply of Brazilian oranges to replace the California fruit which everyone told us would not last more than a day or two. As a matter of fact the imported outlasted the native oranges and we enjoyed them until December 4. I do not think we lost a dozen out of three cases.

All these things considered we feel definitely that ship's stores from S. S. Pierce are cheaper and better than any we have ever had.

Food such as we serve in *Wander Bird* costs one dollar per day per man, including fresh foods bought in ports. This figure can be reduced considerably by eliminating delicacies we enjoy, but it is questionable if such economy is wise in the long run.

REFRIGERATION AT SEA.

Refrigeration at sea is a modern and quite unnecessary luxury. Without it, true, fresh meats will not last beyond a week, even though cooked the first day out and thereafter reheated or served cold, but fresh meats are not at all essential. Eggs will last through two summer months very nicely if packed in dry salt. Canned chickens, bacon, ham and egg dishes do very well in place of meats. Carrots, turnips, tomatoes, onions, potatoes, oranges, apples, lemons, and grapefruit will last two or three weeks if kept in shade and bought with care, and few ships are often at sea much longer than this. Butter, and mighty good butter, comes nowadays in tins. Our babies grew up on *Pet Milk*, the most satisfactory canned milk we ever found.

If you must have refrigeration, build in a well-insulated icebox or ice room; don't fall for the first plausible salesman of a mechanical box who gets on your trail. The old type of box, once thoroughly chilled and opened but once a day, will hold ice for a month or six weeks, and so long as a chunk as big as your fist lasts your stores are preserved. Mechanical freezers cannot be recommended for sea use. They consume a great amount of electricity (or gas) and they are not reliable. If one breaks down (and motion and climatic conditions for which they are not planned makes breakdown likely) early in a voyage, an entire stock of essential food will spoil. With the old-fashioned ice-chest a sailor knows definitely how long his ice will last, and there are few places where he can't replenish his stock. A family-sized ice-box, designed to hold supplies over a week-end, is also unsuited to large-scale buying, and its first cost exceeds that of a bigger and safer built-in ice room.

THE MORE MECHANICAL GADGETS THERE ARE ABOARD THE MORE GRIEF!

This is no pipe-dream!

CLOTHING FOR THE SAILOR.

Tropical sailing presents few clothing problems, although it is well to know that even a slight drop below normal warmth in those regions can seem very cold indeed to bodies acclimated to heat, and then heavy sweaters can feel very good even on The Line.

Long woolen underwear is essential for comfort in cold weather. A light wool garment next to the skin is worth three sweaters over other clothing, and light underwear is less cramping to movement, which is an important consideration.

Sweaters worn immediately over underwear, or even next to the skin, serve their purpose far better than when worn as usual.

Rubber clothing is far superior to oilskins. It actually keeps its wearer dry, which oilers do only when new and then not too well. Rubber, costing only slightly more than oilers, outlasts oilskins three to one. White rubber is desirable, since it is cool by day and visible by night. Rubber dries quickly and does not stick or smell. Its only disadvantage is that it is heavy and more cumbersome (but only a little) than oilers. The fragile oiled-silk and cellophane garments useful ashore are not nearly strong enough for sea strains.

A short rubber coat and rubber trousers fitted with stout elastic suspenders (those which come with most rubber pants are no good) seem to make the best rig. The coat should have buckles like those on galoshes and not buttons or snaps, and should be oversize so it will go on easily over other heavy clothing and leave space for a towel around the wearer's neck.

Leather sea boots are so comfortable, safe and strong they are universally the choice of professional sailors. On our Horn voyage we all wore a new type of short leather boot which we got from one *Sherman Ruth,* a Gloucester ship-chandler (Gloucester, Mass., will reach him), for only $5.00 a pair. They were a foot high and as soft, light and comfortable as old shoes. It was safe and easy to go aloft in them and they were so easy to slip on and off that they made vastly easier the frequent dressing and undressing accompanying heavy weather.

If care is exercised by the helmsman and the ship is not overdriven it is not often, even on small ships, that water will top even such low boots. If it does it is a simple matter to slip into another pair, and such thorough preparation seems far more sensible than to go about forever lugging a pair of clumsy and heavy high boots.

Woolen mittens or leather gloves are of little use in cold weather unless they are protected by rubberized mittens which can now be bought at most rubber stores in seaport towns where there is any commercial fishing. These mitts sell for less than a dollar and mean the difference between limber and warm hands and the agony of numbed and aching fingers. Get them large so they go on easily. If they are hung too near the stove for drying it is said they make no pretense at keeping their plight a secret.

Old fedoras make excellent hard-weather hats. They offer more protection than yachting caps (even if they do not look so romantic!) and knock off less easily. (Lord, the number of yachting caps I've seen disappearing in the wake!) Sou'westers give wonderful protection, but deaden hearing and divert wind so that they seriously decrease the sensitivity which a Master or Mate needs on a blinding night.

A careful sailorman endeavors to keep his clothing dry and in good repair and he has plenty of it. Proper clothing is his reply to bad weather. When he is well dressed even a midwinter North Atlantic night or a Horn watch are not half-bad. Otherwise either is sheer hell.

RADIO EQUIPMENT.

In 1936 I equipped the ship with a *Harvey* 50-watt transmitter using an RK20 tube. Her receiver was and remains a *Na-*

tional FB7A with plug-in coils, providing coverage of various bands.

I knew nothing at all about radio, but in five weeks of intensive study learned enough to pass the Government's examination for a Third Class Commercial license. Since a ship station is mobile I could get no amateur license worth having, but on my request I was granted an Expeditionary status which permits communication with either commercial or amateur stations. I have never had occasion to talk with a commercial station; to do so involves a minimum cost of 14 cents a word, neglecting the 7 cents a word supposed to accrue to me if I transmit. Radio amateurs are so keen and so willing to cooperate that excellent communication is possible through them at no cost whatever.

A station such as mine is unfortunately limited to odd frequencies. Mine (6210 kilocycles for calling, 6230 k.c. for working, or about 48 meters wave-length) is just outside the amateur bands, and amateurs ordinarily do not listen on it, so I can work them only on prearranged schedules. Some commercial stations listen on this wave-length and the U. S. Coast Guard maintains a watch on it. A drastic emergency call might reach them.

ANTENNA TROUBLE—Antenna trouble prevented my "getting out" to any worthwhile extent during the Horn cruise. Radiomen, however expert, cannot properly appreciate the multiple difficulties in rigging an aerial on a sailing ship like mine or smaller. They fail to grasp the complicated system of moving sails and lines and the difficulty of leading wires hither and yon amidst a mechanism given to slattings and flappings at frequent intervals.

Wander Bird's aerial is a single vertical wire leading from a deck insulator at the foot of the mainmast to an insulator on the crosstrees and thence to the topmast truck. It thus happens to be almost exactly half my wave-length, which is the desired relation.

Unavoidably such an aerial is in close proximity to the shrouds. Through some blunder my aerial went only to the crosstrees during the Horn passage, and it thus not only operated inefficiently through being too short but the signals were absorbed and reflected by the rigging in such a manner that what feeble signals got out (maximum distance of perhaps 1500 miles) went only astern.

Even such signals could have kept us in touch with South American stations after we left Rio had not the jittery officials of those countries been so afraid of subversive elements that no amateurs would even listen for my signals, much less reply, for fear of being detected in working with someone not on their narrow band. So, for the time covered by this book, I cursed radio and officials and forgot about both, having better things to occupy my time.

In 1937, on our Hawaiian cruise, we maintained daily schedules with Pasadena and Oakland, and at last got some service out of the equipment.

CODE vs. PHONES.

Code signals (C.W. or Continuous Wave) penetrate static much better than radio phone, or modulated, waves, and they are also good for three or four times the distance on the same power. If a man has the patience to master code it is obviously better for long-distance cruising needs than the phone.

This may be heresy, but I think the value of radio communication is vastly overestimated by most people. A situation can be imagined, admittedly, where a radio MIGHT be the difference between life and death (serious illness aboard or some conceivable strange mishap which would spare the radio but leave ship and crew in jeopardy) but the probability of such an occurrence scarcely justifies the expense, time and trouble involved in equipping a ship with radio. It is very likely that in the event of a ship's being in distress the radio would be out of action through loss of its aerial, dampness or exhausted batteries or an operator too busy, sick or otherwise occupied to summon aid even if he knew his position with sufficient accuracy to direct his would-be saviors.

Time signals are the greatest boon granted a navigator since invention of the chronometer. Radio transmission is principally useful for soothing the unreasoning fears of those at home holding firmly the mistaken idea that the sea is a perilous place for good ships and their people. The "news" brought by receivers is usually revolting and most unreal amid the sea peace, and no one wants to hear advertising blurbs ashore, much less at sea.

A good radio direction-finder is probably fine gear for the coasting sailor combating fog. He is wise, even so, if he never trusts it implicitly because radios often fail under the best of conditions, being subject to strange and baffling ills. The sea is far from supplying the best conditions.

If bound on a long deep-water voyage a sturdy receiver for time signals can be carried with possible great profit. There is no other radio gadget worth taking at all, in my opinion.

PAINTS and VARNISHES.

Dulux Paints, a Du Pont product, are in a class by themselves in our experience. They hold their colors, retain their surface and do not discolor. Our Dulux white (semi-gloss) withstood the fumes of both Tallinn (Esthonia) and Los Angeles, the dirtiest and foulest ports we've ever entered. In either place ordinary whites turn dirty brown or black overnight.

Dulux seems an expensive paint to buy, but when the abovementioned features and its remarkable covering power (a gallon will go nearly twice as far as other paints we've used) are considered, it is a most economical paint in the long run. It brought *Wander Bird* into Talcahuano and Los Angeles showing scarcely a sign of her hard Horn voyage, and when it had been merely washed she shone as white as any ship in the harbor, whiter than most.

In recent years varnishes made with the synthetic resins manufactured by *Bakelite Corp.* have entirely superseded those made by natural gums. They are very hard, brilliant and quick-drying. Bakelite Corp. does not manufacture varnish itself, but varnishes made with its materials invariably are marked "Bakelite" along with the manufacturer's name.

SHIPYARDS.

Shipyards are the graveyards of many high hopes and the beginning and end of many voyages. In all my experience I have found but one where I was satisfied that honesty, skilled work, interest in the ship's welfare, fair prices and good equipment were found simultaneously, and that paragon is the old and famous *I. L. Snow Yard* of Rockland, Maine, where it was my great good fortune to refit for the Horn voyage.

Elsewhere the shipmaster must be constantly alert to prevent shoddy work, over-charging and delays unavoidable if a yard has to send someone to town every ten minutes for a handful of nails.

Yard owners say that high prices are usually caused by the failure of yachtsmen promptly to pay bills, and point out with some truth that their difficulties increase progressively as shipwrights die off leaving no apprentices to fill their shoes. In these days of labor unrest, too, the yacht owner should realize that he is apt to be viewed as an over-privileged individual who is quite fair game for a little exploitation. Such downright dishonesty (with its consequent menace to life and limb when the ship is at sea) is not thought so scandalous by many as it was in an earlier day.

COPPER BOTTOMS.

With the price of copper fluctuating wildly it is not possible to compare accurately the cost of a coppered bottom with that of one protected by various non-fouling bottom paints.

Snow's Yard coppered *Wander Bird* for $1000.00 in 1936 and, through failure to properly estimate the labor necessary for stripping off old copper and cleaning the hull, lost $200.00 on the contract. Since then copper has nearly tripled in price. Then its cost was slightly more than one-third of the whole, labor figuring as largely as usual. The old sheathing—"yellow metal," not copper—brought only one cent per pound. *Wander Bird* is now protected positively for eight, nine or ten years (so long as she is kept off rocks), and I believe that her bottom will prove no more expensive and possibly even less costly than if I were hauling, scraping and painting her every three or four months over that period. Convenience must also be reckoned in favor of a copper bottom, since hauling and painting are often difficult in regions where there may be no yards, no labor, no docks and no tides.

Iron and copper together in salt water set up electrolytic action which swiftly destroys iron, so iron-fastened ships are rarely coppered. It is said they may be so sheathed if the fastenings are countersunk and sealed under wooden plugs, but I cannot vouch for the worth of this expedient. Tree-nailed (wood-fastened) and bronze-fastened ships can be coppered.

Cold-rolled copper, buffed on its outside, gives the kind of bottom the old class-racers used, but it materially adds to cost, unnecessarily so as far as a cruiser is concerned. Hot-rolled copper is less brittle (and therefore less apt to split if hit by

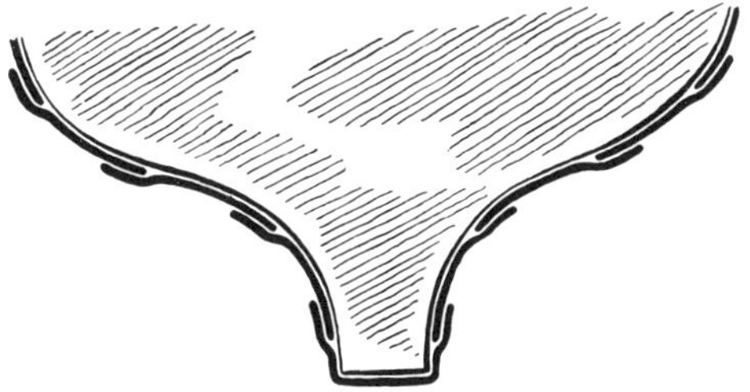

a floating obstruction), cheaper, and easier to handle. Its ordinary surface is quite smooth enough without buffing.

Twenty-ounce (22 B & S gauge) copper girdles *Wander Bird's* waterline; that below is eighteen-ounce (23 B & S gauge), all in standard sheets. It is held on by 650 pounds of copper nails. Lower sheets are lapped over upper plates so that the constant falling of the vessel in a seaway will not rip off the sheets as it will if the copper is lapped the wrong way.

Beneath the copper is a layer of felt stuck to the hull with pitch. Such felt is cheap, costing only $10.00 for the two rolls we used. Its function is to make a pad for the copper and to make the going tougher for such hardy parasites as might get past the sheathing.

Copper, incidentally, is not intended to be watertight. Its presence alone is so distasteful to marine borers that even a handful of copper nails driven scatteringly into a pile will do much to keep it free of marine growths. *Wander Bird's* keel and planking are so impregnated with absorbed copper that they resisted all borers one time when she lay partially exposed in hot Florida waters.

When the ship is on a voyage the copper cleans itself and shines glassy-smooth and red. In port it discolors and takes a dark patina. Copper dissolves very slowly in salt water while making its protective poison; that is why it must be replaced periodically.

Muntz metal and brass, sometimes used for sheathing, last indefinitely but do not stay clean like copper.

WEATHER FORECASTS.

The more I see of weather the less sure I am of my own expectations. When one considers how often official shore meteorologists, with all their multiple aids and checks, are in error it seems unreasonable to expect a lone sailor to forecast with much accuracy what lies in the future.

Possibly it is only because I have not made a sufficiently patient study of my barograph and other aneroid barometers, but I believe that no one on a small ship, working without synoptic reports from many other stations, wet-and-dry thermometers, accurately known index errors of all instruments, etc., can possibly make a better than fifty-fifty guess from a barometer. His chances are better in the tropics where barometric tides are so regular and distinct, but in higher latitudes I think the barometer a vastly over-rated and largely unnecessary instrument.

Radio reports of weather are also of little use generally. The ship is out there and is going to get whatever is coming. Few under sail can run far enough from the effects of the weather even if warned.

In hurricane and typhoon regions every sailor will study the Laws of Storms. The following rules of thumb culled from them are worth remembering:

In the northern hemisphere a vessel on the port tack sails toward the center of a storm and can expect worse weather and a falling barometer.

On the starboard tack the same vessel will sail away from the center and the glass should rise.

A barometer rising when a vessel sails the port tack is an almost certain sign of improving weather, since it indicates that the storm center is moving away from the vessel at greater speed than she sails.

A barometer falling on the starboard tack, conversely, is an equally sure sign of dirt to come.

The familiar old sea jingles relating to colors of dawns and sunsets and the shapes, kinds and forms of clouds, contain the averaged wisdom of ages and are seldom very far wrong.

When wind comes before rain you can almost always luff through it in confidence it will last but briefly and soon moderate. But when wind comes after rain stand by sheets and halliards and get in your kites, for it will blow hard nearly every time.

When you can see under a squall and make out the horizon behind it nothing worse than a puff of wind is apt to be your lot; but a trailing squall which blots out the sea behind it is a menace.

If your ship has sea room and good gear bad weather should mean nothing worse than possible delay and a little discomfort.

NAVIGATION.

I have been using *Ageton Tables* (H.O. 211) ever since it appeared five years ago and find the method excellent. It is treated exhaustively and, I hope, clearly enough for the veriest beginner in my book *Offshore, Navigation* (Kennedy Bros., New York), which is the only volume I know of dealing with this method.

NAVIGATION IS NOT, most decidedly, a difficult or a learned subject. To practice it intelligently a student needs to comprehend possibly a score of the simplest astronomical terms. Thereafter he can go anywhere with only a little practice and the ability to add and subtract.

PILOTING.

The conduct of a vessel along a shore or by means of sea marks is called piloting. It is a far more difficult and momentous problem than deep-water navigation because an error in shoal waters may be followed almost instantly by stranding.

Many methods used, and quite practically, on big ships with a plethora of instruments and observers, are lamentably unsuited for small ships. These methods swell the pages of textbooks until the beginner is apt to give up in despair when he begins to read of them. Those used most frequently on a small ship I have tried to incorporate in another little handbook, *Coastwise Navigation* (Kennedy Bros., New York), which may prove helpful in this regard.

BIG SEAS.

Very little has been done in accurate measurement of the height of storm seas because of the obvious difficulties of applying a tape to fluid beings created by gales and ramping along sometimes a mile a minute. Estimates of wave heights vary upward almost directly with the inexperience of observers. It is a rare ocean passage where some landsman doesn't spot a record-breaking sea or learn from a sympathetic steward that it is the worst voyage the ship has ever made.

Mr. Vaughan Cornish, an eminent English author, has made a fascinating study of waves in his book *Waves of the Sea and Other Water Waves* (published by T. Fisher Unwin, Adelphi Terrace, London, in 1910 and reprinted in a new edition by the Cambridge Press, Cambridge, in 1934), and I am greatly indebted to his publishers for permission to include in this book some of his most interesting conclusions and formulae.

"Measurements of the heights of waves, taken in the usual way by finding the height above the ship's water line from which a neighboring wave-crest just intercepts the horizon, are believed to be accurate to within one foot in ten when made by a practised observer," says Mr. Cornish after explaining that the angle of the ship's heel at the time of observation must of course be considered.

Estimates (or guesses) made from the deck are quite apt to have an error range of 100 per cent, Cornish believes, since there are so many misleading appearances it is quite possible for one man to judge a twenty-foot sea at ten feet and another observer to call it thirty feet high. Regarding the length of seas he states:

"Relation between the wave-length in deep water and the period (or time which elapses between the passages of a fixed point by two succeeding wave crests) has been calculated mathematically and verified by observation as

WAVE-LENGTH = 5½ × Square of Period.

Concerning the Great Lakes, whose storms are notably vicious at times, Cornish quotes Col. Gaillard, of the U. S. Army Engineering Corps, as follows:

"—it seems probable that during unusually severe storms upon Lake Superior, which occur only at intervals of several years, waves may be encountered in deep water at a height of from 20 to 25 feet and a length of 275 to 325 feet."

After deciding that the biggest Mediterranean waves probably run about 27 or 28 feet in height Mr. Cornish says: "Thus the difference in the size of waves in great lakes and in the much larger semi-enclosed seas is less than we should have expected from the observed differences between their size in the smaller and larger lakes. We find, however, a great increase when we go from the semi-enclosed seas to the open oceans."

A most unexpected conclusion, based upon his own studies and those of many merchant officers, is:

"Thus concordant observations indicate that anywhere in the North Atlantic with sea room of from 600 up to certainly 1000 and perhaps 2000 miles the height of the large waves during ordinary strong gales is *practically constant* [italics mine], being not less than 43 feet."

Concerning that favorite of ship-news reporters, the 100-foot sea, Cornish explains:

"Accounts not infrequently appear in the newspapers of some great wave encountered by the fast Atlantic liners.—This height (100 feet) invariably relates to the altitude above the flotation line of the superstructures which have been deluged. This is not, properly speaking, the height of the wave but merely the height to which a body of water is thrown when a wave breaks on board.—This increases with speed.—The recorded heights also tend to increase as the ships are built of larger dimensions on account of the fact that the great height of the navigation bridge and wheel house allows the attainment of a greater altitude being recorded with certainty."

Concerning the North Pacific this conclusion seems surprising:

"—the type of storm was the same as on the North Atlantic routes—the storm waves on the Pacific routes were certainly not higher than those on the Atlantic—"

Studies have indicated also that "at 600 geographical miles from the windward shore waves of the greatest height producible in the Atlantic by the then force of the wind" will be found.

In this connection Thomas Stevenson's empirical formula for deducing the height of waves is given as follows:

$$\text{HEIGHT OF WAVE} = 1.5 \times \text{Square Root of Fetch in geographical miles.}$$

This formula applies to distances offshore of rather more than 100 geographical miles.

(A geographical mile is 6087 feet plus a few inches, being the length of a minute of longitude measured on the equator. It is slightly longer than a minute of latitude because of flattening of the earth at the poles. To all practical intents and purposes it is the same as a nautical mile.)

After agreeing that storm waves are biggest and longest in the Southern Oceans Cornish cites cases of seas measured at from forty to fifty feet high with wave-lengths of 1200 feet. He states that a North Atlantic (and therefore a North Pacific) wave-length of 600 feet would be "enormous."

Two formulas of interest to anyone studying seas are these which Cornish gives, one for the speed of seas and the other for length:

$$\text{PERIOD (in seconds)} = \frac{\text{Speed of wave in feet per second}}{5\tfrac{1}{8}}$$

or, simplified,

$$\text{PERIOD (in seconds)} = \frac{\text{SPEED OF WAVE IN KNOTS}}{3}$$

and

$$\text{PERIOD (in seconds) Squared} = \frac{\text{LENGTH OF WAVE}}{5\tfrac{1}{8}}$$

He points out the interesting fact that these formulae can be applied to figures obtained by timing the breakers on a beach and the results will be accurate, without adjustment, for the speed of the same seas in deep water. The factors involved are not affected by the shallowness of the water where the seas finally break.

In fourteen sailing passages of the Atlantic I have but once seen waves I estimated at more than 45 feet, so my observations agree well with Cornish's studies. In 1929 we were hove-to for nearly a week in *Wander Bird* while a series of furious October gales set us into the Bay of Biscay near Finisterre. After the gales had moderated we encountered terrific swells whose tops rippled but did not break and they seemed at least 50 feet high. They were close together, steep and regular. None who saw them will ever forget the inescapable feeling that the ship must needs roll over on her beam ends if she took them broadside-to. If these seas were as high as we believe, however, their size was doubtless due to the piling up of the waves as they coincidentally encountered shoaling water and the Bay currents.

Our judgment of the seas off the Falklands may have been in error, but I am far from sure such was the case. Cornish (who never was at the Horn and says little about it) would probably question our estimated wave-lengths but my moving pictures rather tend to support us. The altogether puzzling thing about those seas is the speed with which they got up and their size, considering the wind had an offshore fetch of not more than 300 miles, that it blew violently for a relatively short time and that I do not recall there having been any especially noteworthy ground swell beforehand.

Seas we met thereafter at no time seemed much more than 40 feet high.

Regarding the mountainous appearance of waves Cornish gives the following reasonable explanation:

"—this happens when the majority of the crests rise well above the line of sight, especially if the atmosphere be rather thick, so that minute detail is obliterated. Four or five ridges, with the intervening three or four troughs, then fill all the space between the eye and the horizon. Being mounted on a deck, there is a feeling or impression that the horizon is at the distance which it would have on land with such an eye-elevation. This would mean a mile or more from ridge to ridge, which is ten times the actual distance (i.e., for the North Atlantic or Pacific—W.M.T.); and the apparent height is consequently increased in the same ratio, making a wave of 40 feet look as high as a hill of 400."

(In the big blow off the Falklands the atmosphere was brilliant and there was not the slightest loss of detail, all of which strengthens our opinion that those seas were well worth writing home about!)

INSURANCE.

Wealthy people who don't need insurance buy it regardless of cost. But they don't go anywhere. The poor fellows who make the world-voyages invariably discover that—

1. Marine insurance, so far as it covers the case of a yacht on deep water, is apparently written with deliberate disregard of the essential safety of the vessel on deep water as compared to the countless dangers of coastal waters and ports.
2. Minimum-payment clauses are usually so high as to exempt the underwriters from liability for the numerous relatively minor but annoying mishaps apt to be encountered.
3. A worthwhile policy is prohibitively expensive and not worth bothering with anyway, since in the event of total loss only the owner's heirs will collect, and why worry about them?

Knowledge that one's ship is not insured begets proper caution and respect for the sea. Money otherwise spent on premiums is far more effectively put into good gear (how often have I reiterated that phrase!) and an unwritten policy based on good gear and unremitting care is far better than any other.

SHIP'S PAPERS.

The following papers must be at hand and in perfect order whenever an American yacht returns home from abroad:

1. REGISTRY (sometimes called LICENSE).
2. INWARD CARGO MANIFEST.
3. BILLS OF HEALTH.
4. Certificate of FUMIGATION OR DERATIZATION.
5. ALIEN CREW LIST.

Concerning these vital papers let me add a few pointers, since this is a subject little understood by most yachtsmen and it is not easy to dig up the matter from the maze of red tape surrounding the subject.

REGISTERS are issued every yacht of 16 gross tons or more, and vessels of lesser tonnage are advised to carry a bill of sale as evidence of ownership. Yachts bought abroad are granted temporary registers by U. S. Consuls, and such a document is valid until the vessel has reached her home port in America where it must be surrendered within ten days of arrival.

Upon surrender of a temporary document a Permanent Register is issued. Both Temporary and Permanent Registers must be renewed annually.

For complete information on this subject consult *Article 19, U. S. Customs Regulations*, 1937.

INWARD CARGO MANIFESTS—Before leaving America the proper printed Inward Manifest forms should be secured from a customs house broker, since the law requires that the manifests be ready when the boarding Customs Officer visits the newly arrived vessel. Since a yacht is not required to clear when outward bound no outward manifest is necessary.

Inward Cargo Manifests must be made out in triplicate. The law specifies that they shall contain lists of all cargo and stores; practically, since a yacht cannot carry cargo by definition, it is almost invariably sufficient to simply write across the manifest

IN BALLAST; BROKEN STORES

rather than itemizing the ship's supplies.

Each member of the crew and each guest must make out in triplicate (on ordinary paper) a list of his foreign purchases, and one of these declarations is attached to each of the three Inward Manifests. EVERYONE ABOARD A YACHT FALLS INTO ONE OF THESE TWO CATEGORIES, CREW OR GUEST.

If the yacht has any narcotics aboard they must be declared on separate triplicate declarations which state exact amounts and proper names.

If the yacht is bringing home any specimens of any sort none can be released until viewed by the Customs Officer.

No nursery stock, vegetables or fruit from foreign countries should be landed without inspection by the Bureau of Agriculture. Very heavy penalties are provided for failure to comply with this quarantine, and every yachtsman should show the Boarding Officers whatever stores he has of this nature so that the Department of Agriculture Inspector can come aboard to either clear or condemn them.

Such stock, vegetable and fruit (or any other vegetable product such as dried bean jewelry, etc.) if condemned must be BURNED, since it may act as a devastating carrier if thrown overboard to drift ashore.

BILLS OF HEALTH—The Public Health doctor who grants the ship pratique will want a bill of health from every foreign port visited during the cruise, but is primarily concerned with that from the last port of call.

The U. S. Consul in any significant port will issue gratis to American yachtsmen bills of health which I have found perfectly acceptable to the officials of any country I have visited subsequently. If no compatriot consul is available procure a bill of health from the Consul of any friendly power or get a statement of health conditions from the port officials. For these there is generally a fee which is usually not more than $5.00.

ALIEN CREW LIST—The Alien Crew List deals not only with aliens, as its name implies. EVERYONE aboard must appear on this important document.

The Alien Crew List is made out in duplicate on big forms provided by U. S. Consuls, and it must be either *typed* or *printed*. Be sure that each of the many columns, which are concerned with birthplaces and dates, weights, nationalities, etc., is filled out correctly, since errors or omissions are fined at $10.00 each.

The Alien Crew List *must* be visaed by an U. S. Consul. This is supposed to be done in the turn-around port at the outward end of the voyage, but it can equally well be done at the last port before entering American waters. There is no visa fee.

This list must be ready for the Immigration Inspectors who come with the official welcoming party of boarding officers or soon thereafter. Like their official confreres they are apt to be hard and unsympathetic souls who don't care a whoop how glorious your voyage has been if there is a blemish in your papers. They all obviously know nothing of the sea or sail and plainly think little of those who deliberately go to sea for fun. Papers which are in order, coffee and cigars generally affect them pleasantly, but their potential nuisance value is terrific if a yachtsman's ignorance or carelessness complicates their doubtless tedious and unpleasant work.

CERTIFICATE OF FUMIGATION—Every American yacht coming home from abroad is subject to either fumigation or an inspection to discover if she harbors rats. If there are roaches or bedbugs aboard (and there will certainly be if the ship has been in the Mediterranean, West Indies or South Seas) fumigation by hydro-cyanic gas costs generally no more than the inspection, although it involves sealing up the ship for six hours and a considerable airing period thereafter before it is safe to live aboard.

Never, under any circumstances, allow foreign fumigators to use sulphur fumes in your ship. Sulphur is destructive to metals if there is any dampness at all on them and its reeking fumes can be detected six months later in closets and drawers. It too often seems to have an effect aphrodisiacal rather than lethal on hardy insect pests, too. Hydro-cyanic gas, such as is used by the Public Health Service, is odorless and disperses quickly. It does not damage clothing. Undeveloped photographic negatives must be removed or they will be destroyed. Developed negatives and films are unharmed by cyanide gas.

If fumigating must be done, seek to have it performed in a major port by Public Health officials. In minor ports, such as Miami, the work is allotted to local civilian fumigators whose work is often exceedingly careless and whose prices are monstrous.

The Certificate of Fumigation, or the Certificate of Deratization issued in lieu of fumigation, is the concern of the Public Health boarding medico.

LENSES.

Sextants, binoculars, and camera lenses are very susceptible to fouling at sea where the air is frequently filled with flying spray or mist. They are most readily and efficiently cleaned with just such a spray-gun or atomizer as can be bought at any service station where they are used for cleaning windshields. For less than a dollar a gun and a quart can of fluid can be had, enough to last almost a lifetime. This stuff is also wonderfully useful for quickly cleaning ports, skylights, the binnacle or mirrors.

Lenses should be cleaned with lens tissue or old and soft linen cloths which are entirely free of gritty substances.

CAMERA EQUIPMENT.

The pictures in this book were made with Brownie Boxes, a 40-year-old pocket-type Kodak, a Kodak Bantam, a Leica, a Rolliflex, a Graflex, and a Bell-Howell EYEMO. Eastman, Du Pont and Agfa films of all sorts were used, and the pictures were made under every possible kind of weather condition. The author used 35-mm. SUPER X in his EYEMO.

Many of the loveliest shots are the result of incredibly good luck, as so often happens, and, with the exception of John Wright, none of the picture-makers ever took photography very seriously. Hence there is no record of lens apertures, shutter speeds, etc., such as the modern camera fiend would like to have.

The author used a Weston light meter religiously, and carried the following filters:

Harrison Aero 1
Harrison Aero 2
Harrison 23 A
Harrison G
Harrison 72

The Eyemo was equipped with a 47-mm. Taylor-Hobson-Cooke 2.5 lens, and a Dallmeyer 6-inch telephoto lens. The latter, unhappily, was just enough out of adjustment to spoil all the long shots attempted. Since the moving pictures taken were planned for commercial use with the addition of sound and dialogue the object glass of the finder was engraved by the Goerz people in New York to allow for the reduced proportion of the film within which picture composition was permissible. The fee for this engraving was only a couple of dollars.

The exceedingly sensitive film was shipped home from way-ports to avoid anticipated spoiling by the change of temperatures met during the voyage, and none was lost. After leaving Rio in October no film was shipped, and despite the fact that the ship went from the tropics to near-freezing, back through the tropics to more cold San Francisco weather, not an inch of supposedly very perishable negative was lost. The only precautions taken to guard it consisted of storing it, wrapped in black paper, in the hundred-foot tins and keeping the tins in the warm galley when the weather was cold and damp and in an after-cabin bench locker when in the hot climates. No temperature higher than 85° F. in the shade was encountered on the voyage. From this experience it is possibly safe to argue that film is hardier than is generally believed.

The author used and found excellent a $60.00 Mitchell tripod with a most ingenious ball-and-socket type of head. A tripod, alas, is of little use at sea and it is also a terrific handicap in the securing of candid shots where unawareness of the subject is essential.

The American Cinematographer Handbook and Reference Guide was found very useful indeed. It can be had for about one dollar direct from the publishers, *American Cinematographer*, 6331 Hollywood Blvd., Hollywood, Cal.

Anyone going on a long voyage in search of moving pictures should know something about his camera. If he is using a spring-motor movie machine I advise his carrying a couple of spare springs and learning how to install them. I twice broke new springs and lost many pictures through not being able to effect my own repairs. Spare parts, accessible enough at home, are very often exceedingly hard to locate in foreign countries.

The winding key of a brand-new Cinekodak (16 mm.) of the cartridge-loading type broke after brief and careful usage. Examination of its construction indicated possibly that it was too lightly made to be very practicable. That camera went out of action for lack of a spare key.

On the whole, however, modern cameras give remarkable

service under difficult conditions. Keep them as free as possible from salt spray, use good oil frequently but sparingly and they stand up remarkably well and deliver, as this book pretty well proves, delightful results even in the hands of non-expert owners.

VII. GLOSSARY

IN a book where an effort has been made to side-step terms confusing to the layman this glossary makes no pretense at rivaling a sea-dictionary. Its function is merely to interpet expressions possibly not widely understood but nevertheless unavoidable.

BEARINGS—For convenience sailors ordinarily use MAGNETIC BEARINGS. To get these they have only to sight across their compass at another object, be it ship, star or land, and note the compass direction (or bearing) of the object. Unhappily the Compass is dominated by an ever-moving Magnetic Field some distance from the TRUE POLE of the Earth, a spot almost directly below the Pole Star. Since the Magnetic Field is itinerant, magnetic bearings change with the years and they are also almost meaningless to those not knowing the compass error (or variation) for the locality in question. Hence TRUE BEARINGS. They are the direction of objects from an observer with reference to TRUE NORTH, and they are not subject to change with Time.

At the Horn, in 1936, the compass North was 16° West of True North. In 1867 it was 23° West. The angle between True and Magnetic North is called VARIATION. See illustration at top of page 254.

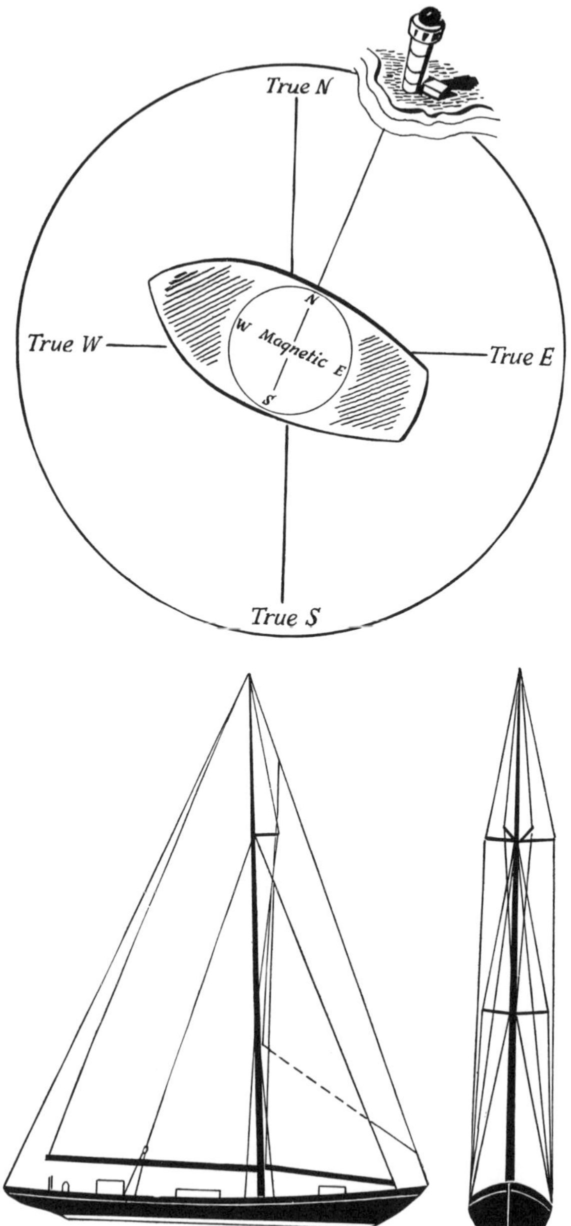
True N
True W
True E
True S
N
W
Magnetic
E
S

BERMUDA RIG—Usage will soon doubtless justify the popular name of MARCONI RIG for the modern yachting system of tall masts and triangular sails. The Bermudians created the mode, however, in their smooth lagoons. Signor Marconi was erecting his tall radio towers at the same time and an enthusiastic public dubbed the Onion Patch invention with the Italian's name.

The Bermuda Rig is distinguished by extremely lofty masts and jib-headed sails. The masts have very little inherent strength, depending almost entirely on supporting rigging. The sails, far longer than gaff sails in the hoist, are more efficient when sailing on the wind. Opposite is shown a Bermuda-rigged cutter yacht.

BOLTROPE—The bordering rope running around sails and carrying much of the strain.

BOOM—The spar extending the foot of a gaff-headed sail. If a sail is laced (as *Wander Bird's* are) the foot is made fast to the boom throughout its length. If a footloose sail is used it is secured to the boom only at the tack and clew. *Wander Bird's* jumbo and jibs carry no booms, although on some ships booms are sometimes fitted to even those sails.

BOWSPRIT—The bowsprit is one of the principal spars of a sailing ship. Originally it was a foremast, but early sailormen discovered that raking this foremast forward improved the sailing of their vessels, and a tendency once started did not end until the mast was nearly horizontal and forming what we call the bowsprit. It extends the sail plan beyond the vessel itself, providing support for the jibs, the hardest-working sails (per unit of area) in a vessel. (See Jibboom.)

BROACH-TO—When a ship has run too long before a gale she may suddenly, through a variety of causes, be thrown broadside to the seas. This usually happens after she has first rolled very deeply, being over-powered by too much canvas aft and the thrust of a big sea. The helmsman loses control and the burdened ship takes charge, coming up part way into the wind and meeting the next sea all unprepared. Countless marine disasters have occurred with breath-taking speed this way.

CLEW—The lower after corner of a fore-and-aft sail is called the Clew. It is the corner to which the sheets lead.

CLEW-UP—When a squaresail is furled its clews are hoisted to the yard as the sheets are eased away. Clewing-up is the first step in furling a squaresail, and the term is frequently used in fore-and-afters when taking in their sails.

CLIPPER SHIP—A term properly applied only to the very beautiful, very fine, fast and over-sparred ships built in the United States between 1850 and 1859 and some of their British prototypes of later date (like *Cutty Sark*, built in 1869) which carried the rarest cargoes at the high freights demanded by high speed. Such square-rigged ships as survive today are rather floating warehouses, supplying long-term storage as well as transportation, and are loosely termed clippers only by very unpoetic license.

CLOSE-HAULED—When a sailing ship is working to windward the clews of her sails are hauled close aboard. In

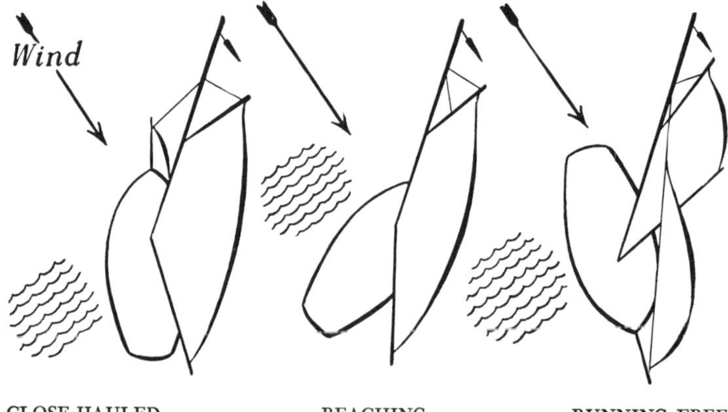

CLOSE-HAULED REACHING RUNNING FREE

a fore-and-after the booms are very nearly amidships, the sheet blocks close together; hence a term indicating that a ship's sails are trimmed for sailing close to the wind. (See REACHING.)

COME-ABOUT—One of the two methods by which a sailing ship offers one side or the other to a wind. In COMING-

ABOUT the vessel swings bow first into the wind, carried by her momentum, until the breeze fills her sails on the new tack and the vessel gains way on her new course.

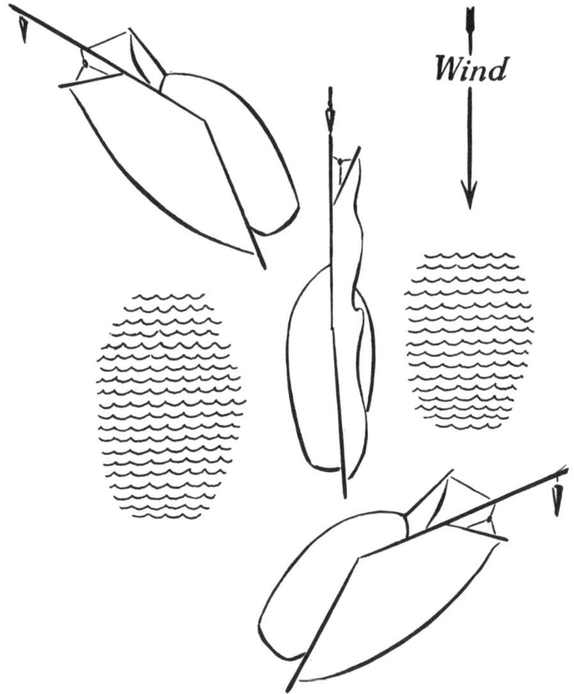

COMING-ABOUT is the common way of changing tacks, but sometimes it is not a feasible maneuver because of a bad sea—which may stop the vessel in that ticklish moment when her sails are not drawing—or a dangerously high wind which imperils slatting canvas. (See GYBE.) When, for these or other reasons, a vessel refuses to come about and hangs head-to-wind she is said (graphically!) to be IN IRONS.

COMPASS—Indisputably the most important navigational device on any ship. It is a virtually foolproof instrument of great antiquity, beauty and simplicity, with the power of indicating the MAGNETIC NORTH. (See BEARINGS.) It consists of a circular cloth disc suspended, very nearly floating, in a covered bowl where it is free to swing about a central pivot. The card supports magnetized needles which afford the directive impulse. It is floated because the liquid dampens oscillations which otherwise would tend to be so wild as to destroy the value of the instrument.

COMPASS POINTS—The compass card is divided into 360 one-degree units, into 32 COMPASS POINTS or a combination of both. In sailing ships POINTS are used almost exclusively, since they cannot attain the course precision possible in long steamers which know nothing of tacks, calms and other things upsetting to navigators.

The sailing ship steers by Points, Half-Points and Quarter-Points. A POINT is 11¼ degrees of arc.

This unit is also used in designating the position of anything with reference to the ship's head. FOUR POINTS ON THE BOW (Port or Starboard) means 45° to left or right of the ship's head; ABEAM indicates midway, 90° or EIGHT POINTS from the bow; ON THE QUARTER indicates twelve points from the bow. These are the commonly used reference points but the intermediate ones are often used for greater accuracy, such as TWO POINTS ON THE BOW, ONE POINT ABAFT THE BEAM, etc.

COUNTER—The after part of a ship, where her lines narrow to form the stern. The design of the counter is of vast importance, for it not only can make or completely mar a ship's beauty but it is a feature of vital concern affecting speed and safety in a seaway. *Wander Bird's* elliptical stern (nowadays so uncommon) is exactly like those developed and proved by the world's great clipper ships.

CRINGLE—When a sail is reefed the strong iron rings set in both the tack and clew no longer bear any of the strain, since they are within the reefed area. On the sail's boltrope, at each end of each band of reef points (which see) sailmakers put secondary irons, held in place by cunningly twisted strands of rope which also seize the boltrope.

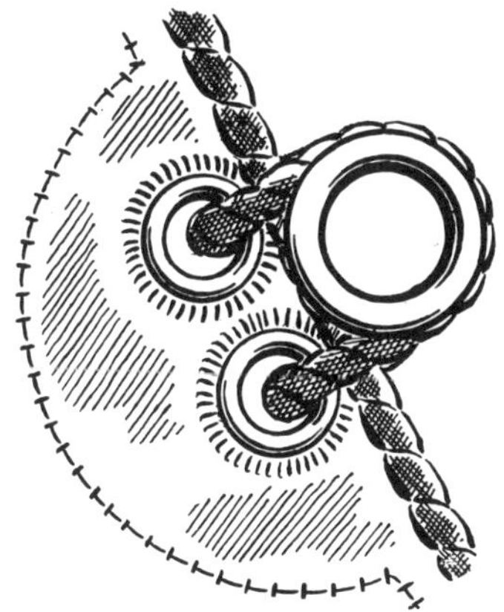

Through these irons, the reef earrings or pennants are passed when putting in a reef.

DOG-DOWN—The lugs used at sea to fasten hatch covers and ports into place (similar ones are found on ice-boxes ashore) are called DOGS. When the DOGS are DOWN the door is closed tight. Hence, anything shut to stay shut is DOGGED DOWN.

DOG-WATCH—When a watch is divided, into any number of portions or for any purpose, it is said to be DOGGED. The purpose of dividing a watch is generally to effect a rotation of the entire watch system, and the EVENING WATCH, from four P.M. to eight, is the watch usually DOGGED. The FIRST DOG is from four to six, and the SECOND DOG from six to eight.

FISHERMAN STAYSAIL—This is an Americanism for what the English term a maintopmast staysail. It is a sail (one of a schooner's most important, too) fitting between the head of the foremast (not foretopmast, mind!) and the truck (or top) of the maintopmast. It is sheeted aft, often to the end of the mainboom, and its tack is held down by a tackline. If it were called "staysail" confusion would often arise, as this is a name frequently used interchangeably to indicate the forestaysail or JUMBO (which see).

FORE-AND-AFT—A term referring to sailing ships whose sails are set on booms and gaffs which, at rest, lie in a

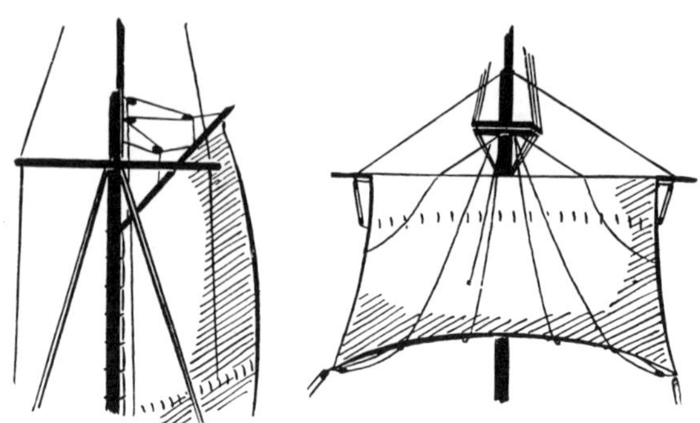

forward and aft direction. It is opposed to SQUARE RIG, although developed from it, and it has the great virtues of being smarter to windward, far easier to handle, cheaper and more efficient in every way except running before the wind.

GAFF—The spar at the top of a four-sided fore-and-aft sail. The throat and peak of such a sail are at the forward and aft ends of the gaff, and the entire head of the sail is lashed to the spar which is hoisted and supported by the throat and peak halliards.

GALLOWS—Or BOOM GALLOWS. A permanent frame designed to support the after end of a boom when the sail is in or is being taken in. It replaces the movable crutch seen sometimes in small vessels. A strong gallows is vitally important at sea, being worth more than a couple of men when it comes to capturing a swinging boom. *Wander Bird's* gallows is rather unique in design. (See Appendix.)

GASKETS—Strips of canvas with lines spliced into each end used for tying up a furled sail. Any line used for this purpose may be called a gasket.

GYBE—Second of the two methods (see COME-ABOUT) by which a ship is put from one tack to another. In gybing the vessel is headed away from the wind, presenting her stern to it instead of her bow.

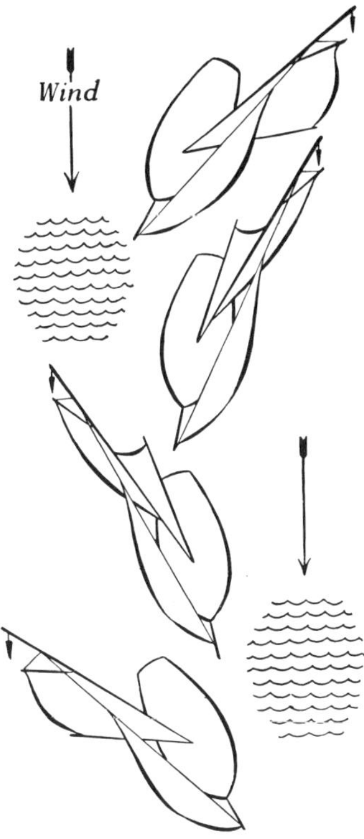

Immediately after she has passed from dead before the wind it will catch her sails on the opposite side to where it was but a second before, and they will fill on the new tack. Gybing costs ground, is slower than coming about, and—unless properly done—contains an element of risk to gear, but it is positive. (See Appendix, GYBING.)

HALLIARDS—When men used to sway yards aloft they called the lines they used for the job HAUL-YARDS. By sea-going ellision the word is now HALLIARD and it means any line used for hoisting a sail or yard aloft.

HELM, UP & DOWN—Students of custom and habit can find no more enthralling example of the power and longevity of popular usage than in this confusing matter of the HELM and HELM ORDERS. Today, after centuries of befuddlement, the maritime powers are at last eliminating a situation which has caused many a shipwreck in the past, one notable one only a year or so ago off the Jersey coast. Here is how it all came about:

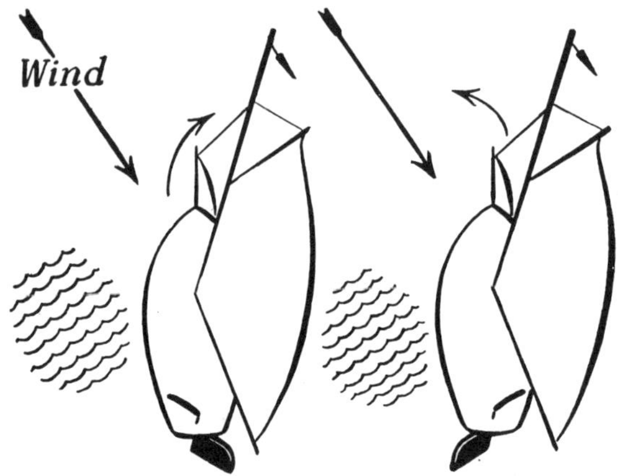

HELM originally meant TILLER, a simple lever stuck through the rudder post to enable the helmsman to swing the rudder from side to side. When the HELM was moved one way the rudder moved to the opposite side. The vessel's bow went to the same side as the rudder. This was all right, and it was also sensible to say that the HELM was UP when it was shoved *toward* the wind, and DOWN when it was moved *away* from the wind. So ships sailed blithely until the wheel replaced the tiller.

It was easy and natural to gear the wheel so it turned in the same direction in which the helmsman wanted to go. Trouble resulted. Now rudder, bow and wheel all moved in the same direction. But things change very slowly at sea, and nothing so vital as helm orders are lightly altered. So the old helm orders survived tenaciously. Helmsmen, often none too bright, had to think of two things every time they heard an order. They had to visualize the movement of a purely imaginary tiller and remember that its ordered motion HELM UP or HELM DOWN was just *opposite* to that in which they must turn the wheel.

The order was also often PORT THE HELM or STARBOARD THE HELM. In the old days a HELM placed to PORT sent a ship to Starboard, and vice-versa, but the giving of the order was the responsibility of the officer in command and the quartermaster had but to obey. With a wheel the sweating helmsman (and don't think they didn't often sweat, too, in narrow waters!) had always to remember that PORT HELM meant spinning his wheel to starboard and STARBOARD HELM put the wheel to Port. Alice in Wonderland found nothing more absurd, and the fact that many ships were rigged with backward wheels is proof of the seriousness of the problem.

With the coming of steam, helm orders with reference to the wind died a natural death. Lately a momentous International Conference has made it an offense, punishable by a stiff fine, for any pilot or officer of a commercial vessel to utter the old helm orders. Today the order PORT THE HELM means to turn the wheel (and hence the ship) to Port. Under Daniels the war-time U. S. Navy went even further for the benefit of its recruits, and banished from helm orders the fine old words of PORT and STARBOARD. In the Navy now it is RIGHT RUDDER or LEFT RUDDER.

Only in sailing yachts do the old terms still linger on. HARD A'LEE (Helm DOWN, or to LEEWARD) indicates a ship is coming UP INTO THE WIND. Conversely, HELM UP warns of a run off, possibly a gybe.

JIBBOOM—Just as masts were extended from single trees to two or three lashed together for greater length, so bowsprits were extended as ships grew. The bowsprit extensions were named jibbooms and flying jibbooms, depending on how many there were. The merit of the multiple

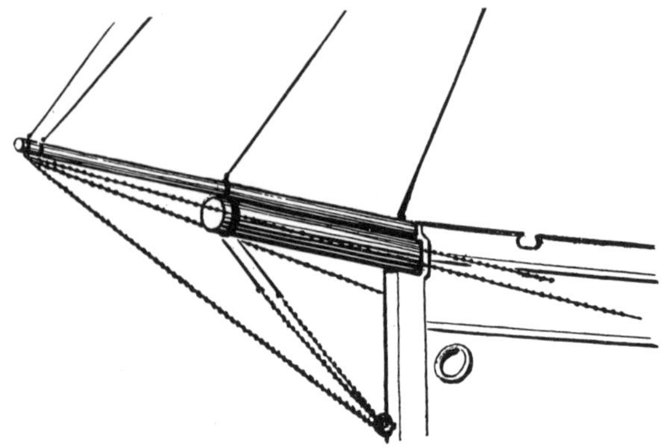

mast and bowsprit is that uppermasts and jibbooms may be lost without crippling the ship.

JUMBO—The American fisherman's name for the forestaysail, used almost entirely on this side of the Atlantic aboard schooners where the foreign abbreviation of "staysail" might be mistaken to mean fisherman staysail.

JURY RIG—Repairs accomplished at sea are referred to as JURY RIGS. A JURY RIG is ordinarily of a temporary nature meant to serve only until the ship can reach port and a more ship-shape repair. Nevertheless many a remarkable voyage has been made under ingenious and strong jury rigs.

KNOT—This much-abused word indicates the WORLD'S STANDARD measure of SPEED. It is not a distance, as most people think. A knot means ONE NAUTICAL MILE PER HOUR. A vessel may make TEN KNOTS but only those ignorant or careless of the precise beauty of sea language say ten knots *per hour*. In one hour a vessel sailing at TEN KNOTS will sail TEN NAUTICAL MILES.

LEECH—Either of the vertical edges of a squaresail. In a fore-and-aft sail the after edge is the leech. (See drawing of SAIL.)

LUFF—The forward or leading edge of a fore-and-aft sail. When close-hauled it is the luff (approximately the forward third of the sail) which does virtually all of the work. It is by increasing the length of the luff through use of high masts that the Bermuda Rig gains windward efficiency.

LUFFING—The shaking of the luff of a sail. This happens when the sail is not properly trimmed to the wind. When sailing close-hauled the helmsman endeavors always to keep his luff just on the verge of trembling, or, in other words, to keep the ship just as close to the wind as she can point and still keep moving ahead. He keeps his sails just FULL and sails BY the wind, shifting his course as it shifts, hence the common sailing term of FULL AND BY, ordinarily referring to sailing close-hauled only.

LUFFING can be deliberate. By pointing a ship too high into the wind the sails are thus emptied and the vessel eased. It is a quick way to meet a sudden squall.

MERIDIANS—Meridians are imaginary circles girdling the globe and passing through both the NORTH and SOUTH POLES. The meridian passing through Greenwich, England, is accepted by most maritime powers as the Prime Meridian from which Longitude is reckoned to East or West.

MILE—A nautical mile is (almost exactly) the length of a minute of arc measured on a meridian or 6080 feet. A degree of latitude is then 60 nautical miles in length.

PALM—A palm is the seaman's substitute for the thimble of a seamstress. It is a leather loop fitted with an iron socket. The hand fits through the loop, the thumb going through a hole in the strap, in such a way as to bring the socket just over the heel of the thumb. The head of the sail needle is set into the socket and the entire strength of the hand, wrist and forearm can then be exerted to drive it through resisting canvas or rope.

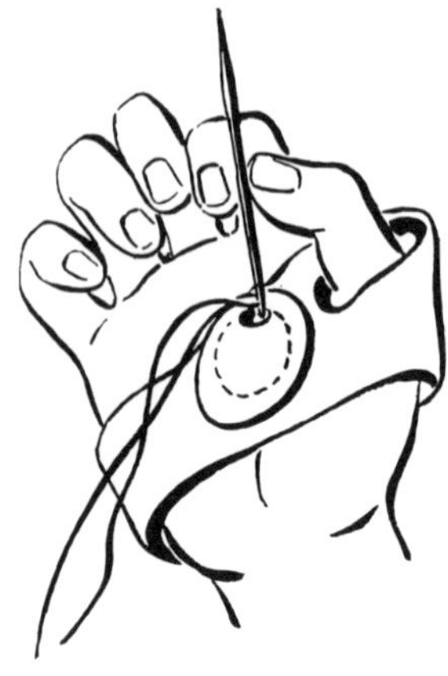

PEAK—The upper after corner of a gaff sail.

PEAK HALLIARD—The halliard which raises the after end of a gaff and hence the peak of a sail.

PORT—The left side of a ship, looking forward. Remember it by this line: JACK LEFT PORT. Left is Port and PORT WINE IS RED, like the port light of a ship.

PORT TACK—When a ship is sailing so that the wind is on her port side she is sailing the Port Tack.

REACH—That pleasant point of sailing when a vessel has eased her sheets just a trifle. She still has the wind well forward of the beam but is not close-hauled. When the wind goes still further aft, but not yet abaft the beam, she is said to be ON A BROAD REACH. (See CLOSE-HAULED.)

REEF—Most sails (barring jibs and light racing sails) are built so they can be reduced in area in heavy weather. The part of the sail which is then not in use is the REEF. Big sails may have provision for as many as three reefs. (See Appendix, REEFING.)

REEF EARRINGS or PENNANTS—Lengths of line passed through the reef cringles to hold the reef in place to the mast and the boom. (See Appendix, REEFING.)

SEXTANT—An angle-measuring device essential in making celestial observations and also often useful in piloting a vessel along shore.

SHEETS—The lines used to trim sails. SHEETS are always made fast either to the clew of a sail or to a boom at a point adjacent to the clew.

SIGHT—An observation made with a sextant on some heavenly body.

SQUARE-RIG—The rigging system where yards are hung from masts, lying (at rest) at right angles to the keel.

STARBOARD—The right side of a ship looking forward. The starboard light is green, STARBOARD LIGHT is the American Navy's poetic name for crème de menthe.

STARBOARD TACK—When a ship is sailing so the wind strikes her on the starboard side she is sailing the Starboard Tack.

STOPPING A SAIL—A handy method of making up a sail in a long roll, securing it with light twine. When a stopped sail is hoisted a jerk on the sheet breaks it out like a suddenly-blooming flower. It is a dodge used continually in racing but it is also of great use at sea in setting a storm sail. (See Appendix, STOPPING SAILS.)

TABLINGS—Heavy reinforcings at the corners of a sail and also at the reefing cringles.

TACK—The lower forward corner of a fore-and-aft sail.

TACKING—Coming-about, getting from one tack to another. (See COME-ABOUT and GYBE.)

THROAT—Upper forward corner of a gaff sail.

THROAT HALLIARD—The halliard raising the throat, and therefore the forward end of a gaff, of a gaff sail.

VARIATION—The amount by which the north point of a compass varies from the True North. Variation is different in different places and in the same places at different times. (See BEARINGS.)

WIND FREE and WIND HEADING—A wind is free when it strikes a vessel abaft (behind) her beam. A wind is heading when it is moving forward, coming ever more from ahead and forcing her away from her course. Conversely, a wind going aft is a FREEING wind.

WIND, ON and OFF the—When a ship is working to windward she is ON THE WIND. When she is sailing as high as she can go she is said to be HARD ON THE WIND. When the course is altered (or the wind shifts) so that sheets may be eased the vessel is OFF THE WIND. PUT HER ON THE WIND, or LET HER OFF, are derivative terms.

WIND, BACKING, VEERING or HAULING—A wind backs when it moves contrary to the established laws for settled weather. In the northern hemisphere an easterly wind which goes northeast, north, northwest, etc., is BACKING. If it "follows the sun," i.e., shifts to southeast, south, southwest, etc., it is said to be VEERING. These rules are just reversed in the southern hemisphere where, to the perplexity of many sailormen, so many things are topsy-turvy. HAULING is a term indicating a shifting wind but affording no clue as to the direction of the shift.